The
Entrepreneurial
PC

The complete guide
to starting a
PC-based business

second edition

Bernard J. David

Windcrest®/ McGraw-Hill

New York   San Francisco   Washington, D.C.   Auckland   Bogotá
Caracas   Lisbon   London   Madrid   Mexico City   Milan
Montreal   New Delhi   San Juan   Singapore
Sydney   Tokyo   Toronto

SECOND EDITION
FIRST PRINTING

Library of Congress Cataloging-in-Publication Data
David, Bernard J.
    The entrepreneurial PC : the complete guide to starting a PC-based
  business / by Bernard J. David.—2nd ed.
        p.   cm.
    Includes index.
    ISBN 0-07-015652-2 (H)   ISBN 0-07-015653-0 (P)
    1. Home-based businesses.   2. IBM Personal Computer.   3. New
  business enterprises.   I. Title.
  HD2333.D38   1993
  004'.068'4—dc20   93-39081
                                                             CIP

Acquisitions editor: Brad J. Schepp
Editorial team: Joanne Slike, Executive Editor
                Susan Wahlman Kagey, Managing Editor
                B.J. Peterson, Editor
                Joann Woy, Indexer
Production team: Katherine G. Brown, Director
                Ollie Harmon, Coding
                Wendy L. Small, Layout
                Joan Wieland, Proofreading
Design team: Jaclyn J. Boone, Designer
                Brian Allison, Associate Designer
Cover design: Lori E. Schlosser   EPC1
Marble paper border courtesy Douglas M. Parks, Blue Ridge Summit, Pa.   4483

This book is dedicated to Lisa, Sam, and Emily David,
my wonderful family.

Contents

Introduction

Scenario 1 You bought a PC (personal computer) for your home. You've played every conceivable game. You've loaded and used Managing Your Money and have realized how small your asset base actually is. Now you're wondering how to justify this very large paperweight that sits in your house.

Scenario 2 You spend four weeks in class learning everything there is to learn about computers. You're obsessed with getting one, but you can't figure out how to justify the expense.

So many people find themselves in the predicament of trying to rationalize buying a computer. In fact, services like Prodigy are playing up the positioning that they are one more thing that can be done on a system.

But you as a present or potential computer user are still looking elsewhere for more reasons. You buy educational software for your children, only to find that your kids lose interest. You join user groups to keep yourself enthusiastic.

Yet the motivation level and best-laid plans to use the computer quickly follow the path of the exercise bicycle. The computer moves from the center of activity in your den, to the bookshelf, and then to the attic. This is the path your computer takes unless you can keep yourself excited about using it.

What better way is there to keep you excited than to zero in on using it to improve your financial position?

You'll find the solution to improving your financial position in this second edition of *The Entrepreneurial PC: The Complete Guide to Starting a PC-Based Business*.

In the pages that follow, you'll learn the nuts and bolts elements of what you need to be successful:

- Are you entrepreneurial?
- Entrepreneurship and the PC industry
- Good PC-based businesses
- PC-based company ideas
- Planning your PC-based company
- Marketing your PC-based company
- Running your PC-based company
- Understanding your company's finances
- How much money do you need?
- Finding capital for your PC-based company
- Potential roadblocks
- Harvesting a computer business

- Choosing computer software, hardware and peripherals
- Help for starting and running your PC-based company
- PC-based companies
- Computer-based companies you can run from your home

The Entrepreneurial PC: The Complete Guide to Starting a PC-Based Business is intended to be a comprehensive nuts-and-bolts guide to selecting, planning, starting, running, and selling a business based on your computer.

Selecting a business

The first thing you must do before getting into business is to select a business to enter. This book assists you in determining how to select a business based on your interests and skills. Added to your own skill set, the book will aid you in determining the appropriate technology you need to start various businesses. Finally, you will get a complete understanding of the financial resources you need to start your PC-based business and of the returns that you can expect from it.

Planning a business

Once you've selected the business, the next step is planning it. This book will explain the merits of planning or not planning your business. It also shows you, through a step-by-step process, how to plan your business.

Starting a business

Sometimes the hardest thing to do is actually start a business. All the best research behind business selection and planning can often be overshadowed by a lack of courage from within, rooted in the basic fear that you might be wrong, and the business might not succeed. You will learn to understand these emotions in the pages you are about to read. And you will learn what skills are necessary to overcome quite natural feelings.

Running a business

Once you've started the business, you need to run it. What you must do in the early survival stages of the business as well as the growth phase of the business are all issues that are covered here.

Harvesting a business

Unfortunately, too few people are really aware of methods for receiving the rewards of the hard work you've put into building the business. You will learn ways of reaping what you've sown.

Selecting, planning, starting, running and selling a business based on your computer can be a very rewarding experience. It also has the potential to be devastating. You must put much care, thought, flexibility, and hard work into the constantly changing process in order to make it a success. This book is intended to make your PC-based business journey a fruitful and rewarding one. Enjoy!

1 Are you entrepreneurial?

This chapter discusses the many attributes of an entrepreneur in the computer industry. A practical checklist of personal goals is presented that allows you to assess your own entrepreneurial tendencies. You can generate a similar set of personal strengths and weaknesses to let you see what skills you already have and what skills you should develop.

Attributes & goals of the entrepreneur

Along with entrepreneurial inclinations, you as an entrepreneur in the computer industry realize that the computer industry is different from many others. You either isolate yourself and your business from the trends in the industry or you must be able to deal with them. One important consideration is the computer industry itself (which is discussed in chapter 2). The most important element in your decision-making process is the set of personal goals that you possess. Your goals and objectives must be compatible with the goals of the business that you now run or will run. Your goals also must operate within the constraints of the computer industry.

What are the goals of an entrepreneur in the computer industry? They vary greatly from person to person. Here are some of the more common ones. Computer industry entrepreneurs might possess any of these goals.

Affect outcomes

Many people become entrepreneurs in the computer industry because they want to affect the outcome of events in their lives. The effect that you can have is certainly more pronounced when you run your own computer-based firm. With that ability comes responsibility. Because you have a great effect on the outcome, you become more responsible for it. If you are correct in your decision, you are a hero. If you are wrong, the effect you have could kill your business.

One division of my company moved information from one computer system to another. Within two years, that division saw its average contract value go from about $1000 per contract to $224 per contract (for the same amount of processing). As the service hit a break-even revenue stream (on reduced revenues), I saw a need to do one of two things: either innovate and change the business or harvest it before revenues fell to nothing.

I first tried to innovate with a dealer program. This action did not prop up prices in the market. Therefore, I made the decision to take the second path, quickly. To find a buyer, I searched for businesses for which this service would make strategic sense. Not able to find any, I quickly changed course to identify competition for the division. Only one competitor had any money to purchase the division, which told me that everyone had experienced the same decline in revenues. The message was clear: harvest quickly. I did and became a hero. Had I waited even two months longer, I doubt I would have done as well in the harvest path. I might have had to just kill that division and liquidate it for a fraction of what I received.

The lesson is simple. When you run your own business you can greatly affect its outcome. With this potential impact comes responsibility.

Desire to build something

If your goal is to build something, the computer industry might be just the place to do it. Much innovation takes place to allow you to build something. Build what, you ask? The number of employees in the firm? The revenues? The assets? Much of the time, the entrepreneur might focus only on one of these items. The classic example is the entrepreneur who boasts that he or she has fifty employees in the firm. A good response to this boast is, "Are you profitable? How profitable?" Another singular building goal is that of revenues. The entrepreneur who does $10 million per year in sales and loses $8 million on those revenues is certainly misdirected. And what about the entrepreneur who has $500,000 worth of computers? How profitable is the firm?

A better goal is to truly want to build long-term value for the firm. This goal can only be achieved with the assurance of long-term profitability of the firm. Some of the other benchmarks for building (number of employees, revenues, or assets) might be completely irrelevant if the underlying profitability and in turn, long-term value, are not there.

Desire to contribute to the world

You might believe that if you set up and run a business, you will be able to contribute to the betterment of the world. To the extent that you have customers and you add positively to their existence, you do contribute to the world. What the definition of *contribution* means to you will determine if you can, in your mind, contribute to the world. Do you want to contribute to the world or change it? There are very few people like Dan Bricklin, Steven Jobs, Bill Gates, and Mitch Kapor (apologies to the tens of people that are omitted). The real question to ask yourself (if you truly ask yourself how you can change the world) is "Do I have an idea for a service or technology for a product that can truly effect change?" If the answer is yes, then you might be able to change the world somehow. If the answer is no, you still might be able to add value to the world and leave a contribution through your business, even though you do not completely shape the way a market functions.

Ego gratification

You might want to start your firm strictly for ego gratification. It is quite a thrill to tell people that you run or own a company. They look upon you with a certain amount of respect and envy. Part of the American dream truly is to run your own show and be your own boss.

This goal can only take you so far. If other goals like building true long-term value are not met, ego gratification might diminish in importance to you.

Family

People also start businesses to build a family. Many people cannot quite understand this sentiment until they start their own firm. Owning a firm can satisfy the urge to have a child because you have already nurtured the growth of a family through your business. Especially in smaller firms, everyone really knows one another. When you work in a smaller firm, it isn't just a job for many of the employees. If you create the appropriate atmosphere, employees feel as if they are a real part of a family.

The corporate culture you create can allow you and your employees to have a lot of enrichment and gain a sense of family. But, you can also feel a great loss every time a family member departs (leaves the company). Be prepared!

Financial independence

If you are an entrepreneur, you feel you will have a greater chance to become financially independent than if you work for someone else. Remember that constraints exist on this notion. Someone asked me, before I formed my business, if I had ever met a payroll. I had not. He cautioned me about the impact a payroll would have on my life. He claimed that it would change it forever. Because I was somewhat naive, I didn't really believe him until I had the experience. In fact, beyond the payroll, I had to meet all of the fixed obligations of the business. I found out that you pay yourself after every other bill you have to pay is paid.

Along the journey of owning your own business, especially when cash is scarce (unless you've been fortunate to have a pile of it dumped upon you), the last thing that you might feel is financial independence. You worry so much about paying all of your bills (especially in the early stages of your business) that you might not have enough cash to pay yourself. Many entrepreneurs have gone without pay to keep our companies afloat and meet a payroll and other fixed costs. Is this financial independence? Hardly.

Where and how does the financial independence come? As you will learn in chapter 12, the independence comes in the form of one of the harvest alternatives. It might come when you are able to take out excess cash from the business or when you sell the entire business. As you read on, remember that financial independence doesn't just happen because you now run your own business. You must plan for it.

Independence from a boss

From the time when you were a child, you probably wanted to do things that your parents never allowed you to do. As you grew up, you learned more about elements of freedom, especially if you live in the United States. Individual freedom is a right of all Americans. Why, then, should you have someone (a boss) tell you what to do? Especially for a major part of your daily life (eight hours a day). Every person likes to do things in his or her own way. Therefore, in order to maximize the freedom you have "to do things your own way," you feel that independence from a boss who tells you what to do is an appropriate goal.

Although this is a commonly held belief, independence from a boss might lead you to other dependencies. You will find that your dependencies change to fit in with the stakeholders—people and organizations—that have an interest in your firm. Who are these stakeholders? For one, they are your employees. You will find that you constantly listen to your employees (as you should). You will realize two elements to this relationship:

- Your employees have good input into the growth of the firm. They give you cause to consider their words carefully. If your employees have functional skills that you might not have, you will listen to them and follow their direction, almost as if your life depended on it. (Isn't that what you wanted to get away from?) Because you will or do probably own a significant portion of your business, you now hang on your employees' every word to ensure your own success. After all, you never really knew a thing about accounting so you must trust your employee who is a certified public accountant.
- If you don't listen to your employees, they will not stay with you very long. You might now do things that you don't want to do (even more so than when you had a boss) because you are concerned that one or more of your employees might desert you if you don't heed their advice.

These examples don't necessarily have to happen the way that they are stated above. Remember that there are many other stakeholders who have a vested interest in the firm. These folks include your investors (if you've sold equity), your banker (if you've borrowed money), your key suppliers, your family (who now believe that they have an outlet for all of their pent-up entrepreneurial urges), and most important, your customers (who can put you out of business if you don't listen to them or give them what they want).

This goal of independence from a boss should be firmly assessed based on the type of job you presently have and the type of computer business you plan to build. You might be jumping from the frying pan into the fire.

Passion

Passion is a strength required among entrepreneurs. It is also a goal. If a love to do something is so strong, it can turn that action into a goal. You love to write software programs. You want to do it all day, but you can't find a job doing it. Passion might lead you to decide to venture out on your own to set up a programming company. As a goal, actualization of a passion can be a tremendous force to motivate you. Given you truly have talents in your arena of passion, you can ultimately be successful.

Unsubstantiated passion can be as devastating as a goal. If you love to write software but don't have any real programming skill, passion might not serve to help you achieve your goal. In fact, the lack of talent might leave you devastated.

Goals of entrepreneurs

To know more about your entrepreneurial goals, complete the following self-assessment. Rank your feelings about each goal from 1 through 10. A rank of 1 means the goal is not important to you; 5 means it is somewhat important; 10 means it is very important.

_____ Affect outcome
_____ Desire to build something
_____ Desire to contribute to world
_____ Ego gratification
_____ Family
_____ Financial independence
_____ Independence from a boss
_____ Passion

_____ Total

A score of 50 or above indicates that you are very entrepreneurial.

Managing your firm's resources

A lot of different skills are involved when you start and run a computer-based business. Accounting, financial, marketing, management and operational, people, and technical skills might all be required. Where can you find each of the needed skills, especially when you need them? There are several things to keep in mind when you deal with this issue.

Fundamentally, there are three resources of any firm. They are people, funds, and technology as shown in FIG. 1-1.

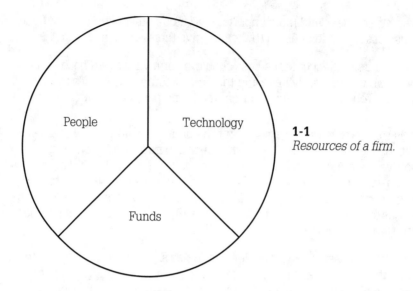

1-1
Resources of a firm.

People resources are those individuals involved in the firm and their skills. The skills people have are important but, so are their personalities, which includes their work ethic. People might be a valuable resource for the firm to give it comparative advantages over competition. People might also be a constraint to the firm if they don't offer what the firm needs.

Funds are the financial resources available to the firm. Everyone has unlimited wants with limited resources, no matter how large the resource base is. Thus, funds are generally viewed as a constraint, although they really are a firm's resource. If you understand that funds are truly a resource to be used wisely, then you can see their value to the firm.

Technology is also a resource of the firm. It includes plant and equipment in a large firm. As it relates to you, it is the computer that you are going to use in your business. It is an asset. Its strengths and capabilities can be viewed as resources and its limitations as constraints.

Any firm's combination of these resources makes up the whole pie. Each one of these resources interacts with the others. Recognize available resources and figure out how you can maximize their utility to the firm.

Often you do not know what resources are available to you because you might not fully understand their value. The best example is the root of your business: your computer. It is one technical resource of the firm. Did you know that you could use it to compose music, to sew, to run your VCR (video-cassette recorder)? Obviously, you are reading this book to learn more about different ways you can use your computer to make money. If you are mindful of all of its uses (and its constraints), you will be able to take full advantage of it. This is true with the people and funds involved in the firm. Fully understand both, and you will be able to take full advantage of them.

People have different sets of skills that can be helpful to your business at different times. How well you understand these skills influences how well you can bring each skill to bear when needed by your business. Naturally, you might have some or many of these skills. And you might be able to satisfy the needs of the business in these areas. The key, though, is to keep in mind your *highest and best use* as well as other people.

Highest and best use can mean one of three things. It can mean that you look at the skills of each person and determine what each can do best. You then have them do these things. The second definition of highest and best use can be what a person wants or likes to do. These tasks might not necessarily be what the person is best at doing, but what he or she likes doing best. The third definition relates to what a person might be needed to do most, even though this is not where his or her skills or interests lie. You need to determine which definition you should choose and for how long. To arrive at a decision, determine what types of skills people have that might be their highest and best use to you. These skills are discussed in the following paragraphs.

Accounting skills refer to how well you can manipulate the numbers that go into the underlying financial information in the firm. Bookkeeping is an accounting skill.

Accounting skills

Financial skills should be differentiated from accounting skills. Financial skills are the ones related to the ability to manage money. To determine when you pay bills, when you borrow money, and when you raise equity, you use financial skills.

Financial skills

Management skills relate to a general ability to manage. Management is rooted in an understanding of the needs of the organization as well as the resources available and not available. Maneuvering the resources of the firm and obtaining those not available are keys to successful management.

Management skills

Marketing skills are the understanding of the market and how to reach the market successfully. Marketing issues that require marketing skills include: Who and where is the market? How large is the market? Who are the competitors? How do you design your product? How do you price, promote, and distribute your product?

Marketing skills

Operational skills are involved at the nuts-and-bolts level of the firm. Running the firm's daily activities and operational processes requires operational skills.

Operational skills

People skills Individuals who have an ability to understand and direct people have *people skills*. Everyone has some degree of people skills. People who can understand individuals and convince others to do what is needed are the ones who have a high degree of people skills.

Selling skills *Selling skills* should not be confused with marketing skills. Selling is the art of convincing someone to buy something. A selling strategy is a part of a marketing plan. It doesn't take selling skills to develop a marketing plan. Nor does it take marketing skills to implement a selling strategy. In order to have good selling skills, you must:

- Understand the product or service that you are selling
- Understand the needs and wants of the potential customer
- Understand how to satisfy the needs and wants of the potential customer with the product or service offered
- Understand how to convince the potential customer to purchase the product or service

Selling takes place at a micro level with a specific client or customer. Marketing involves issues that multiple clients or customers face.

Technical skills *Technical skills* are what you think of when someone has learned a trade. If you are an engineer, you have engineering technical skills. If you are a computer scientist, you have computer-based technical skills. Someone has technical skills if he or she has gone to a trade or professional school to acquire them. Technical skills might be acquired on the job or can be self-taught. Technical skills are skills that someone has in a specific functional area that somehow involves technology.

You must know what skills you have, where your highest and best use is to the firm, and where, when and how you should bring other skills to it. This art is often tempered by the available financial resources of the firm. After all, if you can't afford the resources, you might have to get them in other ways. Financial, technological, and people resources must be kept in a proper balance based on the needs of the firm, or the firm won't grow properly. As a present or potential entrepreneur in the computer industry, you will recognize this fact and be aware of how you fit into this mix. One way to understand how you fit into the mix is to understand your own strengths and weaknesses.

Skills To evaluate your skills, complete the following self-assessment. Rank your feelings about each skill from 1 through 10. A rank of 1 means you feel you are not very strong in this skill; 5 means you have an average capability in the skill; 10 means you have strength in this skill.

_____ Accounting skills
_____ Financial skills

_____ Management skills
_____ Marketing skills
_____ Operational skills
_____ People skills
_____ Selling skills
_____ Technical skills

A score of 7 or greater on any attribute is probably a skill area where you should focus your efforts. For those attributes where you rank less than 7, find a way to enhance your understanding of these areas and have someone else oversee them.

Common attributes of entrepreneurs are described in the following paragraphs. These attributes can be either strengths or weaknesses. Read each description and determine which apply to you.

Common attributes

Hands-on nature

If you prefer a hands-on approach in those areas where you either excel or are needed to fill gaps within your company, this characteristic is a strength. If you are superficially aware of all elements of the business and how they function, then again this characteristic might be a strength. If you are so detail-oriented that you practically have to do everything yourself, you can hinder the way your company functions. If you are so involved in everything that goes on with the business, no one else will feel as if they can play any part in it. As a consequence, they might decide not to play. The nature of being a hands-on person is a balancing act. How far you go is dependent on the resources available to your company as well as your own personal functional strengths.

One of the guys

Being "one of the guys" can foster a spirit of camaraderie. If your company is small, it can probably accept this behavior. If your company is larger (more than 10 employees), you might not always be able to be one of the guys. Your company will require leadership that can't always be achieved with a one of the guys attitude. Sometimes a boss has to be a boss, not one of the guys.

Withdrawn

If you are withdrawn and are good at tasks that can be completed by someone who is withdrawn, you might be able to run a successful company. You will need to employ people who can come forward with the needed cheerleading and promotion. Software programmers are often withdrawn. They might be shy or dislike dealing with people. Your choice, should you fall into this category, is not only to have someone serve as your front, but work on the reasons why you are withdrawn. You might want to change them so that you can come out of your shell.

Ability to follow   You can still be an entrepreneur and be a follower. You might need to hire a person who can lead the troops when necessary (unless you decide to employ only one person—yourself).

Argumentative   A person who is argumentative without foundation is annoying. Arguing is a vehicle to persuade people to see your point of view. If you argue without cause, it is generally apparent that you are argumentative. It will probably not get you where you want to go, unless the other side is so annoyed that you can wear them down.

Cheerleading ability   If an entrepreneur is a good cheerleader, he or she has a good chance of building morale among the troops. If the idea or company is so strong that the market creates momentum, then this skill is not as critical. In most instances, the market is not a strong enough force to boost the spirits of employees to the high level that they can feel from an enthusiastic leader. If your personality is not that of a cheerleader, you might want to either hire someone who is, send your people to seminars that boost morale, or bring in other entrepreneurs who are cheerleaders to help you rally the squad.

Commitment   Commitment is absolutely necessary for success, especially in an entrepreneurial pursuit in the computer industry. You can't enter into something as a part-time pursuit and expect it to succeed. An entrepreneurial venture needs the nurturing that you would give to a young child to develop properly. Just as you can't be a part-time parent, you can't be a part-time entrepreneur.

Too much commitment can also be detrimental. When I founded my first business, I was working twenty hour days. An average work week was one hundred hours. I was crazed by my company! In fact, I worked such long hours that I sacrificed some very important things: sleep, exercise, and outside interests. Sleep is necessary. It wasn't until I was so exhausted and I almost ended up in the hospital that I realized that I had to sleep. Sometimes you can become so committed to a cause that you forget about food and exercise. I didn't sacrifice food. In fact, I used food to keep myself going, especially coffee (and anything that contained large amounts of sugar). Many entrepreneurs do sacrifice food and lose weight. Neither extreme is good. Exercise is important to keep your body and mind physically fit. A fit body helps to make a fit mind. Physical conditioning can extend your level of commitment. Outside interests can give you a renewed perspective on your own business. They, too, are necessary for the entire mix needed to maintain your commitment. Commitment, just like the other attributes, must be kept in balance. The balance relates to your own abilities as well as the needs of the business.

Confidence

Confidence is always a strength. The only time it isn't a strength is if it turns into cockiness, which is a negative quality in any pursuit where other people are involved. Quiet confidence is an attribute that leaves the one who possesses it an admired individual.

Consensus-building ability

A peacemaker's trait is that of consensus building. If people agree on an idea, then they will support it. Sometimes, building a consensus on some items might be near impossible. If consensus can't be built, nothing happens in the interim, and the organization might suffer as a result.

Creativity

Creativity is another invaluable strength of an entrepreneur. If you see a lemon and are creative, you will be able to figure out how to make lemonade. If you look at an opportunity in a creative fashion, you might create an entirely new market niche. Paraphrasing Robert Kennedy, "Some people see things as they are and say why? I dream dreams that never were and say, why not?" This thought applies to you if you are capable of dreaming. Creative dreaming must be tempered with reality. If you are creative and fabricate a fantasy, your creative value will end up having little value. Dream, but keep your feet on the ground.

Impatience

Impatience can be a strength or a weakness. If impatience is used as a tool to get a job done quickly and well, it definitely can be a strength. If impatience causes you to do a task in a shoddy fashion to get that task done quickly, it can be a weakness. If you stand over your employees in order to speed them up, impatience is again a weakness. If you can use your impatience to instill a sense of urgency in your employees, it can be a strength.

Insecurity

Insecurity can work for or against you. The insecure entrepreneur who works hard to compensate for the perceived or real deficiencies can end up a much stronger person. This person often has much more to offer the firm as a result of working on these weaknesses. The openly insecure person who never overcomes any perceived or real deficiencies can truly mar the reputation of the firm. If you are insecure, try to understand why you are insecure and address the underlying reasons in order to overcome them. Turn your weaknesses into strengths.

Leadership

Leadership is an invaluable management skill. Getting people to follow your direction can help you build a loyal and dedicated team who can and will want to get the job done for you. Are leaders born? To a certain extent, yes. But if you are capable of seizing control over a situation, truly rising to the occasion, you can become a leader. Leadership is a trait that is not around for a fleeting moment. To use leadership to its fullest extent, you need to be able to endure time.

Leveraging financial resources

Leveraging financial resources is another skill that, if practiced prudently, can be invaluable. You must know how far to go. If you go too far, you can jeopardize the health of your firm. If you don't use this concept at all, you might not take advantage of all of the resources to maximize the return you get from your organization. Leveraging is very often in the form of *bootstrapping* or, as my grandmother used to say, "doing it on a straw."

The concept of *bootstrapping* is marvelous. You start with nothing and somehow build a real asset base. My grandfather started his bootstrapping by telling one art dealer that he believed he could sell one of his paintings. The art dealer would then give it to my grandfather to sell on consignment. My grandfather would then walk practically next door and sell that painting to another art dealer for an increased price. My grandfather had nothing to begin with and something (money) after the transaction was completed. This leveraging occurred through his creative thinking. This concept is also referred to as using OPM (other people's money). Who took all the risk in the transaction just described? The art dealer from whom my grandfather got the painting. My grandfather used this art dealer's money (the collateral tied up in the painting) to make a profit for himself. If this concept is taken too far, you won't be perceived as a straightforward player. The key is to understand the concept and practice it in moderation.

Logical thinking

Logical thinking is beneficial. If you can logically reason through a problem, it works to your advantage. You can use this skill to do such things as outsmart a competitor or decide when is the best time to buy a second computer system. There really is no substitute for good logical reasoning.

Motivation

Motivation is an attribute closely related to your commitment to do something. If you are committed to your business, you are generally motivated on its behalf.

Multiple talents

If you are multi-talented, you can do a lot of things well. If you use this skill to judge other people who work for you, this ability is then a strength. If you are multi-talented and use this capability to fill in when necessary in the organization, this is a strength. If you interfere with the way that people do their jobs because you feel that you can do them better, you might run into problems.

Opportunity-sensing ability

The ability to sense opportunities is critical to success. A good entrepreneur will take a lemon and squeeze it, making lemonade. Creativity is key for sniffing out opportunities. Look at things differently than someone else has, and you might find great success. Consider Fred Smith with his hub setup for Federal Express. By sending all packages through his Memphis processing center, Mr. Smith exerted much more control and expedience over his shipments and created a billion-dollar corporation. Sensing opportunities does not have to be this grand in order to be successful. If you live in an area of the country where people admire embroidery and want to get personalized embroidered items, why not seize that opportunity and set up a facility to create embroidery through a computerized process? It's a small, yet potentially successful, way to sense an opportunity and succeed.

Passion is a strength because it can serve as a tremendous driving force to achieve something. The old cliché, "If you truly enjoy something, you'll do well at it" is certainly rooted in reality. Don't do something just for money. If you do, and you don't enjoy what you are doing, you are limiting your chances of success. Conversely, if you are blinded by your passion, you might also be jeopardizing yourself. You might become so enamored by something that you might no longer be able to see its flaws.

Passion

People skills are always a strength. As you have read, managing people is one third of the resource management equation. This strength should never be underestimated.

People skills

Perception is one of the most valuable strengths of an entrepreneur, especially in the computer market. The more you can perceive about the market, your people, and your clients, the better off you will be. Being perceptive leads to understanding a situation more completely. If you are perceptive and use the information you glean to take appropriate actions, you can develop tremendous advantages in the market. This might include making your clients happy, keeping your employees employed, and your company focused on the correct market opportunities. If you are perceptive and don't translate it into action, you will lose the impact of your skill. If you are perceptive, act on your knowledge.

Perception

Persuasiveness is always a strength. Getting internal and external stakeholders of your firm to see and follow your point of view can help you get what you want.

Persuasiveness

Promotional ability doesn't mean you are the *Music Man* type but that you can encourage sales and financial investment. If a promoter has no substance, he or she is generally viewed as a fraud. Over time, people will realize this fact. If the promoter has substance, he or she is generally viewed as a good salesman.

Promotional ability

Being a quick thinker can work both as an advantage and a disadvantage. If you are a thorough quick thinker, you can leave the competition behind. If you are an incomplete quick thinker, you might do something that is detrimental to the firm. Analyze where you fit in.

Quick thinking

Risk-taking ability

Willingness to take risks is one of the keys to entrepreneurship. Do you have the guts to take the first risk? Do you have the knowledge and sense to minimize all risks after the first risk (of launching the business), yet maximizing the value of your business? Risk taking, albeit a constant undertaking, is not as scary as you might think it is. To continue with the job that you dislike, you actually take a much bigger risk with your life than if you leave it and start a company to do something that you love. After all, passion to do something is one of the most critical success factors.

Sense of urgency

An entrepreneur almost always has a great sense of urgency. Although this trait might look a lot like impatience, it is not.

Speaking ability

If you are a speaker, you can use this vehicle as a means to get the word out about yourself. Again, the "good" speaker will have substance and add credibility to the firm. The "bad" speaker will lack substance and have the same effect that the superficial promoter has on the firm.

Steadfastness

Steadfastness is often associated with being stubborn. The line is certainly a fine one. A steadfast personality who is completely uncompromising will probably have a hard time, over time, getting a spirit of cooperation from other individuals. Knowing when to compromise and when to be steadfast will allow you to get what you want to get most often. Balance is key in this attribute.

Team-building ability

Team builders are generally good managers. They want many people to be in on the act to ensure a greater amount of success. This strategy also diversifies the people resources so that an organization is not overly dependent on one individual.

Thoroughness

Thoroughness is good if not taken to excess. Some people are so thorough that it either takes them forever to make a decision or they never reach one. Either way, it is no good to the organization. If your decision-making process is too delayed, it might interfere with an opportunity that you have available to you. Time is a key element in today's competitive environment. If you are tardy, you might lose an opportunity. Thoroughness can be a strength in that you might be able to avoid opportunities that don't make sense and find new ones that do.

Vision

Vision is extremely important in the computer industry. With the short product life cycles of both products and services, you have to know what your next move will be. If you have a vision of where your particular segment of the computer business is going, this vision can help you direct your business. If you understand trends in the industry, you can be there ready and waiting for them to hit. Acting too soon, though, can be detrimental to your business. Vision must be tempered with market realities. You might have thought that in 1993 your high-resolution television yielded the best possible picture, and it might have done so. You also have to take into consideration that the market reality is that United States broadcasting cannot yet take advantage of your improved picture quality. Vision must be tempered by reality. The real skill is turning your vision into market realities.

A good working knowledge of technology is definitely a strength. Understanding yet another resource of the firm can only bode well. In even the largest of computer firms, the president should still understand the underlying technology. This understanding will lead to new, creative ways to apply it.

Technological knowledge

If an entrepreneur is a writer, he or she can use this skill as a valuable promotional tool for the business. If you are not a writer, you might want to find yourself a *ghost writer* (someone who can write for you) because writing can be one of the most credible promotional tools. For some strange reason, most people believe what they read in print. If it weren't valid, how could it pass muster through an editorial staff? Writing to the exclusion of doing, though, can be detrimental to the performance of your business, unless your business is writing. You must strike some balance between writing and doing.

Writing ability

To evaluate those attributes than can be either strengths or weaknesses, complete the following self-assessment. Check all attributes that apply. The intent of this assessment is to give you a clearer perspective of the type of person you are. Be honest with yourself!

Attributes

_____ Hands-on nature
_____ One of the guys
_____ Withdrawn
_____ Ability to follow
_____ Argumentative
_____ Cheerleading ability
_____ Commitment
_____ Confidence
_____ Consensus-building ability
_____ Creativity
_____ Impatience
_____ Insecurity
_____ Leadership
_____ Leveraging financial resources
_____ Logical thinking
_____ Motivation
_____ Multiple talents
_____ Opportunity-sensing ability
_____ Passion

_____ People skills
_____ Perception
_____ Persuasiveness
_____ Promotional ability
_____ Quick thinking
_____ Risk-taking ability
_____ Sense of urgency
_____ Speaking ability
_____ Steadfastness
_____ Team building ability
_____ Thoroughness
_____ Vision
_____ Technological knowledge
_____ Writing ability

Conclusion

Entrepreneurs have many attributes, as does any subset of the population. Depending on the type of business you are running, different strengths and weaknesses will matter less or more. Pick a business to run that is compatible with your goals, harnesses your strengths, and doesn't suffer from your weaknesses.

2 Entrepreneurship & the PC industry

In order to understand attributes of an entrepreneur in the computer industry, you must first understand the computer industry. The computer industry is one of the most dynamic industries in today's marketplace. With the innovation that takes place daily, many patterns and issues arise. Some of the most important attributes of the PC industry are:

- Rapid change
- Short development horizons
- Need for quality products and services
- Short product life cycles
- Constant innovation

The computer industry encompasses so many different products and services that it is nearly impossible to explain them all. The industry changes so rapidly that between the time of writing and printing this book, the computer industry will have changed a multitude of times.

The fundamental root of the computer industry is the computer. As *The Computer Dictionary* by Charles J. Sippl and Roger J. Sippl (Howard W. Sains & Co., Inc., Indianapolis, IN) defines it, the computer is "a device capable of accepting information, applying prescribed processes to the information, and supplying the results of these processes. It usually consists of input and output devices, storage, arithmetic and logical units, and a control unit." The computer is analogous to your brain in that it accepts information, processes it, and supplies the results of the processing.

In the computer industry today, all of the devices used in processing are constantly being enhanced. Today, the industry sees new processing chips that serve as critical components to the CPU (central processing unit) such as the Pentium 586, Motorola 68040 and Power PC chips. Optical disk storage is a reality, and experiments with light/color storage continue. Enhanced input/output devices speed processing of information.

The intent of this book is not to reiterate trends in the computer industry today. The popular trade press serves this role. Rather, this book is intended to help you understand general components of the industry that remain constant from product to product and service to service over time. The understanding will help you deal with any product or service that you might encounter.

Development cycle

Before what is commonly recognized as the introductory phase of a product life cycle (the introduction of the product to the market), the product must go from idea to reality. This development process can take minutes for simple service-based businesses to years for technically complex products. Until there is a readied product, though, the market-based product life cycle doesn't officially begin.

In the computer industry, development must proceed completely, from a quality standpoint, and swiftly.

Completeness

If a product is incomplete when it is introduced in the marketplace, it will appear to be riddled with what are commonly called *bugs*, a term that originated when the first computer—the ENIAC computer at the University of Pennsylvania—became inhabited by a moth. The moth caused the computer to malfunction and it wasn't until the system was *debugged* that it worked properly again. If the product is software and one of the lines of code causes the computer system to crash, the software must be debugged to solve this problem. A board assembled with a new computer chip burns out after 12 hours of continuous use. The new chip is isolated to be the problem. Then, a new chip must either be used in place of this one, or this new chip must be repaired. A peripheral device, such as a computer printer, is introduced into the market. It was only tested with one type of microcomputer. If it is to be used with other types of microcomputers, it must be thoroughly tested with them to determine performance standards. If, after thorough testing, it only works with one brand of microcomputer, that fact must be advertised. Or, the computer printer must be reconfigured to enable it to work with a host of different microcomputers.

Quality is another extremely important point to be considered in the development process. You build a microcomputer that has latches to hold the chassis together. These latches fall apart after you've opened the system five times. Your latch quality isn't good enough for general market use. If you make a computer case whose zipper breaks after 17 uses, you've got a quality problem. If you run a desktop publishing service that creates output only on a low-quality printer, you've got a quality problem. All products or services you develop must be able to withstand all market tests of endurance.

A good test of quality is to include, as a part of the development cycle, something called *alpha* and *beta* testing. *Alpha* testing might be no more than concept testing, especially in service-based businesses. Is the service a valid service? One good way to perform this concept test is to put together a simplified example or prototype of the service or product. At this point, you think that the product or service will appear as you've shaped it. You are using modeling clay to create it. If you are incorrect as to its attributes, you can change them through remodeling. Had you built this alpha prototype out of concrete at this stage, it would not be malleable. Because it is malleable, you can shape it into a product or service based on what the market wants.

Once you've remodeled the initial thoughts behind the product or service, you can go into further development. When you feel that the product or service works, yet still needs some refinement, you probably have a product or service ready for beta testing. *Beta* testing uses a working example to refine its attributes. In the alpha test, you defined the attributes of a product or service. Here, you have defined the attributes and you are simply refining them based on the market testing of the product or service. You should take all feedback into account. Feedback includes comments such as "yes it works" as well as "yes these are the attributes that I feel should be included."

The amount of effort involved in the development process should relate to the degree of complexity in your product or service. The more straightforward a product or service, the less effort required to develop it. Effort should also correlate quite closely with time you have available.

If you ensure that you have a quality product or service, through these correct development steps, you have a much greater chance for market success.

Swiftness, speed, and time are all really the same thing. There is a tremendous amount of competitive pressure in the computer industry. The advantages go to not only the more complete, high-quality product or service but to those that reach the market first. You, as a consumer, want a résumé printed immediately. It will take one day for a service to typeset and print it. With a one-day delay, you might lose out on the job opportunity advertised in this morning's paper. In contrast, you go to a competing résumé service. They can produce a high-quality résumé for you while you wait. You will patronize the second service, even if it costs more than the first. This second résumé service has found a way to reduce time involved in its process. In today's fast-paced environment, time reduction creates a competitive advantage.

On May 10, 1993, WordPerfect announced that its product will run on the Apple Macintosh Power PC implementation at the release date. This will give WordPerfect a first-mover advantage, it hopes, over all other competition. This way, WordPerfect hopes to gain a predominant market share on the Power PC platform, because it acted more rapidly than others.

Product life cycle

Once you've gone through the development process and you feel confident that you have a product or service that is complete, you can then take it to market. One of the biggest issues that you must face in the computer industry is the length of time a product or service lives in the marketplace. This life is commonly referred to as the *product life cycle* (this expression also is applicable to service-based businesses). Here again, speed plays a vital role in the product market life. In the computer industry, because of the great amounts of innovation, the time that a product lives is very short, especially in relation to technical products. Technology is quickly replaced by new technology.

This product life cycle begins with its introduction into the market. At introduction, the product is not known nor has it generated any revenues. For it to succeed, people must be aware of a product or service in order to buy it. The ultimate level of awareness that you must create is with the end consumer. For the consumer to find out about a product or service, word must get out that it does exist. Word of mouth is the most effective means of communicating the attributes and benefits of a product or service. Time, again, becomes a consideration in reaching everyone in the target market. How quickly can the word be spread? Obviously, the faster, the better.

Once the product or service has been introduced, people who try it first are the innovators. Even if the product or service is thought of as a low-risk product or service, people like to stay with the status quo. Generally they like to buy what they think are low-risk or safe purchases.

It is not until a fair number of people feel that the purchase decision for a product is safe that the market begins to accept it. Once this happens, though, you see the second phase of the product life cycle begin to emerge. This stage is commonly referred to as the *growth phase*. During the growth phase, sales of the product or service begin to increase. More acceptance of the product is seen. It is less of a risk to purchase.

After a while, all of those people who want to try the product or service have probably tried it. The third phase of the product life cycle, the *maturity phase*, begins. Growth in sales peaks and then sales begin to level off. A majority of people who were interested in purchasing have probably done so by now.

Finally, demand for the product or service will begin to decline. The market will have been satisfied and demand will no longer remain constant. It will dwindle. This phase of the product life cycle is called the *decline phase*. The product life cycle is shown in FIG. 2-1.

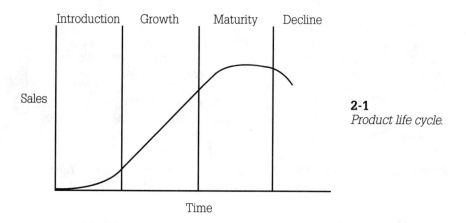

2-1
Product life cycle.

Product or service pricing in each of these phases correlates to the phase itself. It also relates to competitive forces. In the introductory phase, especially for a new product, you might be able to command premium prices for the product because of lack of competition. As demand grows, the price will probably decline, especially as new entrants appear in the market. Price as a function of time in the product life cycle is shown in FIG. 2-2.

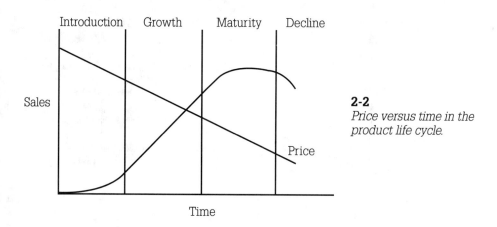

2-2
Price versus time in the product life cycle.

A key element of success in the computer market is an understanding of where you are in the life cycle of a product or service so that you can determine what actions to take. Actions might be pricing decisions (for example, lower prices) or product or service innovations (for example, a competitor has just added sound capabilities to its word processing program that could reduce the amount of life that you have left in the product life cycle unless you can meet or beat this competitive action).

Time is critical in the product life cycle because so many innovations take place so rapidly in the computer industry.

Dependencies

There are many dependencies for products and services in the computer industry. These dependencies have a direct impact on the product or service competitive position as well as its place in the product life cycle. Some examples will help illustrate these impacts.

You write a macro to execute accounting functions for sailboat businesses. You write this macro to run with Lotus Improv. Your dependencies take on the profile seen in FIG 2-3.

Specific product dependency   **General level of product dependency**

Sailboat accounting	Application macro
Lotus Improv	Application
Program language	Program language
MS-DOS	Operating system
Pentium-586 based microcomputer	Hardware platform

2-3
Product dependencies in the computer industry.

Sailboat Accounting has four levels of dependencies. From the top level down, Sailboat Accounting depends upon Lotus Improv. Sailboat Accounting drives a Lotus Improv operation, and as such, depends on Improv. Improv depends on the program language in which it was written. The program language depends on the operating system in which it was written. Finally, the operating system is dependent upon the hardware platform, the Pentium 586-based microcomputer.

This example shows how fragile these layers become, especially when you have greater number of dependencies involved. If any one of the layers should change, it can affect any of the layers above it. Therefore, if the MS-DOS operating system should change, it could impact on the programming language in which Improv was written, Improv itself, and Sailboat Accounting. Obviously, the more layers on which your product or service rests, the more sensitive it is to change. This sensitivity is an example of a technical dependency.

A second type of dependency is market dependency. This market dependency, though, is inextricably linked to a technical dependency.

Just as Sailboat Accounting is layered, technically, these layers affect the market dependencies. If Lotus Improv doesn't sell, Sailboat Accounting won't sell. The more layers on which you rest, the more sensitive you are to market issues at these layers.

Conclusion

To be successful in the computer industry, you need to recognize technical and market dependencies. You need to understand how short product life cycles create a continuous need to innovate with more development. And you must understand how the development horizon must be short, complete, and of the highest quality. All of these factors are interrelated. To run a business in the computer industry, you must be nimble enough to change course whenever you spot a shift in the course of the market. Along with being nimble, you should have an ability to provide the innovation required to satisfy the market shifts as quickly as humanly possible. This process is continuous. You might guess right once and head down a path successfully for a period of time. Yet, the dynamic marketplace in the computer industry demands that you must shift course and innovate again and again and again. Do you have the skills necessary for the journey?

3 Good PC-based businesses

If you are planning to open a PC-based business, look for the following characteristics. Your chance of success is greater if you find a business with many or all of these characteristics.

- A business that interests you
- A definable product or service
- Easily identifiable customers
- A growing market
- Easily reachable customers
- A product or service with a competitive advantage
- A business you can run
- A business that has few identifiable roadblocks
- A business that you can fund
- A business where technology is available to you

To determine if a PC-based business is a good one, you need to figure out the suitability of the business to you, the market, the proposed operation you're putting together, as well as your available financial resources. In essence, you must be able to appropriately screen opportunities to decide the one which is most appropriate for you.

To screen PC-based businesses, you need to ask some fundamental questions.

Does the business interest you?   You must be honest with yourself. Is this a business in which you want to be actively involved? Often, opportunities look appealing because of some ridiculous factor, like money. Don't be attracted to a business strictly because you think you can make a lot of money. If you are not interested in the business, you won't do well, the business won't do well, and you probably won't make money. Be driven by your passion to do something and you will perform well at it.

What will you sell?   When you've identified a business that interests you, you must clearly define the company's offering. The product or service must have bounds. The bounds are necessary for both your focus and your customers' understanding. If you consult, what type of services do you offer? If you program, what markets do you serve with what program languages? If you sell software, do you sell software you've created or are you a remarketer of other developers' products? Clarify your vision of your product or service. It makes it much easier to identify your customers.

Who are your customers?   The customers are the people or businesses to whom you want to sell your product or service—your target market. As an example, in a computerized payroll service, the target market is business owners, payroll department managers, controllers, and chief financial officers of firms, depending on the size of the corporation. If the company is small, your target market is probably a business owner. As the firm increases in size, you can move through the above list until you reach the chief financial officers in the firm.

If you misdefine the target market, you will never be able to reach the people who want your product or service. One way to define the market is to survey the market you think is the target market. Ask questions, via a mail, telephone or in-person questionnaire, to determine if it is your target market. Don't be shy about this survey; you can get valuable information from people. More frequently than not, they are quite willing to share it with you.

How do you know if you've properly defined the target market? If you have surveyed those who you believe to be the target market and you get a positive response about your product or service, you can guess that you have defined the market correctly. If you get no positive reactions, you probably have not defined it correctly; you should reconsider the target market's definition.

How many customers are there?   Are customers increasing in number? Once you've defined the target market, you should assess its size. If the market size isn't large enough to support your business, you don't want to spend the time pursuing it. For example, you determine there is a market for computer-based embroidery. After surveying 1,000 potential customers, you discover that only one is interested in the product. You don't have a large enough customer base to make the opportunity appealing. If you survey the market and discover that there are enough customers to support your business, that's fine for now. But will they still be there tomorrow? And will there be as many tomorrow as today? You want a growing number of customers. You can often tell if the market is growing by an increase in the number of competitors. Go to the yellow pages in old telephone books and look up the category of your company. Follow the chronology from an early telephone book to present. If you find an increase in the number of companies that serve the market, you can bet that the market is growing. There is, though, a potential that the businesses are all on the brink of disaster. Check out the competition thoroughly.

Where do you find customers?   Once you've defined your target market and assessed its size, it should be easy to find them because you know who they are. If you've defined them within a geographic boundary, you can use telephone books to locate them. If you've isolated them to specific industry segments (for example, candy manufacturers), you can use sources like the *Thomas' Register* (available in most libraries) to find them. Depending on how specialized your market segment is, you can go to trade associations. They often sell their membership lists. You can even contact mailing list brokers who sell lists with almost any criteria you establish.

How do you get your message out?   Reaching customers can be another story. You have to ensure that you know the proper promotional channels that will reach them. In order to figure them out, you need to understand your customers.

Where do customers look to purchase?   Ask your potential customers, as a part of your survey, where they look when they want to purchase your service. Do they look in the newspaper, do they look in the yellow pages, do they ask a friend, or what? Then, when you tally the responses, you will know where to place your emphasis.

What do customers read?   If you understand what they read, you can either place advertisements in these publications or write editorial copy for them. You will be amazed at how starved for copy most trade publications are—you can write articles, even get paid for them, and raise the level of awareness of your product or service.

Are telephone calls effective?   Are customers inundated with telephone calls or do they like them? How many times have you received a telephone solicitation? Although these solicitations can be annoying if performed incorrectly, they can be one of the most cost-effective ways to reach a potential customer. Call early or late in the day if you want to reach someone at their office. They are often in and more relaxed because the hectic pace hasn't yet begun. I often call people at the Pentagon at 6:30 A.M.

If your target market is the government, as an example, some employees don't like telephone calls but they do enjoy visitors. If you want to do business with these folks, you'll have to visit them.

Is direct mail effective?   Direct mail, along with direct telephone solicitation, can be a very effective channel. Yet, the channel is so effective that many use it. Unless you can somehow distinguish yourself from the other mail, people will not read it. Can you create a floppy disk with an advertisement on it that people will want to pop in their computer? Can you produce a videotape that people will view in their VCRs? Determine if the business can differentiate itself using direct mail.

Who are your competitors?   You should understand who is your direct and indirect competition. Direct competition is a firm that offers the same exact service or product that you offer. Indirect competition offers a product or service that is competitive to your offering but not exactly the same. For example, a word processing service bureau's direct competition is another word processing service bureau. An indirect competitor is an individual who is capable of doing his or her own typing. You should assess your competition and make certain decisions. First, you should decide if there is room for another competitor. Secondly, you should determine the competitive strengths and weaknesses of your direct and indirect competition and decide if you can compete against them. These strengths and weaknesses include financial, technological, and people resources. You need to ask questions like, "can a competitor or competitors react so quickly and so well as to make the business opportunity unattractive?" Does the competitor have some type of proprietary technology or process whereby there is great value to what they have?

What are your advantages over competition?   You need to assess how your product or service is better than the competition. Can you deliver a better product at a lower price in less time? Can you deliver a product that can completely change the industry? Did you hear about the business that can produce and sell a battery that will let an electric car run 1,000 miles on a single charge? And take a nanosecond to recharge? And be completely recycling? This business opportunity has the potential to completely restructure the way the industry is now functioning. Very few businesses actually have this type of potential, though. Although rare, if you can gain this type of competitive advantage, you can truly own the market.

What talents will you need?   Carefully determine the special skills that are required to run the business. Make sure that these skills can not only be covered, initially in your business, but on a continuous basis. And at a price that is affordable to the business. One of my businesses used to require people to understand a host of computer platforms (for example, Apple, DEC, HP, IBM, and Wang). The business required an understanding of many of these platforms. It was easy to find people who understood one platform.

Finding someone who understood a second platform got a little harder. The third became much more difficult. Even if these people understood a host of platforms initially, ensuring that they wanted to keep up with each platform was another thing altogether.

If you can't easily find or train people with the appropriate skills to run your business, the task of running the company can become very difficult.

Who should you hire? Management is the most necessary element to running a business. You need the right people for the business opportunity. If you don't have the right people resources, making an operation run can be very difficult. People who fund companies are enamored with stating that the three critical success factors in any firm are management, management, and management. These same folks are often quoted as saying that it is better to have a good management team implement a bad idea than to have a good idea implemented by a bad management team. The proper team for the company is absolutely critical.

Who is necessary and when they are necessary are important questions. Not only should you be sure that you have people involved in the business when you need them, but you should also make sure that you don't have incorrect people on the team "just because." An example is the business that is formed in the bar room with all of your buddies. Your buddies might have completely inappropriate skills but "just because" they were there, they were included in the team.

When to hire people is another question. When you need someone on a short-term basis or if you are uncertain as to what the future might bring, you might want to hire someone as an independent contractor. Independent contractors are not employees, but they do work for you on contract. Only when you see that you pay them as much as you would if they were a salaried employee, should you consider bringing them on board.

How will the business run? You need to look at all of the different operational facets of the business to see what is necessary. Every business produces something. A service business provides a service. A product business produces a product. What will it take to optimally complete this production? Can you use the people, funds and technology that you have in-house or should you subcontract a portion of the process? Subcontracting might be the best way to handle your process on an ongoing basis, as long as you can put the proper controls in place to ensure that you get the needed quality to be competitive in the marketplace.

An example of subcontracting is found with a product produced by one of my firms, Milestone Planning for Successful Ventures™. We developed, internally, design specifications for the product and subcontracted the Macintosh and Windows development. The contractors are both top-notch programmers in these environments. Once given a completed product (which was quality controlled), we took the rough copy of the manual to an individual who specialized in writing and refining computer manuals. Once given a final manual, we completed a quality control evaluation of it. We needed to create proper packaging and graphic designs for the product so we licensed the product to another company and let them do it. Our license agreement requires this firm to sell a certain amount of the product each year. For this right, the licensee pays my company a fee.

Analyze what it will take to have the business produce the product or service the way you want it to. Figure out what you want and can do. Assess the profitability of each step that you undertake and compare self performance to subcontracting. Don't forsake quality. Optimize on the self-performance and subcontracting mix.

Part of the production is technology support. Technology support capability is the ability to maintain, support and develop the existing technology needed to be and remain competitive in the market. If you've outlined the needed technology support for the business but can't afford it, that might not necessarily mean that there isn't a fit. Here, again, you might be able to find a way to subcontract for the needed technical resources if they are not presently available to you.

What are the potential roadblocks?   What are all of the risks that you face if you are to start this business? Here it is good to go through the market, operational, management, financial, political and social risks that surround the business.

A critical risk that you might face is the product life cycle of a technology product or service. Anticipate shifts and plan for them to occur.

Another critical risk that you might face is diversification. If you have only one offering (product or service) and something goes awry with it, you might be out of business. Yet, if you have more than one offering too early on, you might not be able to give each one of them the necessary attention because of your limited resources—people, funds and technology. A delicate balance.

How much money will you need?   Once you have determined how you want to run the business, how much money is required of you? The specific amount of money that you have available to you will be your resource base. This is also your constraint. If it takes $500,000 to start a business, and you only have $5000, there might not be a fit. There might be different ways to approach this $500,000 business opportunity that might let you start it for $5000. How can you take advantage of the business opportunity with the amount of money you have available to you? How can you change the business? If, by way of example, you looked at the business and thought that you needed $500,000, $498,000 of which was going towards buying a minicomputer. If you were to timeshare on a minicomputer, even at $50 per hour, you can get 100 hours of computer time for your $5000. Will that get you started?

What are potential yearly sales? This dimension gives you an idea of what your sales volume will be. If the volume is not large enough for you, look at another business.

What are potential yearly income? Yearly profitability will probably be the go/no go decision point. If you can't make enough money from the business, it isn't worth pursuing.

Conclusion

If you have analyzed each one of the areas listed above, you've covered all of the bases to perform a screening of an opportunity. Where you've found problems, can you change anything to make the opportunity more viable? If so, and you've eliminated all potential roadblocks, you probably have a business that will work. Refer to chapter 4 and appendices A and B for ideas on specific PC-based businesses.

4 PC-based company ideas

This chapter discusses some of the more popular businesses that you can actually run with the help of your personal computer. Of the PC-based businesses you can consider, some have increased potential during bad economic times:

- Bookkeeping service
- Collection agency
- Employment agency
- Outplacement business
- Used-computer broker

Other business ideas offer good opportunities regardless of the condition of the economy:

- Application training (word processing, spreadsheet, database, and desktop publishing)
- Desktop publishing service bureau
- Presentation service bureau
- Word processing service bureau
- Writing

In this chapter, each business is described in a standard format so you can compare them. The topics addressed for each business are:

- What is the business?
- Who are its customers?

- Where do you find customers?
- How do you get your message out?
- Who are your competitors?
- What talents do you need?
- Who should you hire?
- What are the potential roadblocks?
- How much money do you need?
- What are the potential yearly sales?
- What is the potential yearly income?
- What equipment do you need?

Bookkeeping service

What is the business?   A bookkeeping service keeps track of the financial books of another business. These books include the money owed the business (*accounts receivable*); money the business owes (*accounts payable*); the goods that the company has on hand (*inventory*); the money the business needs to pay its employees (*payroll*); the goods and services the business needs to buy (*purchasing*); the money it needs to bill its customers (*billing*); the financial forecasting it needs to do (*budgeting*); and the checks on all financial records (*auditing*).

You can run this business as an external service. In this case, you do all work outside of a company and bring your client the results. You can also provide this service on a contract basis. Here, you (or one of your employees) goes into a company to do the bookkeeping.

Although this business is actually good for all economic times, in bad ones, it becomes more critical that the books of the business are managed correctly. In bad times, a business might not be able to keep a bookkeeper on staff because of the expense.

Who are its customers?   The market usually consists of those small businesses that don't want to keep a bookkeeper on staff. The client business normally ranges in size from 0 to 100 employees.

If you have a particular skill in one accounting package, your target market is companies that have that same package, given that you are performing a subcontract service to them.

Where do you find customers?   You can find customers through the yellow pages, newspapers, referrals from CPA (certified public accounting) firms and computer retail stores.

How do you get your message out?   You can take advertisements out in the yellow pages. Write a column for your local newspaper. Tell your customers and your friends to tell other people about you. Stay in touch with CPA firms. Let computer retail stores who sell accounting packages know you exist.

Who are your competitors?   In-house bookkeeping services and similar contract bookkeeping services are the nearest competitors.

What talents do you need?   Marketing skills, a thorough knowledge of the accounting process and computers are all necessary to run the business.

Who should you hire?   Recruit people who can input and review accounting information and people who can sell the service.

What are potential roadblocks?   Potential roadblocks include:

- Finding the right people, in addition to yourself, to do bookkeeping
- Meeting deadlines of clients and tax authorities
- Getting penalized by tax authorities
- Causing a business to take a wrong turn as a result of your efforts. You are dealing with the lifeblood of your client's business, so you need to know what you are doing.

How much money do you need?   You will need enough money to buy a personal computer (with basic accounting software) and a laser printer.

What are the potential yearly sales?   Potential yearly sales are $1000 to $75,000 per person.

What is the potential yearly income?   Potential yearly income can be as high as $25,000 per person.

What equipment will you need?   You'll need a basic accounting and bookkeeping package like Quicken and a microcomputer. To print things out, you'll need a laser printer. A fax machine or modem also is helpful.

Collection agency

What is the business?   A collection agency collects money from people or companies. The money is collected for other companies (*creditors*). In bad times, companies need money to keep the business going. Many companies are not as quick to pay their bills when the economy is down, which is why this business is ideal for bad economic times.

Who are its customers?   Almost any business of any size can be a customer for a collection agency.

Where do you find customers?   You find customers through local Chambers of Commerce, Better Business Bureaus, yellow pages advertising, direct mail, and telephone solicitation.

How do you get your message out?   To help get your message out, join the Chamber of Commerce and talk to the people at the Better Business Bureau. Create a captivating direct mail piece to send to all local businesses. Get on the telephone and call.

Who are your competitors?   Your competition is in-house personnel who collect accounts receivable. In a small company, it might be the owner of the company. In a larger company, it is the accounts receivable clerks. Your competition is also other collection agencies.

What talents do you need?   You can run this business by yourself with the help of a telephone. You need to be persistent, methodical, and able to get someone to pay you.

Who should you hire?   You'll not need to hire anyone, initially. Eventually, you will want to hire people who can sell the service to potential clients or collect money. Someone who can do both is ideal.

What are the potential roadblocks?   One potential roadblock is that you might find that collection is not for you. Also, you might not be able to collect any money. If you bill your client based on your ability to collect, you won't make any money.

How much money do you need?   You could start this business without a computer. It makes a lot more sense to use a database or contact-management program to manage all of the calls you need to make. With a contact-management program, in particular, you can record who you need to call and when. The program will prompt you at the appropriate time to make the calls. ACT! is an ideal contact-management program for this business.

What are the potential yearly sales?   You can bill for your services on a fee or percentage basis. Expect to collect a flat fee only in rare instances. You should develop a schedule that compensates you on the amount collected and the age of the receivable. It is best to price the service based on what other competitors in your geographic area charge. Call them and ask.

What is the potential yearly income?   Yearly income can be from $1000 to millions of dollars (if you collect large enough receivables).

What equipment do you need?   You can run this business with a contact-management program like ACT!, and a personal computer. To print invoices and keep your books, you need to buy a package like Quicken. In order to print things out, you'll need a laser printer. A fax (facsimile) machine or modem also is helpful.

Employment agency

What is the business?   An employment agency is a business that helps people find jobs. Those agencies that deal with higher-paying jobs call themselves *search firms* or *executive* search firms.

Employment agencies or search firms can specialize in finding people jobs within specific industries (for example, the computer or pharmaceutical fields) or within specific job functions (for example, attorneys, accountants, or artists).

Who are its customers?   The agency's customers can either be the employers (companies in a certain industry of a certain size) or the potential job applicant. The customer is the person or company that pays your fee.

In poor economic times, many more people are looking for jobs than are available. Therefore, there is a greater number of people who want jobs than are available. In good economic times, the converse can be true. More employers have jobs available than people looking for them. This business is good for both poor and good economic times.

Where do you find customers?   Make cold calls to individuals who might want jobs and to employers who might need employees. When an employer's need is matched with a qualified individual, a match is made. You need to pursue a constant flow of both new jobs and new potential employees.

How do you get your message out?   Telemarketing is an effective way to get the message out. So is radio, newspaper, and magazine advertising. You can find both candidates and potential jobs through these vehicles. Pick your media based on the types of employers and prospective employees you are targeting.

Who are your competitors?   Competitors are local boutiques (other individuals like you), large regional and national franchises, and international firms.

What talents do you need?   You need persistence and understanding. Knowing when there is an opportunity for a match to be made is important as is knowing what will make an appropriate marriage between prospective employer and employee.

Who should you hire?   Initially, you can run this business yourself. You might want to hire an assistant to help you organize yourself if you aren't already organized. When you have too much business for you to handle, hire another individual. Or contemplate a partnership, if you know there is a valuable fit.

What are the potential roadblocks?   Roadblocks occur if you are unable to find potential job openings, unable to find individuals to fill the job openings you find or unable to make marriages.

How much money do you need?   You need enough money to buy yourself some time to make a marriage and get paid. Depending on how good you are, this phase might take 3 to 6 months of living expenses.

What are the potential yearly sales?   Annual sales depend on your target market and your own persistence. Sales can range from $0 to millions of dollars per year.

Fees are either a flat number (generally of lower salaries) or a percentage of the first year's salary (up to 33%). Check with competitors in your specific niche before you price your service.

What is the potential yearly income?   You can expect to pocket as much as 70% of your gross sales, depending upon your fixed costs.

What equipment do you need?   You can start this business without a computer. If you use contact-management software (like ACT!), it can aid you in keeping track of your operations. You'll simply need a computer to run it on. To print invoices and keep your books, you want to purchase a package like Quicken. Finally, in order to print things out, you'll need a laser printer. A fax machine or modem also is helpful.

Profile

Bill Vick
Vick & Associates doing business as Solo Systems
3325 Landershire Lane
Plano, Texas 75023-6218
214/612-8425 (Telephone)
214/612-1924 (Facsimile)
CompuServe User ID: 72106,17

What is your business?   I conduct two businesses. The first is Vick & Associates, an executive search firm that I have owned and run full time since 1987. The second is a software publisher and VAR (value-added retailer) named Solo Systems that sells software and other solutions to recruiters. I have run this business in addition to Vick & Associates since late 1992.

Who are your customers?   My search business helps companies in the microcomputer industry find and hire mid- and senior-level marketing and sales people. Solo is sold to executive recruiters.

Where do you find customers?   Lots and lots of phone calls. When I'm marketing, I make between 50 and 80 calls a day. I have run my first advertisement on Solo and have over 40 responses to follow up on.

How do you get the message out?   Many ways! Trade shows, fax-grams, sales letters, postcards, newsletters, and phone, phone, phone.

Who are your competitors?   The recruiting marketplace is large ($30 billion in 1992) with over 28,000 offices. My billings place me in the top 1% of all recruiters in personal production that exceeds $250,000 per year. My software venture is now number three on the Macintosh platform (but I am one of three products versus over 130 products on the PC/Windows platform).

What talents do you need?   Courage, confidence, commitment, and the ability to be at the right place at the right time.

Who do you hire?   I don't.

What are the potential roadblocks?   Very, very intense competition; the difference between success and failure is a very thin line.

How much money do you need?   Three months living expense, plus working capital to cover equipment and operating cost. Equipment cost will run between $3000 and $5000 and operating cost (telephone, advertising, etc.) will run close to $4000 per month.

What are your potential yearly sales?   My search business generates over $250,000 per year in sales and income. My software business will gross around $100,000 this year.

What is your potential yearly income?   Enough to smell the roses whenever and wherever I want.

What equipment do you need?   Computer (I have a Mac Powerbook 160, FP monitor, laser printer, FaxModem) software, and a telephone.

Outplacement agency

What is the business?   The outplacement agency provides counseling and assistance to people who have lost their jobs. In poor economic times, business booms for outplacement agencies.

Who are its customers?   The customers for this business are primarily medium and large companies. Some companies have in-house outplacement operations, but most don't.

Where do you find customers?   You find customers by approaching the human resources department of medium and large companies.

How do you get your message out?   The best way to get the message out is through telephone solicitation, direct mail, and personal solicitation. This is a business where you have to stay in touch with your potential or present clients. If you do a good job for them, they'll keep you around. Everyone tries to get outplacement business when firms lay off large numbers of people. If you've been there all along (even when they weren't laying off people), you will have a better chance for success.

Who are your competitors?   Your competitors are outplacement firms of all sizes and forms. Small, medium, and large firms are in this business. So is everyone from psychologists to physicists (yes, physicists!).

What talents do you need?   You should have some type of human relations or resources background. Good education and previous experience give you a leg up. If you don't have the education or experience, try to get it.

You need to be able to relate to people who have lost their job and are under a lot of stress.

Who should you hire?   You can start this business yourself. If you don't have a background in this area, you might want to team up with someone who does. You can sell the work and the other person can deliver on it.

What are the potential roadblocks?   Potential roadblocks are an incorrect background, a very good economy where there are no layoffs, and your poor performance and consequent bad reputation.

How much money do you need?   This business requires that you have enough money to carry you until your first client pays you. You might need three to six months of living expenses.

What are the potential yearly sales?   There are firms that bill millions of dollars in outplacement services. Before you price your own services, call all of the local competitors to see what they charge. Fees can range from a monthly retainer ($3000 to hundreds of thousands of dollars) to a per-employee fee.

What is the potential yearly income?   If you are successful at this business, you can reasonably make $50,000 to $150,000 each year.

What equipment do you need?   You don't need a computer for this business. But, as with the employment agency, you can use contact-management software (like ACT!) to aid you in keeping track of your life. You'll need a computer to run it. An accounting package like Quicken will allow you to keep your books. You can print things out with a letter-quality or laser printer. A fax machine or modem also is helpful.

Used-computer broker

What is the business?   In this business, you buy and sell used computers. In poor economic times, individuals and businesses look for all possible ways to save money. Buying used computers is one way. They also look for increased revenue sources. Selling old computers is one vehicle.

Who are its customers?   Your customers can either be individuals or businesses. As customers, individuals will take a lot of effort for you to make a small sale. When you deal with a business (especially a larger business), you can either purchase or sell them a larger number of systems. Although your gross margin might not be as great as an individual sale, you can make a greater amount of money with this larger sale.

Where do you find customers?   You can find customers through computer user groups, direct solicitations, and newspaper and trade publication advertising. Don't forget to contact computer dealers and leasing companies.

How do you get your message out?   Many people who belong to user groups do so because they want to get good deals on computers. These individuals often meet monthly. You can find out who they are and where they meet by looking in either your local computer newspaper or the events section of your local paper.

If you can identify specific companies as potential customers, call the purchasing department. They will know both when they want to purchase and sell used computers.

You can take out advertisements in both local newspapers and targeted trade publications. You might advertise in *Chemical Engineering News* or *Train* magazine. Most suppliers advertise in computer publications.

Not all computer dealers want to sell used computers. When they sell a new system to an individual or a company, that customer might ask the dealer to either buy or sell their old computers. If you work directly with computer dealers, they can often sell you a lot of used equipment.

Leasing companies often look for ways to dispose of old computers that come off leases. If you have a good relationship with a leasing company, the leasing company could be a constant source of used computers.

Who are your competitors?　Your competitors are computer dealers and used-equipment dealers. Most of these firms are regional. There are two national computer exchanges that specialize in selling, on consignment, used computers. They are the American and Boston Computer Exchanges. Although they are competition, they can also be a source of used computers for you.

What talents do you need?　You need a quick mind to negotiate, an ability to buy low and sell high, and persistence.

Who should you hire?　You can run this business yourself. As you grow, you might consider hiring an assistant.

What are the potential roadblocks?　Roadblocks will happen if you can't get used computers or if you can't sell those you get. Also, it is possible that you will get such a large order that you can't finance it. You might have to strike a deal to get paid up front or negotiate terms with your supplier.

How much money do you need?　You might need only enough money to cover you until you reach a cash breakeven. If you never take title of the equipment and are paid a fee at the sale, you'll never need capital to finance the equipment. If you do take possession of the equipment, you'll need inventory financing.

What are the potential yearly sales?　Sales can be anywhere from nothing to millions of dollars.

What is the potential yearly income?　As with yearly sales, income can be up to millions of dollars.

What equipment do you need? You can run this business without a computer. Just like the employment agency, if you use contact-management software (like ACT!), you will have help in keeping track of your life. You'll simply need a computer to run it on. To print invoices and keep your books, you want to purchase a package like Quicken. Finally, in order to print things out, you'll need a laser printer. A fax machine or modem also is helpful.

Application training

You can offer your clients application training in the typical applications (word processing, spreadsheet, database, or desktop publishing) or in many more specialized applications.

What is the business? Application training is a business that trains people on how to use different computer application software on microcomputers, minicomputers, or mainframes. Computer training in this area varies from on-site training (at a company's own facility) to off-site training (at a facility that is owned or rented by the training company). Often, special facilities are rented just for the training.

Training courses vary in theme, based upon the underlying software itself. For example, a company might offer two courses in WordPerfect: Introduction to WordPerfect and Advanced WordPerfect 5. Sample curriculum for a two-day introductory class might include:

- Creating and editing documents
- Cursor control
- Setting tabs and margins
- Block commands
- Formatting the document
- Printing
- File management
- Using the spell check and thesaurus

A one-day advanced WordPerfect class might include:

- Mail merge
- Macros
- Creating columns
- Math functions
- Sorting
- Footnotes
- Creating and using forms
- Generating a table of contents

The same company might offer two courses in Microsoft Word. The curriculum for the one-day introductory course might include:

- Introduction to Microsoft Word
- Creating and editing documents

- Paragraph formatting
- Cut/copy/paste text
- Using the spelling checker
- Search & replace function
- Using fonts and style attributes
- Text alignment
- Page setup and printing

A one-day advanced Microsoft Word course might include:

- Mail merge
- Multiple column formatting
- Creating headers & footnotes
- Using the glossary feature
- Outlines and table of contents
- Creating style sheets
- Custom dictionaries and menus
- Advanced document formatting

Generally, application software training follows some type of outline format.

Who are its customers?   The target market for computer application software training includes people who:

- Just purchased application software packages
- Just entered a new job where they now need to use a new application software package
- Need to learn more than the basic features of an application software package
- Know how to use one application software package but, because of an upgrade, now need to learn the features on the upgraded package

Where do you find customers?   You can target small clients (where you might train one person in the entire organization) or you can target large-scale organizations (where you might land a training contract for the whole group).

You can find people in this target market in small and large companies, in small and large towns, and in all types of professions. In essence, anyone who could possibly use application software is a potential customer.

How do you get your message out?   For the smaller training clients, you can reach them through the yellow pages (make sure you call your local telephone company to find out the deadline for submittal) and the Donnelly Directories (which enable you to perform dynamic updates of your advertisements throughout the year). You can take out advertisements in your community newspapers, local business newspapers, and metropolitan newspapers. You can inform computer dealers in your area that you offer this service and give them a referral fee (for sending you business). You can also reach them through local user groups.

The large training clients might require some of the vehicles that are used to attract any of the larger clients. You will need to sell these businesses through telephone solicitation, direct mail, and even direct sales calls.

Who are your competitors?   Competition ranges from one-person training companies that perform computer application training to large training firms that perform a host of different computer-based application training. There is a geographic bent to training firms. You are best served to look up *computer training* in the yellow pages of your telephone book to see what competition is located in your area.

What talents do you need?   You will need the ability to market, both proactively and reactively. You will also need the ability to train people on different applications. You must also know how to use these applications yourself.

Who should you hire?   Consider hiring one person who can market the training service and perform it. If volume increases, you might want to hire another person so that one can perform the training and one can do the marketing.

What are the potential roadblocks?   There might not be a market for this service in your area. If you don't use the correct promotional channels, you might not think you have a market for your service. The customer might refuse to pay for training

How much money do you need?   You will need money for marketing and working capital. If you train on-site, you will not need any computer systems or overhead projectors.

What are the potential yearly sales?   Application software training is generally priced by the course. There are some training operations that price the courses based on the number of days involved in the course and the type of system on which the training will take place. There are different rates for on-site and off-site training. Check out local competition before you set your prices.

On-site training might take on a schedule such as $600 per day plus $25 per student (within a 25 mile radius of your company).

Gross receipts will vary greatly. If you can book one course a week, in an on-site class with five students 50 times each year, you can expect to bill $36,250 each year. The only cost you have associated with this revenue are your instructor's salary, travel, and marketing costs.

If you can book an off-site classroom five days a week with 10 students for 50 weeks each year, you can expect revenues of $312,500 per year. Costs associated with this revenue are your instructor's salary, marketing cost, rental of the classroom, and the cost of the 10 systems that you are either renting, leasing, or paying off.

What is the potential yearly income?   Profitability will vary greatly. If you are doing all training on-site, yourself, your profitability might be $20,000 on the $36,250 of revenue. If you are booking a classroom, paying instructors, and renting both equipment and space, your profitability might be $60,000–$90,000 on $312,500 of revenue. In this scenario, though, you might be one of the instructors you are paying.

What equipment do you need?   If you're setting up a training site, you'll need enough computers for the number of students you'll have. You'll also need an overhead projector.

What is the business?   This business creates quality published output for advertising, newsletters, newspapers, magazines, and books.

Who are its customers?   Customers are individuals and companies who need to have high-quality output for producing printed material.

Where do you find customers?   You can find customers through advertising, word of mouth, and by contacting commercial printers.

How do you get your message out?   You can advertise in local, regional, or national publications. Printers who produce finished output can be one of your best referral sources. Show them your work and let them begin working for you. Most important, your satisfied customers will refer other people to you.

Who are your competitors?   Local, regional, and national desktop publishers are your main competition. Other competition includes advertising agencies and commercial printers that offer desktop publishing services.

What talents do you need?   A background in art and design is imperative. Most people feel that they can do desktop publishing if they purchase PageMaker or Quark. This belief is similar to believing that you can practice medicine because you own a stethoscope.

You'll also need to be adept at marketing and production. Workflow management might become a critical problem. If you are inundated with work and can't perform, you might never see more.

Who should you hire?   If you have the appropriate design and layout capabilities, you can operate the business yourself. If you don't have these skills, you'll need to hire someone who does.

Desktop publishing service bureau

What are the potential roadblocks?   You might not be able to sell work. Also, you might not be able to satisfy the client with your performance, and you don't get paid. In some areas, there could be so much competition that the market becomes extremely price conscious.

How much money do you need?   You'll need enough money to survive the purchase of equipment, cost of marketing, and living expenses for at least six months with no income flowing in.

What are the potential yearly sales?   Realistically, this service can do several hundred thousand dollars in revenue if you are talented. If you can find a slew of top-notch desktop publishers to work for you, you can push revenues up to the millions of dollars.

What is the potential yearly income?   Potential income is at least 10% of gross sales.

What equipment do you need?   You'll need a desktop publishing program (like PageMaker or Quark), a computer to run it on, and a high-quality laser printer. A fax machine and a modem might also be helpful. You will need a bookkeeping software package.

Presentation service bureau

What is the business?   It's a service bureau that helps companies develop presentations, usually for use on overhead projectors or projected from a computer screen.

Who are its customers?   Customers can be companies of any size.

Where do you find customers?   Use direct mail, telephone solicitation, advertising, and schmooze to find customers.

How do you get your message out?   Send out many letters about your service. Call everyone you know in business. If they don't need your service now, send them a letter with information about it. Ask them if they have friends who you can contact. Advertise in any publication you can afford that reaches people who need help putting together presentations. Schmooze with anyone and everyone who you can find.

Who are your competitors?   In-house presentation (art) departments, advertising agencies, and individuals who need the presentations and put them together themselves.

What talents do you need?   Above all, you need to know how to create computer-based presentations. You need creative skills. You need to be able to listen to and work with your clients to produce what they want for the presentation. You'll also need to be able to cultivate clients through your marketing efforts.

Who should you hire?   If you have the talent to create presentations, do them yourself. If not, hire someone who can or subcontract to someone who can.

What are the potential roadblocks?   Some potential roadblocks could be an inability to sell work or an inability to satisfy your client with a presentation and, in turn, an inability to get paid.

How much money do you need?   You need enough to purchase the equipment needed and enough to live on for at least three to six months.

What are the potential yearly sales?   Potential sales can be anywhere from zero to several hundred thousand dollars, depending upon your own marketing skill and ability to deliver high-quality presentations.

What is the potential yearly income?   Potential income is as high as 40% of yearly sales.

What equipment do you need?   You'll need desk-top presentation software like PowerPoint and Director, a computer with enough memory to run these programs, and a printer with a high enough resolution output to print the presentations. If you will assist your client in giving the presentation, you'll need a projection unit that attaches to the computer.

What is the business?   A word processing service bureau business is an outgrowth of the typing services of yesterday. In its purest form, the service is nothing more than a transcription service that takes textual information that is not in any computer media and puts it into a computer medium. Input formats are in four basic varieties:

Word processing service bureau

Handwritten or hand printed   Given that you accept input in this format, you will have to be sure that you are able to read what is given to you. When you accept input in this format, you spend a lot of time trying to figure out what other people wrote. Therefore, be sure that you have a good quality-control mechanism in place if you are going to accept both handwritten and hand-printed input.

Verbal   In order to accept verbal input, you need some type of dictation system. With the decline in cost of dictation systems, you can use one inexpensively as a way to differentiate yourself. You can set up systems to accept dictation that people transcribe over the telephone into your office or dictation that people create on microcassette tapes and give to you to transcribe.

Typewritten   There are people who use either manual or electric typewriters. They want their output to be generated with higher quality than they can get from a typewriter. You probably want to have some type of an optical character reader to capture as many of the keystrokes as possible to avoid retyping.

Computer-based electronic media You can also receive input via computer-based electronic media, including telecommunications, floppy disk, hard disk, or magnetic tape.

Output formats for word processing include:

Computer-based electronic media Quite often people want to have information delivered to them, to their printers, or to their clients on an electronic medium. Electronic media includes all of the media mentioned on the input side of the equation: telecommunications, floppy disk, hard disk, and magnetic tape.

Telecommunications With the use of modems, you can send output to your clients or designated sites. This type of delivery vehicle is becoming more popular as more people have modems. No information is committed to paper and the output can be automatically incorporated into your client's work. I work this way with many of my employees and subcontractors.

Facsimile transmissions With the proliferation of facsimile machines and facsimile boards for microcomputers, this delivery is becoming more accessible and usable. Information is word processed and then facsimile transmitted directly to the recipient.

Hard copy, draft quality Many people want to see a "rough" copy of the output of the word processing service, and draft-quality printing is the acceptable delivery vehicle. If you choose to offer this delivery mechanism, you will need a draft-quality printer.

Hard copy, letter quality Letter-quality output requires either a near-letter quality or actual letter-quality printer. With today's acceptance of laser printers, laser-quality printing has come to be known as the acceptable letter-quality standard of the 1990s.

Hard copy, typeset quality If your client wants typeset-quality output, you will need an extremely high-resolution laser printer. Requirements for typeset quality are more often encountered in desk-top publishing than in word processing.

Who are its customers? The target market ranges from anyone who wants to have a résumé word processed to a corporation that wants to off-load its excess word processing for which it doesn't have capacity in-house. Essentially, anyone who has word processing needs is a candidate for this type of service. The target market can either be viewed as a low-volume, high number of customers target market or a high-volume, low number of customers market.

Where do you find customers?   You can look for customers in organizations such as AISP (The Association of Information Systems Professionals), in special interest groups devoted to word processing, and in the telephone book.

How do you get your message out?   Depending on which target market you are attempting to reach, you will obviously find customers in different places and will use different means of getting your message out.

The low-volume of transactions business is found primarily through retail-type vehicles such as advertisements in the yellow pages, local newspapers, college campus postings, and retail foot traffic. In this low-volume segment, you will find little repeat business. You will spend a lot of time and money to find a supply of new customers, and you will find that you have to complete a tremendous number of transactions in order to make any money. The allied cost of doing business is now associated with a transaction dollar value that might be very small. For example, you might have a transaction that is valued at $2 (word processing a résumé). Yet you still have incurred an advertising, client selling and development, job processing, job completion, job acceptance and collection expense.

A lot of these expenses do not seem to actually cost anything because time is the only dimension that you seem to have invested. But realize that time does have a value and an allied expense associated with it. If you spend time doing one thing, then you can't spend time doing something else. So if you are processing someone's résumé (at $2 total job cost) you can't be processing a massive word processing overflow client that might yield you $4000 for the entire job.

Doesn't it make more sense to allocate time across potentially larger volume contracts?

The moderate- and high-volume of transactions segments have pretty much the same attributes. The higher volume will in turn yield a higher gross revenue figure. You should also see higher profit.

The moderate- and high-volume of transactions segments might be reachable through the same vehicles as the low-volume segments— advertisements in the yellow pages, local newspapers, college campus postings, and retail foot traffic. If you reach them through these channels, it will be more the exception than the rule. Normally, the high-volume segments have to be reached through direct mail, telemarketing, and direct selling with a specific target in mind—the corporations, law firms, accounting firms, insurance firms, and word processing administrators or managers. The goal, after all, in these market segments is to try to get overflow work.

Who are your competitors?   In each city in the United States, there are companies that list themselves as word processing service bureaus or typing services. Look in the telephone book to see who your direct competitors are.

What talents do you need?   You need the ability to market, both proactively and reactively, a word processing service. You also need the skill to complete your projects accurately.

Who should you hire?   Hire one person who can market the service and who is skilled at word processing. If volume increases, you might want to hire another person so that one can perform the word processing and one can do the marketing.

What are the potential roadblocks?   Potential roadblocks are:

- Lack of a market for your service
- Rejection of your work by a customer
- Customer refuses to pay for work done
- Your computer or laser printer breaks down in the midst of a heavy workload

How much money do you need?   You'll need enough money to buy equipment, pay for your initial direct marketing costs, and cover your living expenses for three to six months.

What are the potential yearly sales?   Word processing service bureau work can be priced either on a per-contract basis or an hourly basis. No matter what, the contract should be priced using an hourly billable rate and an estimate of the number of hours required. Billable hourly rates that are reasonable range from $10 to $45. Sales volume, if you are billing 40 hours per week and 50 weeks a year ranges from $20,000 to $90,000.

What is the potential yearly income?   Income is yearly sales volume less the operating costs of the business. Using the gross sales volume figures above, expected profitability should be 60% of volume (given that you pay yourself out of profits of the business). Profit should range between $16,000 and $54,000, given that you can sustain the above volume of business.

What equipment do you need?   You can start this business with a computer and word processing software. To print output for your clients, you'll need a dot matrix or laser printer. A fax machine or modem also is helpful. To keep your books, you might use a package like Quicken.

Writing

What is the business?   Writing is one of the oldest professions in the world. Much of the information that has been passed on from generation to generation has been conveyed through this medium. Beginning in Biblical times, history was recorded and subsequently studied through the written word. Communication has been facilitated through writing, accomplished by matching one verbal language to a written form.

Who are its customers?   Writing can be done with three sets of audiences in mind: a given target language, a special-interest group, or a type of publication.

Language is defined by the American Heritage Dictionary as "The aspect of human behavior that involves the use of vocal sounds in meaningful patterns and, when they exist, corresponding written symbols to form, express, and communicate thoughts and feelings." In the world as you know it today, there are a host of spoken and written languages. As a writer, you can choose any one of these written languages in which to communicate.

Based on the language you choose, you will then segment your target market. As an example, if you choose to write in the English language, you will limit your market to those people who read English. If you write in French, German, or Spanish, your maximum target market is all (or some) of those people who read French, German, or Spanish, respectively. These languages are some of the most common languages in which you can write.

One of the interesting elements of human beings is that they have different interests. When you write for humans who speak any one language, you might address a subset of the potential market. Thus, you have to look at the special interests that human beings have in order to help determine what target market you might address.

General-interest items are considered to be the first type of segmentation that you can isolate. *World events*—events that impact on the entire world fall into this category. Items that relate to food, health care, sleep (something of which I don't get much), and physical fitness are all considered to be general-interest items.

There are two other major categories of segmentation of human interest: recreational and vocational. *Recreational segmentation* includes all of those items that humans do for enjoyment, such as sports, hobbies, and travel.

Vocational segmentation incorporates all of those dimensions by which humans classically engage in and consider to be "work." Here you commonly think of professions like medicine, accounting, the law and teaching.

Vocational and recreational segmentation have many crossovers. If you do something without pay, it probably falls into the category of recreation (except for volunteer work). If you do that same thing for pay, it probably falls into the category of being vocational. Consider my woodworking hobby. I enjoy woodworking (but seldom have the time to do it). I've never done it for pay. In fact, I put money into this hobby. There are many people who use woodworking to earn money to support themselves. This crossover is seen in many different areas. These different interests might create different target audiences for you as a writer.

To follow through on the woodworking example, if you were writing to a vocationally oriented woodworking audience, you might write to them with ideas on how to make more money in their woodworking. If you were to write to the woodworking hobbyist, you might write to them about casual woodworking creations that they might make. Again, there might be a crossover between the recreational- and the vocation-oriented woodworker. Each might be interested in what was written for the other.

Once you've chosen your target language and human-interest group, you then need to choose your target publication. Choosing your target publication is not necessarily choosing the way you will reach your target market. In this instance, choosing your target publication might be a choice between a newspaper, newsletter, magazine, soft- or hard-cover book format.

When writers evaluate these attributes, they prioritize them by human-interest group first, then target publication, and finally target language. Most of the time, the chosen language is set by the language that the author is most comfortable with. A second target language is often added when there is an initial level of success with the first target language.

Where do you find customers?   Once you've somewhat decided on a publication type for your focus, where do you find out what the different publications are in a specific category? Follow through with an example based on this book. I went to the bookstore to learn just who the publishers are for business and computer (human-interest segmentation—both vocational and recreational) books (target publication) in the English language (language segmentation). I made a list of these publishers (with the help of a reference publication titled *Books in Print*). Then came the question of how to reach the publishers.

How do you get your message out?   If you want to write a book, buy the book titled *Writers Market*. Begin contacting all of the editors you can. If you want to write for a specific trade publication, contact the editor-in-chief of the publication. Ask if you can write for that publication. Make sure you have an article idea already in mind. At this point, you might even want to have an outline of the article to help you sell it.

Depending upon your human-interest segment, target and language segmentation, how you find and reach the correct people to publish your writing will vary. Libraries are a good source of target publications (be they newspapers, newsletters, magazines, or books). Generally, a publication has an editor and a publisher. Contact the editor of the publication. For any of these types of publications, you can use an agent (get names from *Writers Market*) or you can contact the editor yourself. In either case, you can take two approaches.

The first approach is to put together an outline of what you want to write. Submit this outline, along with a writing sample, to the editor. Contact the editor via telephone or in writing. A telephone call works best to "pitch" the editor on the article. Again, though, if you are a better written communicator than you are a verbal one, you might want to write to the editor.

The second way that you can approach an editor is to write whatever you plan to write in its entirety. Once it is completed, you then contact the editor, either by telephone or in writing, and pitch your completed work.

The difference between these two approaches is a matter of risk factors. In the second scenario, you bear all of the risk. You might expend a tremendous amount of time and not have your writing accepted. In the first situation, very often you can get an acceptance on your article but the editor might still reserve the right to reject your work once you have submitted it. So, in essence you still face a risk, but mentally it might not seem to be as great.

Who are your competitors?   Virtually anyone who is capable of writing or is presently writing is your competition. If you have a certain baseline of skill, you can get published. Most every human-interest subsegment seems to be starved for people who can create usable editorial information. Therefore, if you keep trying, you will probably get published.

What talents do you need?   You must either have some expertise in a human-interest segment or subsegment or the ability to write.

Human-interest segment expertise   Very often people who have a special expertise in a given human-interest segment write books or articles. They might not be able to write but hire a *ghost writer* to assist them in writing. The expertise that these people have is then conveyed to the ghost writer. The ghost writer does the writing.

Research & writing ability   People who have no special human-interest segment expertise but do have writing ability will often write articles or even books on topics for which they know very little. In this instance, the author needs to research and analyze a topic to be able to write about it.

Human-interest expertise & writing ability   Another combination of skills that an author might have is both human-interest segment expertise and the ability to write. Research skills might still be required to augment the author's expertise.

Who should you hire?   Hire yourself. You might want to augment yourself with a worthy assistant who can perform research for you, do some of the writing, or both. If you are writing on a human-interest segment with which you have no familiarity, you might augment your own skills with someone who has expertise in the given segment.

What are the potential roadblocks?   As roadblocks, you might not find a market for your work. It is possible that your work will be rejected by a publisher or that you get writers' block or cannot meet a deadline.

How much money do you need?   You will need enough money to cover your equipment. Unless you get a huge advance, you'll also need to do something else to make money while you are trying to get published.

What are the potential yearly sales?   Yearly sales volume will vary depending upon the human-interest segment you write for, your experience and reputation, as well as how much the target publication pays for manuscripts. Some examples of various levels of expectation are:

Magazines   Free advertising for your company or $0.15 to $1.50 per word.

Books $1,000 to $2,000,000 advance against royalties that range from 7.5 to 15% of the wholesale selling price of the book.

What is the potential yearly income?   Potential income is yearly sales volume less the cost of paper, electricity, and (if you lease it) the lease cost of a computer.

What equipment do you need?   You will need either a simple memory typewriter, a dedicated word processor, or a computer running a word processing program. You also need a dot matrix, letter quality or laser printer and a modem accompanied by communications software (if your publisher accepts copy communicated electronically).

Profile

Tom Hudock
Systemax Computer Graphics
New York, New York

What is the business?   The business designs disk-based marketing and advertising. It is primarily involved in creating self-running demonstrations that fit on a single floppy diskette. Companies use such presentations primarily to promote products or services although they have also been used as electronic newsletters, greeting cards, tutorials and surveys.

Who are its customers?   Primarily software and hardware companies are the customers. Some of the clients include Hewlett Packard, Price Waterhouse, Contact Software International (makers of ACT!), LaserMaster Corporation, and Sears Roebuck.

Where do you find customers?   Tom has found the most effective way for obtaining new clients is actually doing top-notch work for his current clients. Because his company's name and phone number appear in the opening credit and copyright screen of every presentation, which are distributed on disk by the thousands by his clients, many potential clients get to see his work.

How do you get your message out?   If you are new in the business, it is a chicken or egg (or Catch-22) dilemma. You need to have some work for people to see in order to get more work. You can start out by creating your own electronic portfolio of your best graphics and animation work (it must be very good work) to send to potential clients. Pricing your work much lower than the competition initially is another way to attract clients, especially when you're bidding against larger and more established competitors for a project.

Who are your competitors?   Competition comes primarily from companies who are in the same business. Competition is not necessarily advertising agencies, although your company will function in a similar vein.

What talents do you need?   You need a background in graphics design, advertising, and marketing as your top talents. You need to be able to write good catchy copy. And, you need the ability to sell your own services and to persevere. Strong computer skills and some programming experience are also necessary if you're going to be a one-person shop initially.

Who should you hire?   Hire people who have the skills you don't have or who can augment your own skills. When Tom gets extremely busy, he subcontracts to graphics artists, illustrators, and to Grasp (Graphic Animation System for Professionals) programmers for particular projects. (Grasp is published by Paul Mace Software.)

What are the potential roadblocks?   Potential roadblocks are:

- Getting your first client
- Coping with the peaks and valleys of work flow; it doesn't all come in when you want or need it
- Ensuring you get work
- Making sure you can perform the work when you have it; finding the right subcontractors when you need them

How much money do you need?   You will need a minimum of $15,000–$25,000 for the equipment, software, and materials. You'll also need sales and marketing money and enough to live on until you get paid by your first client.

What are the potential yearly sales?   Potential sales are $30,000–$500,000. With contracts in value from $15,000 to $35,000, you need a lot of work to keep you going.

What is the potential yearly income?   You can anticipate an income of approximately 15 to 20% of your yearly sales.

What equipment do you need? A very powerful PC (fast processor with lots of memory and hard disk space), a color flatbed scanner (hand scanner won't do), a digitizing tablet, laser printer, high-speed modem (to transmit graphics and files to distant clients), and a fax machine or board. This set of hardware is a good start.

5 Planning your company

Successful businesses begin with a business plan. Effective business plans have the following characteristics:

- Contain strategic and tactical elements
- Set business goals and objectives
- Factor in personal goals and objectives
- Set forth the strategic direction of the firm
- Establish the tactical elements needed to implement the plan
- Are based on a thorough outline that becomes the table of contents
- Are thorough and complete
- Are succinct
- Are credible

This chapter introduces you to the pitfalls of planning and of not planning a business. You are shown that the expression "The harder you work, the luckier you get" probably is true. Well thought out plans can help your luck along the way. You are introduced to the executive summary, market, operational, financial, and management sections of a workable business plan. Marketing versus operational business plans are discussed. You can learn how to write a brief business plan in one day and how to expand on that plan over a period of useful information-gathering sessions.

Particular note is given to the dynamic nature of business plans in the computer industry. Rapid industry and technological change introduce short product lives. You need to react extremely quickly to survive and grow in the industry.

The pitfalls of planning

Probably the largest pitfall in planning is overplanning. I know someone who wants to be so sure that he is always right, that he falls into an endless research and planning loop. External forces can't even move him out of the loop. He is so busy researching and planning that he never does anything.

The key with any business plan is to be thorough enough so that you draw proper conclusions. You don't want to be so thorough that you lose sight of what you want to accomplish. Often, insecurity about "doing" something can leave you in an endless planning loop mentioned above. After all, isn't it easy to rationalize the fact that you don't want to make a mistake? Isn't that why its important that you research just this one more item? Often people who exhibit this behavior are so scared of the "doing" that this seemingly good trait—thoroughness—is used as a wall to hide behind.

People can get caught up in improper planning. This syndrome is rooted in looking at the wrong things because of the desire to be thorough or a lack of knowledge about what is truly needed for proper planning. In the first instance, where you have gathered too much information, it is important to understand the issue of relevance. Information that is relevant to run (or sell the business to potential investors) is appropriate to use for planning. Superfluous information only confuses you. It might seem relevant to include 30 different prices for the word processing software package that you are going to purchase for your word processing service bureau. Three (at most) probably would suffice. On the second point, improper information can show a lack of knowledge as to how to run the business. More important, it can show a lack of the ability to think through a situation. For example, there is no reason to include a list of clients you have had in a retail food service business if you are planning a computer database programming business. You'd only include them if for some reason they are a part of your potential new market. For example, the retail food customers would be a potential market for the new business if they all have or will purchase computers because they have database programming needs.

Another pitfall of planning is a byproduct of it—putting so much credence in the plan itself that you will not deviate from it, no matter what happens. You might take the approach that you spent so much time planning that it must be right. If this approach creates inflexibility, you can set yourself up for failure. Organizations survive because they are flexible when external factors cause them to be flexible. Deviate from even the best plan, if it makes sense to do so. Situations do change!

You can underplan yet think you have planned adequately. You've gone through all of the motions. You've prepared a written business plan. You couldn't find out information on your target market size, so you guessed rather than spent any more time performing market research. For example, you never have hired a secretary. Rather than look in the want ads of the local paper, you estimated a secretary's salary to be $50,000 plus benefits. You hire a secretary at this salary. You skew what you have to pay everyone else in the business. Quickly, you go out of business because your expenses are so high. Underplanning can surface on those "Well, if I only had more time to research it" issues. The result is that you can be completely misled on the direction you take.

Floundering, with no real goals, is another pitfall in planning. If you have no real goals for your business plan, you probably have no real goals in the business. A way to correct this situation is to set some concrete goals that make sense at the time. Don't set goals that are extremely vague. Goals that are vague are almost as bad as no goals at all. Make sure that your goals are specific and measurable with certain actions required to meet them. The goals should follow a sequence. You should outline what must be done first, second, third, and so forth.

If you don't set certain milestones, you can find yourself procrastinating over many important issues that you should address. It is easy to be so busy that you put off addressing issues that might be absolutely critical to your business. These milestones should be developed around certain target elements that go into each milestone. Once you've completed all the elements for a specific milestone, the milestone is complete.

It is critical that you constantly reassess your milestones. As you reach a milestone, you must evaluate whether or not it comprised all the things that you initially thought. If not, what are the elements of the milestone that have changed? How do they impact future milestones that you have set forth? You must constantly reassess all of the milestones that you establish. At the beginning and end of the milestone, you must ask two questions: 1) Is the milestone achievable and realistic based on all of the information that I now have? and, 2) Are the elements, events and assumptions within the milestone, reasonable? If you constantly ask these two questions, you will most certainly be on the right track.

Another pitfall of planning is a failure to anticipate obstacles. If you are extremely optimistic that your plan will work, you might not have set forth any other alternatives to it. What happens if you are wrong? If you have not established some type of decision trees, you might find yourself at a dead end. As an example, assume that you start a computer business that will develop computer graphics software for a Sun Microsystems workstation. You set forth the following critical path:

Milestone	Resources
Product Specification	John Doe, Graphics Programmer
Product Design	John Doe, Graphics Programmer
Product Development	John Doe, Graphics Programmer
Product Testing	John Doe, Graphics Programmer
Product Manual Develop	You
Product Packaging Design	You
Product Marketing	You

After the product specification, you have a fight with John Doe and can no longer use his services. You realize that he is the only graphics programmer where you live. He is also the only person who owns a Sun workstation in your area. Now what are you going to do? He has left with your product specification. Because you two had never signed a contract for the software development, it was all quite legal that he went off with his property (the software). The problem is that you failed to anticipate these obstacles. You now have nowhere to turn.

Although this example is a little farfetched, the basic point still holds true. You must anticipate as many obstacles as possible, or you can find yourself at a dead end.

Yet another pitfall of planning is a lack of commitment. Unless you follow the aspects necessary to achieve your milestones, the plan is worthless. You must be committed to following your plan. You must be able to modify it as you go along. You can't become overcommitted to a bad plan, either. This might leave you with a lemon begging to be squeezed to make lemonade out of it. If you find yourself in a bad situation, you must reassess why you are in it, where you went wrong, and most important, how you can get out of it.

The final pitfall of planning is an inability to learn from your mistakes. One of the companies that my firm does business with has developed a virtual object database engine. It should, if it is successful, replace all other types of database structures. The president of the company has a favorite saying that I will paraphrase. He states that he makes a lot of mistakes, but he attempts to make those mistakes only once. He tries to learn from all of them so they will not be repeated.

To avoid making mistakes twice, you must first acknowledge that what you did was a mistake. A mistake is perceptual. If you feel what you did was wrong or inappropriate, it is probably a mistake. There are mistakes that you might not acknowledge to be mistakes but others might. First understand that an external source perceives what you've done to be a mistake. Then you must acknowledge, for yourself, that your action was a mistake. When you reach this point, then you can set forth to correct and learn from it.

What conclusions can be drawn about planning as it relates to a business? Be complete enough to fully understand the situation but not so thorough that you never act. Always make sure that your research is proper, well substantiated, and founded in reality. It should be riddled with milestones that make sense and are amendable. Finally you need to be committed to the entire process of planning, revising your plans and learning from your mistakes.

The pitfalls of not planning

Have you ever driven somewhere that you've never been before without a road map? How difficult was it for you to find your way? How difficult would it have been to find your way without a road map and without street signs? If you answered "difficult" to either of these last two questions, you can begin to see the reason to create a business plan. If you don't plan your business, you can wander around aimlessly, not knowing where to go. Through this wandering, you waste one of the most valuable resources you have—time. If your competition has effectively planned, you are at a great competitive disadvantage.

There are two types of business plans you can create. The first type—the *strategic plan*—deals with the overall goals and objectives of your company as well as their implementation strategies. The second type of plan—the *tactical plan*—takes the results of the strategic plan and uses it to develop a nuts-and-bolts plan. The plan might be used as a marketing vehicle (to find investors) or as an operational plan (to actually run the business). Strategic plans must be done first, no matter what the size of your business actually is or will become. The first step in the strategic plan is business goal and objective setting.

Strategic & tactical plans

Before you even sit down to write a business plan, you must outline the goals and objectives of the business. At the outset of a business, the goals and objectives coincide with those of the founder. What do you want the business to look like? What do you want it to do? What level of sales do you want it to achieve? What do you want its geographic scope to be—local, regional, or national? How large, in terms of employees, do you want the business to become? What type of financial results do you want the business to achieve? How do you feel the business should be developed to lead to the most beneficial harvest options? What are the most beneficial harvest options in your mind?

Business goal & objective setting

These are goals that you set before you even begin to plan. They are the global direction that you set for the business, the same way you do for yourself in your life. Look at some of the questions raised and see how they relate to specific goals and objectives for a computer-based multimedia production company that you might want to start.

What do you want the business to look like?   Multimedia Company, Inc., has the goal of creating a firm that gives the market the highest quality multimedia production found anywhere. The firm will be more responsive to customers' needs in the marketplace than any other competitor. The firm will also use time as its critical element of competitive advantage. It will complete work more rapidly than any other competitor.

Multimedia Company, Inc. Goals & objectives

What do you want it to do?   The firm will create high-quality multimedia presentations for its clients.

What level of sales do you want it to achieve?   The firm will be a multimillion dollar company in three years.

What do you want its geographic scope to be? Local, regional, or national? The firm will serve the New York City through Washington, D.C. corridor.

How large do you want the business to be? The firm will have low overhead and will employ as few people as possible.

What type of financial results do you want? The company will achieve a return on sales of 25% per year by year three (a net income of 25% of its sales, before tax). It will have a return on investment of 30% (a return of 30% of the amount invested in the business initially) by the fourth year.

What are the most beneficial harvest options? (What are the best ways to cash in on the business?) The business will go public at the end of the fifth year.

How should the business develop for best harvest? The business should focus on getting the greatest share of the market possible to increase sales for the harvest. Expenses must also be monitored closely in order to maximize profitability.

Personal goal & objective setting

Where do you want to take the business? What do you want out of the business? At the inception of a business, ask yourself and the other founding members what each of you wants to get out of the firm. If you are a solo entrepreneur, your goals will coincide with the goals of the firm. If you are a part of a team, your goals might diverge from those of the other members of the founding team. Know where you and other members of the founding team will fit into the business as it progresses. Ensure that each of you sits down and contemplates your personal goals and objectives. See where, when, and how they fit into what you have arrived upon to be the business goals and objectives. You might find, through this exercise, that personal goals and objectives do not match the business goals and objectives. Something must change. Either a business goal and objective must change, or the role of an individual within the business might have to change.

Both business and personal goals and objectives should undergo a continual review. Just as the business plan is iterative, constantly reassess both business and personal goals and objectives.

Set forth general strategic direction

Once the general goals of the business are set, a strategic dimension must be added to each one of them. This strategic element is the ideology behind the goals. Revisit the example to see how the strategy fits into the business goals and objectives.

Multimedia Company, Inc., strategies

What do you want the business to look like? Multimedia Company, Inc.'s goal is to create a firm that gives the market the highest quality multimedia production found anywhere.

Strategy The strategy is to create the highest quality multimedia production and employ the most talented individuals with the most experience who have the highest creative flair and can use the highest quality equipment available.

The firm will be more responsive to customer's needs in the marketplace than any other competitor.

Strategy The strategy is to ensure that everyone in the firm is trained to listen to the customer. Deliver the product that meets and exceeds the customer's needs.

The firm will also use time as its critical element of competitive advantage.

Strategy The strategy is to complete all tasks in the shortest time frame possible. Don't sacrifice quality in the process.

What do you want it to do? The firm will create high-quality multimedia presentations for its clients.

Strategy The strategy is to act in an extremely professional manner in order to serve the clients' needs.

What level of sales do you want it to achieve? The firm will be a multimillion dollar company in three years.

Strategy The firm will increase sales through an aggressive advertising and promotional campaign implemented by knowledge-based salespeople.

What do you want its geographic scope to be? The firm will serve the New York City through Washington, D.C. corridor marketplace.

Strategy The strategy is to open offices throughout the corridor to serve these major markets at the lowest cost.

How large do you want the business to be? Keep overhead low and employ as few people as possible.

Strategy The company will grow to no more employees than absolutely needed to run an effective firm. Contract workers will be used, when required, to achieve an even higher quality than could be afforded by hiring permanent employees.

What type of financial results do you want? The company will achieve a return on sales of 25% per year by year three and a return on investment of 30% by the fourth year.

Strategy The strategy is to achieve a 25% return on sales by ensuring that our gross margin remains at 85% of revenues and that our fixed expenses are no more than 60% of expenses. Throughout the initial start-up phase, purchase as little plant and equipment as possible. Purchases should generate 30 cents to the bottom line for each dollar invested.

What are the most beneficial harvest options?   The business will be taken public at the end of the fifth year.

Strategy   Every action taken in the first five years of business will be geared towards an initial public offering in the fifth year. We will retain and consult advisors with experience in accounting, banking, investment banking and the law.

How should the business develop for best harvest?   The business should focus on getting the greatest share of the market possible to increase sales for the harvest. Expenses must also be monitored closely in order to maximize profitability.

Strategy   Market share will be monitored by a marketing director. Expenses will be monitored initially by the president of the company. When the company can afford to hire one, a controller will monitor expenses.

Establishing tactical elements

Once you have set forth the general goals and objectives of the business and outlined strategic issues affecting each of them, you can then use both of these elements to write a tactical plan for the firm. The tactical plan is often referred to as the *business plan*.

Writing a business plan

The business plan should mirror the goals and objectives of the business. It should adhere to the strategic direction for each of those goals and objectives. The goals and objectives should encompass each of the areas outlined in the business plan table of contents. These areas should also be covered at the strategic and tactical levels of the business plan.

The key to writing a proper business plan is to include information that is relevant to your business. Present it in a succinct fashion yet one that substantiates all of the points you make.

The cover page

The first page of a business plan is the cover page. This page should include the company name and address. The name you choose can be very telling as to the nature of your business. For example, if you chose *Computer Business Solutions, Inc.*:

- You won't be wed to any specific computer business
- The company appears larger than it actually might be. If you chose John Doe & Associate, the connotation is of a much smaller firm. Yet had the

name of choice been *The Desktop Publishing Company*, customers have a much better idea of what the company actually does.

You might want to include a registration block on the cover page that lets you keep track of the copy number, recipient, authorization, and purpose of the plan distribution. This feature lets you know how many copies you've given out.

If you want to raise money, you want to limit the number of people who look at your business plan. If too many people see the plan, it will look as if you couldn't easily fund the business, especially if those people operate in the same circles. Therefore, be cautious as to how many plans you actually give out.

You might also want to include a confidentiality notice on the cover page. Although this warning might not stop some people from copying the plan, it should deter a great many.

A good business plan should start with a good outline. This outline will probably become the plan table of contents. Although your plan might not include all of the exhibits mentioned, it should definitely cover the eight major topics, as well as a set of pro forma income and cash flow statements and balance sheets. A typical table of contents is:

The table of contents

Table of Contents

I. Executive summary
II. The industry, company, and service
III. Marketing research and analysis
IV. Economics of the business
V. Operations plan
VI. The management team
VII. Overall schedule
VIII. Critical risks and problems
IX. The financial plan

Exhibits

1. Pro forma income statements
2. Pro forma cash flow statements
3. Pro forma balance sheets
4. Market survey
5. Résumés
6. Target market breakdown
7. Competition breakdown

Sections of the plan

Executive summary   The *executive summary* is a complete summary of the business. It is a summary of the marketing, operational, financial, and management sections of the business plan. It should be brief enough to give the reader a snapshot of the business. Yet, it must be complete enough to describe everything that the reader will hopefully read in the plan. The executive summary is your one shot to capture a reader's attention. If you do not succeed in this summary, your reader will probably not read the rest of the plan. It should span no more than several pages.

The business   In this section of the business plan, you should describe the industry, the company, the company's products or services, and the entry and growth strategies of the firm.

The industry   The industry section of the plan describes the target industry. Generally included in this description is a qualitative description of the industry with some historical background.

The company   A general description of the company should be included in this section of the plan. The information offered in this area should be different from that presented in the executive summary. If you have an existing business, discuss background information on the history of the company here. Products or services with which the company deals, markets the company serves, and clients for which the company does work all belong here.

The products or services   This segment of the plan references the products or services that the firm presently or will provide to the market. A description of the products or services in general terms is important at this point. The reader of the plan must be able to understand what the company offers. This section might also include some product differentiation among the competition. It is good, first, to describe the products or services. Once you've described them, point out their comparative or proprietary advantage. Also show the future direction of the product and company that will keep that proprietary position intact.

Entry & growth strategy   Any potential investor wants to know how you will grow. This is the place in the plan where growth plans should be elucidated. Remember that when you seek investors, you should look for individuals or institutions that are compatible with you. Don't be bashful to express your growth strategy. If it is compatible with potential investors' philosophies, they are more likely to be better partners throughout the process. If the strategy is not compatible, then you probably didn't want them as a part of your firm anyway.

Entry strategies are relevant where a new product or service is concerned. If you have a new company, by definition you will have an entry strategy that encompasses the entire firm.

Market research & analysis   The market research and analysis section of the business plan answers some very critical questions. It addresses the question, "Is there a market for the product or service?" It defines the market to whom the product or service will be targeted. Substantiation for the target market is achieved through either primary or secondary market research. With primary market research you actually go out into the market and ask questions to learn more about the market and its attributes. With secondary market research, you use already explored information on a given topic to get a general idea of the market attributes. Secondary market research sources include newspapers, magazines, books, research reports, and market research firms.

Once the target market is defined and you give reasons as to why the target market is what it is, discuss the market size. How large the market is and its growth factors will help convince you or an investor that there is enough potential to support the business opportunity. Substantiation of the market size might be accomplished through the same primary or secondary market research sources you used in the target market definition.

Now look at trends in the market. You might explore a hot market today for your business, but is this trend expected to continue? What factors are or will come to bear on the market to continue or change the trends that are now surfacing? Will technological innovations change the market? Will new competitors reshape the market? Will your own employees potentially become your competitors? These issues must be researched thoroughly and substantiated as a part of your plan, or you won't know what to expect.

Competitive products   Understand your competition. The more you know about your competition, the better you will be able to react to their moves in the market. This section of your plan should include information on:

- Who is your competition
- What are their products
- What do their products do
- What are their products competitive advantages
- What is the financial strength of the company
- What are the operational strengths of the company (as described from both a process standpoint—how well do they get the job done—and a management standpoint—who are the key employees).
- Summarize the competitive section in the body of your plan. Place the lengthy information on the competition in an appendix or an exhibit at the back of the plan.

Comparative advantages   Comparative advantages are those items that you can do better than your competition. Comparative advantages can include product capabilities, marketing, sales, operational, managerial, or financial strengths. This section of the plan should outline all of your comparative advantages that you feel you have over competition.

Estimated market share & sales   Look at the competitors. Observe what portion of the market each one of them now has captured. Then, look at the marketing and sales vehicles that you intend to put into place. Then, estimate how much of the market you can capture. One way to translate this number into market share is to look at the potential sales that you feel that you can generate based on certain marketing activities.

Ongoing market evaluation   This section shows your commitment to understand a dynamic marketplace and change with it, as necessary. Sources of the market evaluation are particularly good to mention in that it shows your understanding of the market as it now exists.

Economics of the business   In the economics of the business section, you should show the profitability of the business. Show the gross and operating margins of the business (see chapter 8 for further explanation). They should be realistic figures that you have gotten from the financials of the business. This section could also include a general discussion of the profit margins of the business and their longevity.

Operations plan   This part of the plan outlines how the business will operate. Elements such as geographic location, facilities, and the operating plan of attack are included in this phase.

The management team   The key component of the business is its management team. This section should outline who they are, what their particular strengths are, and how they work together to make up a reasonable business. Be sure to include only those elements of a person's résumé that are somehow relevant to the business. It is not necessary to describe the paper route you held when you were a youth. As a part of the management team, you might want to round out the skills of the team with a board of directors. Realize that they might be used as a group of advisors, especially in areas where there are voids in the management team.

Overall schedule   Critical path charts or overall schedules of activity are extremely beneficial to the potential investor as well as the management team of the business. This component gives a graphical perspective on events. From this component, you can judge what events must occur, and when, in order to reach certain milestones within the business development process.

Critical risks involved in the business   This section of the business plan, if included, shows a lot about the people who are or will run the business. If virtually all conceivable critical risks of the business are listed in this section, it demonstrates a thoroughness of thought. It shows an understanding of the business as well as a certain honesty if the risks listed are accurate and might even negatively impact on the financeability of the business. It also demonstrates an ability to think situations through that might arise and plan for contingencies in case they actually do occur.

The financial plan   The financial plan comes from the rest of the business plan. The marketing plan shows what is needed to garner the sales shown in the plan. The operational section shows what it will take to perform in a fashion to complete the work behind the sale. Thus, the financial plan shows the sales (revenues) and allied operational expenses (both variable and fixed) that result. A detailed description of the assumptions behind all of the numbers should be quite easy, given the marketing and operational sections of the plan are well thought out. These assumptions are truly the substantiation of the numbers that are found in the income and cash flow statements and balance sheets for the company.

In the financial statements, a good format to take is to cast profit and loss (income) and cash flow statements on a monthly basis for the first year, a quarterly basis for the second and third years, and an annual basis for the fourth and fifth years. As you project further out in time, you will have less of an idea as to what will actually happen. Therefore, you are most accurate at estimating the first year and less so for years two through five.

All of the supporting material that is either too long or strictly supportive should be placed in exhibits or appendices.

Exhibits

There are two ways in which you might write your business plan—as a marketing or an operational plan. A marketing business plan has many more adjectives in it than does an operational plan.

Marketing versus operational plans

The marketing plan has a dual purpose—to sell potential investors on the business as well as to describe how the business will be run.

An operational business plan is written solely as a guide to management to actually run the business. It is extremely detail oriented and lacks the adjectives found in the marketing plan.

- Thoroughness and substantiation—When you write a business plan, it should be thorough enough to get your ideas across, completely. Those ideas should also be thoroughly substantiated. Use credible sources as a basis of your substantiation.
- Succinctness—Get your points across succinctly. Do not ramble on idly. Clarity is best achieved through succinctness.
- Credibility—If your plan is a marketing plan, it is particularly important that it convinces. Your substantiation will help the plan's credibility. Make sure your statements and sources to back them up are all real.

Critical plan elements

When I went to start a high-end luxury commuter rail service between Philadelphia and New York City, I wrote a business plan for the company in one day. The way I did it was to simply write an outline of all of the points that I wanted to cover. This document became the table of contents for the

How to write a business plan in a day

plan. I only wanted to put meat on each of the topics outlined. My immediate concern was not, necessarily, to substantiate all of the points that I made. This substantiation would come later. It did.

The plan hit all the major points that needed to be covered. It showed the areas where further research was needed. This further research led to the validation or dispelling of assumptions that were in the plan. This substantiated what had been already written.

So how do you write a business plan in one day?

- Create an outline for the plan
- Put the meat on the outline, making assumptions about the points being made
- Validate or dispel assumptions made through further research performed once your initial plan has been completed

This plan should be recognized only as a starting point for more work to come.

How to write a valuable & thorough plan

One way to write a valuable and thorough plan is to follow the format outlined in this chapter. Then, comb the completed plan and ask certain questions:

- Is the information contained in separate parts of the plan thorough?
- Is the information thorough enough to be convincing?
- Is the information completely substantiated so that it is convincing?
- Is the plan succinct in its statement of ideas to get the information across, simply?
- Is the plan credible?

If you can honestly answer yes to all of these questions, then you have written a valuable and thorough business plan.

The need for ongoing planning

Based on the fact that the computer industry is dynamic, you must constantly revisit the plan that you've created. This review might occur on a monthly basis. It is completely dependent on the market segment in which your product or service-based business operates. If you do annual planning in the computer business, you could be out of business in a very short time.

The ongoing planning in the industry is event-driven planning. Any time there is an event that could possibly affect your business, you had better start to plan around the actual or possible event.

Now two issues surface. The first is a simple monitoring question. How can you possibly monitor all events that occur in the computer industry so that you can factor them into your planning horizon? The answer is simple—read a lot! If you don't have the time to read a lot, then you should have someone in your business assigned to the task. I read about twenty trade publications a week. As a result, I have been able to anticipate trends and find new opportunities for my companies. In fact, every time I don't keep up on what is going on in the computer industry, I begin to wonder what opportunities I am missing.

The second issue is quality control. How, even if you keep up on the dynamic changes in the industry, do you know what to follow? Do you read and try to absorb everything that is going on? Or do you try to select only those items that are relevant to you and your business? This question is a tough one. I never quite know when one aspect of technology will become relevant to me and my business.

A sensible way to deal with the problem of keeping up with all segments of the computer industry is to assign topical areas to certain people in your firm. This assignment ensures that you will be able to know what is going on the moment you need information. If you don't have a large enough firm, you can pool with some of your friends. Each one of you can keep up with a different area of the industry.

On-line computer services can help you learn about what is going on in all segments of the industry. Even though on-line computer services don't give you the access to people that a trade show might, you might possibly find that you can be just as effective with this tool. With an on-line computer service, you can search through a reference database that gives you background information about a particular topic. You can then read articles in many of the trade journals with key-word searches. Finally, you can join in forum discussions and query people who have the same special interest that you are researching.

You can spend a lot of time planning and researching your business and out of nowhere comes an opportunity that completely changes your business direction and plan. A good example of luck is the story of Microsoft. Had Digital Research, who was writing the CPM operating system for IBM, followed through on the deal, Bill Gates would never have had the opportunity to write the Microsoft Disk Operating System (MS-DOS) for IBM. And had Bill Gates not been at the right place at the right time, do you think he would have been asked to write the disk operating system? Probably not. How well can you plan for an event like this one to occur? The answer is "not well or easily." But it is important to recognize that there are many opportunities in the marketplace ready and waiting for you to seize. You can definitely layer these optimistic elements into your plan, but only as outside chances. In some cases, like Microsoft's, probably not even Gates could have anticipated IBM's request much in advance of when it happened. The lesson—plan, work hard, and ensure that you have the right resources either as a part of your organization or as readily available to you, just in case a golden opportunity comes your way.

The element of luck in planning

To give you a better sense, a sample business plan follows that you can use as a model for your own plan.

Computer Business Solutions, Inc.
Business plan

Computer Business Solutions, Inc.
Main Street
Any city, USA 00000

Copy Number_____
Recipient _____
Authorization _____
Purpose _____

This business plan has been submitted on a confidential basis solely for the benefit of selected, highly qualified investors, company principals, and board members. It is not for use by any other persons, and may not be reproduced, stored, or copied in any other form without express permission of the company president. By accepting delivery of this plan, the recipient agrees to return this copy to the corporation at the address listed above if the recipient does not undertake to subscribe to the offering. Do not copy, fax, reproduce, or distribute without permission.

Table of contents

1. Executive summary

A. The business   Computer Business Solutions (CBS) offers desktop publishing services and consulting to save costs for our clients. By automating repetitive and complex tasks and facilitating a greater range of information management abilities, CBS adds permanent concrete value to our client's businesses. Our service is unique in that our consultants are experts in current computer desktop publishing technology, the business of the client, and are highly proficient teachers. CBS will engage in long term relationships, keeping our clients on the leading edge of technology.

B. The opportunity   CBS represents an unusual combination of complementary skills and experience across its management team. In light of the increasing trend to computerize many functions of business and publishing, CBS has the resources to provide complete desktop publishing consulting service at a lower cost than our competitors. We have a large market of potential clients who have expressed a need for our services.

C. Competitive advantage   With average prices of desktop publishing consulting at $90 per hour in the Philadelphia area, CBS is able to offer superior services at $60 per hour due to lower overhead, unique talent of management team, and a long-term philosophy that inspires repeat customers.

D. Profitability   Direct market research and experience has led to the conservative projection that CBS will be able to generate positive cash flow after three months and achieve over $1 million in sales after four years. Gross margins are projected to increase steadily while fixed costs will taper off, bringing increasing long-term profitability.

E. The team   The management team has years of experience in technical and business capacities. They have individually run computer consulting firms; programmed; edited for publications; run advertising agencies, retail sales, computer repair, accounting, and financial analysis businesses, and managed a restaurant. Their varied experience provides for powerful synergies.

F. Offering   CBS seeks $45,000 in debt to cover the start-up costs. Repayment is to occur within one year. Equity negotiations will also be considered.

A. The industry   The prospects for our entry in the desktop publishing service and consulting industry are promising. As the computer becomes more pervasive in the regular conducting of business, the demand for desktop publishing will increase. The hardware used by CBS (Apple, IBM, and compatibles) makes up the majority of the microcomputer market in the United States. The goal of a successful consulting firm is to implement desktop publishing service and systems for business sectors that are in the early stages of computer implementation or integration of new technological standards. CBS has found such market segments, and will seek to integrate desktop publishing therein.

II. The industry, the company, & the services

B. The company & the concept   Desktop publishing simply encompasses computer and printing machine systems that give their users the in-house ability to convert written material, ideas, and graphics into professional publications.

Computer Business Solutions offers solutions to desktop publishing related problems incorporating Apple Macintosh and IBM computer systems and a variety of software. CBS consultants combine expertise both in business and desktop publishing systems, to design intelligent solutions to our client's problems. Also central in the CBS method are efficiency, reliability, and instilling in the customer the comfort of knowing that their desktop publishing problems will be solved at reasonable cost in a way that they can understand. Our clients will benefit both by increased efficiency, and an increased scope of tasks that can be undertaken with the systems we design.

The general process of our desktop publishing consulting service is to first work with a client to determine their business problems. Second, we analyze solution options with the client with regard to benefits, costs, length of time to implement, and the long-term implications of the particular solutions. Third, the decided system is designed, implemented, and the client is trained in its use by our consultant(s) or support team. Finally, we remain in periodic contact with the client over the long term, both to ensure the system's reliable utilization and maintain a business relationship with the client.

CBS will serve a variety of types and sizes of firms, with the primary focus being medium-size firms requiring desktop publishing systems.

Computer Business Solutions will begin business as a Sub-chapter S corporation on January 1, 1993. The two principals of the company, John Doe and Stanley Doe, will be synthesizing their respective private computer consulting practices and their joint partnership firm, C & C Consulting into Computer Business Solutions on that date. John Doe's individual consulting practice began business in September 1986, offering management of information systems consulting, desktop publishing, and technical programming. Stanley Doe's individual consulting practice began business in March 1985, offering information systems consulting and programming. The C & C Consulting partnership began business in July 1986, offering the same services as the individual practices.

The new concept that CBS brings in this synthesis is the dual outlook on desktop publishing problems from a business and technical perspective. Also new is the added emphasis on developing and maintaining long-term relationships with clients.

C. The services   Desktop Publishing Services of Computer Business Solutions

- Publishing
  ~Layout

~Technical publishing
- Presentations
  ~Graphics
  ~Charting
  ~On-screen presentation
  ~Slide Shows

The clients for CBS services will in general be medium-size firms with yearly sales ranging from $300,000 to $50,000,000. These firms will be significantly dependent on either management of information related to their purposes or involved in publishing.

The primary desktop publishing tasks will be to facilitate the process by which our clients collect, edit, assemble information, and produce written newspapers and periodicals. These newspapers and periodicals will have the following attributes:

- Articles from many sources
- Combine text and graphics
- Use nonlocal information (need phone lines)
- Many users share printing machines
- Keep large bases of information

Some sample client engagements will include:

- Publishing companies that collect their articles from many sources are susceptible to the data and communication breakdowns discussed above, causing missed deadlines and loss of credibility in the field in which they publish and with their advertisers. To rectify these problems, we create and implement database systems that are specifically designed to manage textual and graphical information—the essence of publishing. These systems will map the status of articles as they progress through the editing process to their publishable form, keeping the publisher aware of the big picture with regard to the ability to meet deadlines. Some clients will require communication systems that allow articles written in one place to be transferred to another where it becomes incorporated and published. Accordingly, our systems will feature the ability to pull articles from the telephone lines through which they are sent and placed directly into the editing and layout processes.
- The combination of text and graphics into one document is a requirement in most forms of publication. The efficiency of our clients is directly proportional to the quality of the system they use. By designing systems that are tailor-made to our clients' layout and editing needs, we afford them greater efficiency and an enhanced ability to meet deadlines. The majority of our work in these cases is advising on software and hardware purchasing, configuration of the system and training in its use. In cases where larger numbers of people are working together, networked systems

allowing combined use of one printing machine or database are designed and implemented.

There are additional features of CBS' services beyond those described thus far that make it unique. First is our emphasis on communication with clients and our ability to teach people how to use systems rather than merely design and build them. Many companies are good at designing computer systems, but few are able to combine training and general business expertise into one desktop publishing and consulting service as CBS does. The second feature of our uniqueness is our policy of developing long term relationships, and the use of our whole consultant team to maintain the relationships.

Perhaps the most important consideration of the service comes from the clients' point of view. The payback period for CBS's consulting areas are calculated and substantiated in Exhibit 7 (FIG. 5-12). The payback period for a standard CBS implemented desktop publishing system is five months. The fact that the costs saved by our clients will on average recoup their expenses for our fees in only five months is an extremely attractive feature. After the payback period, our publishing clients will be adding about $60,000 per year to their annual cash flow. Because changes in computer technology require major system upgrades on the order of three years, our clients will enjoy more than 2.5 years of the increased cash flow before we will design and implement a new upgraded system, congruous to our long term relationship philosophy.

Working in a dynamic industry such as computer desktop publishing system consulting carries several important responsibilities with regard to the service. If we are to stay competitive for the long term, we must continually stay abreast with the latest developments in hardware and software technology, as well as conventional changes in communications media. Accordingly we will maintain an up-to-date library of products and require our consultants to spend regular time becoming proficient in using and implementing the new technology that benefits our clients. Thus, our service is an evolving entity.

D. Entry & growth strategies   The key success variables will be relatively low cost of service, innovative integration of business and technical expertise, and establishing and maintaining credibility. Our growth will be dependent on our ability to increase our credibility and convince our target market. The pace of our growth is intended to be steady, with a five-year goal of $1.2 million in sales (substantiated in upcoming sales forecasts). Faster growth is not desirable because learning the client's business in addition to technical ability is a fundamental company mission. The basis for our entry and growth in this industry is the cost effectiveness of our service and the excess demand over supply for such a service.

III. Market research & analysis

A. Customers   The customers to whom CBS will be providing services in the first year of operations are detailed below, with the reasons why each particular customer group was chosen. The reasons are assigned a code for convenience as follows:

Target Market Segments: First Year of Operations

A:	Good accessibility	C:	Special contacts in industry
ED:	CBS Desktop publishing	N:	Need for CBS expertise
EG:	CBS Graphics expertise	F:	Financially solvent client
EA:	Decision analysis expertise	T:	New technology involved

Customer Group	Reasons for Choice Code
Advertising Agencies	EG, EM, N, F
Newspaper Publishers	ED, N, T, C, F
Periodical Publishers	ED, N, T, C, A, F

These three market segments have the combination of attributes that makes them best suited for our target market in the early years of our operation. The first requirement in selecting these markets was the existence of a client need for which we have expertise. Medium-size firms were selected, providing a balance between accessibility to a new consulting firm and financial solvency (i.e., ability to pay consulting bills). Additionally, the periodical and newspaper publishing segments will be particularly conducive to our services, given our proprietary advantage in the latest technological advances in color imaging and processing.

Our target customers in these segments have been located through Dun and Bradstreet's on-line marketing research system at the Wharton School's business library. The firms are scattered throughout the Philadelphia area, including its suburbs. Exhibit 1 (FIG. 5-1) contains charts showing the breakdown of sample portions of the target market by sales and number of employees.

5-1   Target market sizes by segment for 1993

Market segment	Average hours/job	Additional hours	Total hours	$/hour	Number of potential clients	Market size
Advertising agencies	194	25	219	55	50	$602,250
Publishers	194	25	219	55	54	$650,430
					Total market size:	$1,252,680
					Average $/sale:	$7,488

An important factor in selecting and recruiting from our target market was the ease with which the people in these firms who make consultant hiring decisions could be reached for negotiations. The table below shows the level of difficulty in making this contact by segment, and the means by which it has primarily been made.

Market Segment	Ease of Contact	Means of Contact
Advertising agencies	Challenging	Mail
Newspaper publishers	Moderate	Mail, phone
Periodical publishers	Easy	Mail, phone, inside contacts

B. Market size & trends   Information regarding the numbers of potential clients is broken down by segment shown in Exhibit 1 (FIG. 5-1) for the first year of operations. This information comes from Dun & Bradstreet's on-line system. The data is for Philadelphia. The number of hours required to service these clients and the price per hour for CBS services are also used to calculate the market size in dollars. (Information showing how many consulting hours are required to service a client are contained in the operations section.) Starting in 1993 through 1998, the target market will be expanded to include medium-size companies in these segments in the entire Delaware Valley area. Additional segments will be added periodically to facilitate growth.

C. Competition & competitive edges   There are about 90 firms in the Philadelphia area that offer some form of desktop publishing consulting. These firms vary greatly in the scope and quality of services offered. Information about the competitors was gathered in three ways—(1) The Dun & Bradstreet on-line market research system was used to determine who was in the industry in the area, and their profitability, size, number of accounts and employees, and other information. (2) CBS sent a mailing to these firms in the form of a generic firm requesting information about their companies, services, and prices. (3) A sample of the firms were called to get a feel for the level of comfort felt by a caller trying to seek their services.

The on-line research was used to compile a ranking of the firms that would consider the competitors' ability to generate revenue in a manner that did not necessarily require a particular size. By using the quotient: (Sales/# of employees) as a general ranking criteria, we can gauge the ability of these firms to generate profits. Assumably, this ranking will encompass both technical expertise and people skills, because they are both required to generate revenues. A sample of 25 firms in the Philadelphia and surrounding area (for which sales and employee numerical data was available) ranked in this manner, are listed below along with the services they offer. See Exhibit 2 (FIG. 5-2).

This information is useful both in understanding how our competitors perform as well as what range of values employees bring to various firms. For our competitors, the average revenue generated for each employee is $113,000, a key figure that CBS will plan to exceed by offering high-quality expert services to the markets that most need them. Breakdowns of the competition by sales and number of employees are contained in exhibit 2.

5-2 Competition ranked by revenue-generating ability

Perf. rank	Competition firm	Area 1	Area 2	Area 3	Sales/employee(s)
1	Easy Business Solutions, Inc.	A	O		300
2	Consolidated Data Services, Inc.	C	DP	S	273
3	American Computer Services, Inc.	C			267
4	Bernstein Ted Associates	P			250
5	Iverson Associates, Inc.	C			160
6	IMA, Inc.	C			143
7	Programming Consulting, Inc.	C	DP		125
8	Fastech, Inc.	C			120
9	Total Consulting Services, Inc.	C			111
10	Software Support Services, Inc.	C	B	S	105
11	International Software P.	C	DP		94
12	American Phoenix Comp. Service	C			89
13	American Computer Educ., Inc.	C			86
14	XRT, Inc.	C	DP		83
15	Macro Corporation	C	O		82
16	Professional Data Solutions	DP			77
17	Ezware Corporation	C	DP		71
18	Comtech Resources, Inc.	C			67
19	Micro Endeavors, Inc.	A	C		60
20	Dinkerton Computer Cons., Inc.	C			58
21	Product Research, Inc.	C	DP		57
22	Maxima Office Systems, Inc.	C			50
23	Professional Training Service	C	T		43
24	Comprehensive Management, Inc.	C			43
25	Cone Software Lab, Inc.	DP			20
				Ave S/E:	113.39

Service codes: C=computer (general), DP=data processing, A=accounting, O=office automation, T=technical programming, S=systems design, B=billing

The mailings that were sent to these companies requesting information and pricing structure were met by three types of responses—(1) A form letter requesting a personal meeting to find the "exact nature" of the client's needs. (2) A profile sheet detailing the company's services. (3) A profile sheet attached to expensive glossy advertising brochures put out by the software companies whose products they implement. (This seems to be an effective marketing tactic that CBS will utilize to save on advertising costs in the first two years.) About 50% of the companies did not respond to the request for information. About 30% refused to send information through the mail and instead requested a personal meeting. The remaining 20% sent information. The phone sample was used on 25 firms and generally resulted in cheerful conversation. All the firms wanted a personal meeting, and nine were willing to send information through the mail.

Comparative advantages   From the research, the following strengths and weaknesses of the competition were determined:

Strengths

- Wide varieties of services offered
- Established and solvent
- Reputable client base
- Well respected in technical community

Weaknesses

- Business and technical expertise not emphasized
- Inaccessible (some elitist characteristics)
- Lack of consulting on presentations
- Services not well understood by target market

Our ability to provide complete desktop publishing services that are sensitive to both business and technical issues is the basis of our market niche. Additionally, we understand that computers are a source of uncertainty for many of our potential clients and accordingly emphasize communication and training skills. We will frame our services into terms that can be understood by noncomputer experts, and emphasize the concrete benefits to be received.

The fundamental value added by our services to our client's companies comes in the form of saved costs. By increasing efficiency and removing work from business and publishing processes, we bring long term sustained cash flow increases to our clients. A detailed payback analysis has been performed. Through consultation with previous clients and our desktop publishing director's publishing company who have implemented systems like CBS offers, we have determined exact savings figures. The detailed calculations of the time required for clients to recover their expenses are presented in Exhibit 7 (FIG. 5-12) at the end of this plan) for the publishing services. The results are presented in FIG. 5-3.

These payback periods are strong marketing tools in convincing clients to contract for a system, because they demonstrate concrete benefits. They will be used as the core of the CBS sales pitch to interested clients. Upon this base will be built the more human benefits of our service such as the long-term relationship and the ability to teach.

D. The market survey   A sample of 90 was taken from our target markets to determine the kind of services needed, desired attributes of the firm

5-3 Payback analysis—CBS services

Service	Total costs	Average savings/month	Payback period*
Publishing consult.	$17,800	$4,295 after proficient	5 months

*Payback period includes learning time

providing those services, and willingness to pay various prices. The results of the survey are as follows:

- Sample size: 90
- Return rate: 19.7%
- Services needed: Desktop publishing (large variety of specifics)
- Desired qualities:
  - ~(1) Computer and business expertise
  - ~(2) Teaches and communicates well
  - ~(3) Reliability
- Price willingness average: $68/hour

E. Forecasting sales & market share   The market survey and prior experience is the base for the CBS sales forecast that, in turn, is the basis for the projected financial statements. It is important to put significant amounts of effort into projecting sales in a substantiated manner because many things depend on this forecast. With this consideration, the following model was used to forecast sales.

CBS sales will be generated through three channels—(1) Contacts achieved through direct-mail surveying and advertising. (2) Word-of-mouth diffused from previous clients. (3) Contracts with previous clients to update their previously designed systems to take advantage of technological developments. Experience of the principals in the operation of C & C Consulting has shown that once contact has been made and a presentation given to the person having authority to make consultant hiring decisions in firms of comparable size to the ones considered above, decisions to hire have been rendered within three days. About 30% of clients with the need for our services contracted for full scale system design and implementation; about 10% of such potential clients contracted for less involved services (for example, small mailing systems or purchase recommendations); an additional 20% did not contract for services initially, but contracted later for services (usually within one year). A diagram of this breakdown is shown with direct mail considered in FIG. 5-4.

This model can be used to predict the expected value of contact with clients through direct mail and word of mouth. Direct mail is the channel considered explicitly above, showing the predicted results of each survey sent including

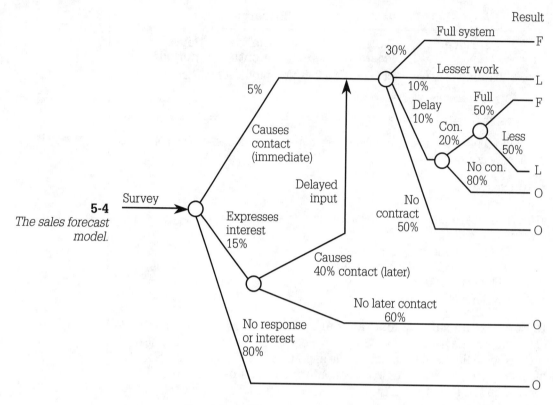

5-4
The sales forecast model.

Result key: F = Billable hours for full system
L = Billable hours for lesser work
O = No payoff

the effects of direct and delayed response. The payoffs listed at the end of each branch are multiplied by the probabilities of reaching each payoff that is determined by the probability function that models the tree. Word of mouth can be modeled by thinking of it as a mechanism by which CBS is contacted with interested clients—completely analogous to being contacted with interested direct-mail respondents. Thus projected word of mouth contacts can be fed into the tree at the point following direct-mail response.

Word of mouth is estimated as follows—Twenty percent of all clients who contracted for work the prior year will generate some contact that might result in another contract with probability given by the tree function. Fifteen percent of all clients who contracted for work two years prior will generate some contact that might result in another contract as given by the tree function. Ten percent of clients for whom work was done three years prior, will generate the same new contract potential.

Jobs for previous clients are estimated as follows—Twenty-five percent of clients who received a full system three years prior will contract for a new system to take advantage of the 3–4 year technological cycle of computer systems. Fifteen percent of clients who received a system four years prior will contract for a new system. Five percent of clients who received a system five years prior will contract for a new system. This method in conjunction with the average prices and hours (see operations) of full desktop publishing systems and lesser consulting lead to the following sales in FIG. 5-5.

5-5 Sales forecast 1993–1998

Year	1993	1994	1995	1996	1997	1998
Direct mail sent	2400	2400	2000	1500	1200	1000
Mail-generated (full)	67	67	56	42	33	28
Mail-generated (less)	24	24	20	15	12	10
Word-of-mouth (full)	0	6	11	16	19	21
Word-of-mouth (less)	0	2	4	6	7	7
Jobs for prev. clients (full)	0	0	0	17	28	55
Jobs for prev. clients (less)	0	14	43	51	58	62
Total full contracts	67	73	67	75	80	104
Total lesser contracts	24	40	67	72	77	79
Total jobs done	91	113	134	147	157	183
Full contract rate	$ 7488	$ 7488	$ 8237	$ 9060	$ 9695	$ 10,276
Lesser contract rate	$ 1250	$ 1250	$ 1375	$ 1513	$ 1618	$ 1715
Projected sales	$531,696	$595,999	$643,784	$786,783	$902,342	$1,202,709

This forecast utilizes the methods described to estimate the number of full desktop publishing systems and lesser consulting (that is, purchase recommendations and small programs) to be completed by year. The prices of this work starts in 1993 at $55 per hour and increases at 10% over 1994 and 1995, and increases thereafter only to cover inflation (5–8% average). This sales forecast is nice in that it is based on logic and experience. The tree diagram also allows for easier identification of problem areas and subsequent fine tuning of marketing methods and forecasting. The survey method of advertising also allows CBS to stay in contact with its target markets and thereby evolve with the market needs. It is important to maintain this market contact after initial successes to be able to integrate markets and technology for the long term.

A. Gross & operating margins   The gross margins available to cover fixed costs are graphed in FIG. 5-6 to show the prospective profitability trends.

Both gross margins and variable costs of the company rise semilinearly through the first six years of operation. By mid-1995 the gap begins to widen

IV. The economics of the business

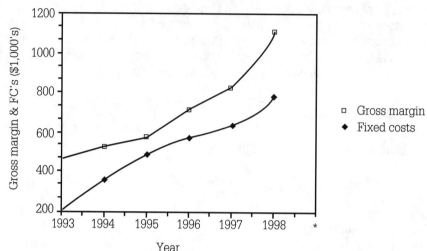

Gross margins and fixed costs 1993–1998

5-6
Gross margins and fixed costs 1993–1998.

□ Gross margin
◆ Fixed costs

slowly as economies of scale set in, bringing greater returns on the fixed costs due to experience and better opportunities.

B. Profit potential & durability   The market research and financial projections have shown that the business will be able to achieve steadily growing profits through healthy expansion plans and increasing market share. With a 1 year period to retire debt, and a three-month period to reach positive cash flow (see financials—Exhibits 4 and 5 near the end of this plan) the business is a viable venture economically.

V. Operations plan

A. The operating cycle   Although there is no basis for any patterns of consulting demand correlated to certain times of the year, there is an operating cycle dependent upon technological developments. Major developments in software tend to follow major hardware innovations because software packages are typically designed around hardware specifications. The demand for consulting services will tend to surge after hardware and software advance, because new benefits can be exploited that place the new technology users in relatively advantageous positions. Through participation in hardware manufacturers consultant's relations programs (such as Apple's ACR program), close ties with software producers, user group participation, and technological trade magazine authoring (*Computerworld*), CBS will stay abreast of innovations that will bring a surge of new clients and previous clients seeking new systems based on new technologies.

B. Geographical location   In 1993 and 1994, CBS will be located in a West Philadelphia apartment, probably somewhere on the 4100–4600 blocks of Pine Street. Such a location provides centralized access to our target market that is situated in Center City Philadelphia and the surrounding suburbs. The combination of convenient location and low cost make this choice optimal for the early phases. In 1995 the business will move to a more "high profile" location such as the University City Science Center to increase credibility and to associate the business with a technologically connotative location, while still maintaining close proximity to the clients. The fact that clients rarely will enter the CBS office, makes the site choice flexible, allowing the company to focus on its own needs in making this decision.

C. Facilities & improvements   The office will be a large room attached to three smaller rooms in a modest house. The smaller rooms will serve as offices for the principals, and the larger room will serve as an administrative and design area. Consultants will have work spaces in the larger room in reasonably close proximity to the company's resource library. Overall, the layout is intended to foster a close team atmosphere. Facility improvements will consist largely of security measures such as window bars and an alarm system.

D. The consulting job   The consulting job consists of several phases. The first phase is the initial determination of needs, presentation of CBS services, cost/benefit analysis, and a price quotation. This phase is always executed by either John Doe, Stanley Doe, or Jane Doe. This takes four billable hours and is only charged to the client if a contract is made. As the company establishes more credibility, this free initial consultation policy might be removed to prevent potential clients from getting a "free" needs analysis.

The second phase of the process is to observe operations, make a purchase recommendation for hardware and software, and design the desktop publishing system. This phase will again be executed by one of the three principals in conjunction with contract consultants in order to assure that the system will encompass the client's needed benefits, and to give each principal the contact necessary to manage the contract consultants. (The principal will participate mainly in observation and recommendations, and the contract consultants will be primarily responsible for design.)

The third phase consists of implementing the system into the environment of the client and testing its full range of functions. Any problems are corrected. This phase will be executed by the contract consultants because they are most familiar with the tailor-made systems that have been designed. The principal will be well connected enough with the job to step in for emergency problems.

The fourth phase consists of training and final modifications. This phase will be executed by the contract consultant that designed and implemented the system. The publishing training phase is intensive due to the large number of specialized tasks that must be taught.

The final phase is follow up work that occurs after the formal completion of the system. This will usually involve additional training and correction of errors that take a longer time to surface. Although CBS representatives will tend to work on discrete portions of jobs, there will be a team atmosphere whereby assistance can be obtained from fellow consultants. The principals will serve as a general support staff to the contract consultants. There might, on occasion, be a job that is inherently more important than other jobs (for example, big contracts, clients with large word-of-mouth potential, etc.). These jobs will usually be executed in their entirety by the principal most associated with the client and the specifics of the job. This strategy will help keep the control of important situations in the hands of those people most disposed to act in the company's best interests. A feedback policy will also allow clients to express their level of satisfaction with CBS services as they are being received, so that the principals can make necessary adjustments in service.

VI. The management team

The CBS management team was selected by John Doe to reflect a complete set of complementary skills and management ability. Presented below are profiles of each member of the team. Exhibits 3a, 3b, 3c, and 3d below are complete résumés for each member.

John Doe, President, CEO

Education:
    B.S. Wharton School, Univ. of Pennsylvania, Entrepreneurial Management
    B.S.E. Univ. of Pennsylvania, Electrical Engineering
    B.A. Univ. of Pennsylvania, Physics, History & Soc. of Science
    Prior Study: Harvard University

Prior Work:
    Implementation of computer systems for distributors, real estate managers, software developers, retail businesses, banks, graphics design firms, and art galleries (California, Florida, Boston)
    Assistant Manager: Wendy's food service
    Technician: Computerland

Responsibilities:
    Manage CBS, keep firm competitive both on technological and business fronts, establish and maintain contacts with clients and target industries, consult clients, give talks, and write articles for trade periodicals.

Initial CBS Salary: $25,000/year

Stock Ownership: 51%

Stanley Doe, Vice President, Operations

Education
    B.S. Univ. of Florida, Economics
    Prior Study: Harvard University

Prior Work:

Design and implementation of MIS systems for hospitals, software developers, interior designers, retailers, distributors, and fitness centers. Worked as a salesman and instructor for a computer retailer. Ran successful advertising firm.

Responsibilities:

Direct the desktop publishing consulting activities of the firm, maintain high quality service standards, consult clients, keep firm abreast of technological developments, give talks and write articles for trade periodicals.

Initial CBS Salary: $25,000/year

Stock Ownership: 25%

Jane Doe, Director of Desktop Publishing

Education:

B.A. Univ. of Pennsylvania, Mathematics

Prior Work:

Assistant for SIAM News, graphics layout utilizing computer based systems, Managed advertising division of SIAM.

Responsibilities:

Consult desktop publishing clients, keep firm abreast of desktop publishing and presentation developments, produce CBS newsletter, write articles for trade periodicals.

Initial CBS Salary: $20,000/year

Stock Ownership: 10%

Harry Doe, VP, Finance

Education:

B.S. Wharton School, Univ. of Pennsylvania, Accounting, Economics

Prior Work:

Accountant for Spicer & Oppenheim, Manages the Doe Fund, prepared financial statements and rendered financial advice for a variety of clients.

Responsibilities:

Preparation of CBS financial statements, financial and legal advisor, liaison to New York markets, work on CBS designed accounting and financial related systems.

Stock Ownership: 4%

Compensation:

Percent of year-end retained earnings plus personal expenses.

The board of directors

John Doe:

 Chairman of the Board. Mr. Doe is chief operating officer of Computer Business Solutions.

Harry Doe:

 Managing Partner, The Doe Fund; Auditor, Spicer and Oppenheim. Mr. Doe will serve as a financial and legal advisor to Computer Business Solutions.

VII. Overall schedule

Presented below is a time line detailing what will be done prior to the start of operations, and when each event is projected to occur. This gives a greater feel for the "big picture." See FIG. 5-7.

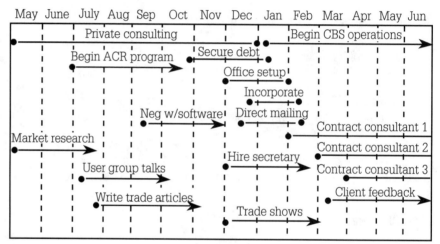

5-7
Overall schedule May 1993–June 1994.

The CBS principals will act as private consultants throughout the summer, seeking to both expand their technical expertise and come in contact with new people and potential clients. Additionally, the principals will seek to integrate themselves into the technical community by way of user group talks and trade magazine article writing. Integration into the communities of the particular industries of our target markets will be accomplished in a similar manner. Participation in the Apple Consultant Relations program will begin three months prior to the start of operations to provide an optimal balance between consulting technique benefits offered, and our capacity to service clients that are referred as a result of the program. Negotiations with software producers will begin at midsummer, to establish a working relationship. This will keep us abreast of software developments, enhancing our competitiveness.

Start-up and initial operations costs will be covered by the $45,000 short-term debt secured at the end of 1992. Office setup, secretary hiring, and trade show attendance start in January 1993, as the business officially incorporates and begins consulting under the CBS name. The first year consulting staff is completed as three contract consultants are hired in the first quarter of 1993. A direct-mail survey/advertisement (2400 count) will be sent in January 1993.

Much effort will be expended to ensure that the schedule is followed in a timely manner. Particular emphasis will be placed on the items that are not immediately pressing such as the user group talks and articles. These items do not reap immediate benefit, but are essential to the company's goal of being a respected member of both the technical and business communities, that brings greater long-term rewards.

VIII. Critical risks & problems

1. Sales expectations are not reached.
   Resolution: Reduce rates to increase client base. Increase recruitment efforts through increased direct-mail advertising and higher involvement with our potential clients.

2. Service becomes obsolete fast.
   Resolution: Spend significant company effort keeping abreast of latest technological developments, through contact with computer manufacturers (Apple), software manufacturers, and our own developing consulting library.

3. Collection of fees.
   Resolution: Collect up-front portions of total fees before job, and make provisions in the service contract for additional collections as milestones are reached in the project.

4. Our consultants try to become independent.
   Resolution: Reward consultants generously and consistently, making their relationship to the company mutually beneficial by keeping the consultant up to date with technology. Provide incentives with stock ownership plans and contracts.

5. Cash flow problems.
   Resolution: Financial planning has indicated the appropriate amount of debt to incur, but we need to operate in a manner that will ensure that this quantity is sufficient and in the event that it is not, we must have a back-up source. Accordingly, we will purchase fixed assets only as they are needed, and will rely on our personal savings and additional short-term borrowing in the event of a cash flow emergency.

6. Competitors try to jump in.
   Consulting, being a somewhat egotistical industry, is conducive to having a competitor intervene and convince clients that they could receive better deals elsewhere.

Resolution: The only way to prevent this is to develop and maintain close ties with the client in a relationship of mutual reliance. Fortunately, this is a founding philosophy of CBS.

IX. The financial plan

A. Pro forma income statements 1993–1998

Exhibit 4 (near the end of this plan) presents projected income statements for the years 1993–1998, with an operations start date of 1 January 1993. The assumptions and substantiation for these statements are as follows:

Revenues: Projected from the sales derivation covered in detail in the marketing section. The monthly projections for the first year are interpolated as a linear function achieving the average monthly value based on the sales forecast at midyear.

Salaries of principals: Flat rates starting low to cut costs and demonstrate commitment. Later they grow to reflect the firm's increasing profitability.

Salaries of contract consultants: Number of contract hours required is taken as the difference between the total projected demand for hours (sales forecast) minus the principals' capacity. Wages start at $35 per hour and increases with the cost of living (5–7%). One consultant is added each month for three months during the first year, and one consultant is added each year thereafter, to meet demand.

Benefits and insurance: Estimated to be on the order of typical values found by research with insurance firms and governmental regulations.

Interest expense: Assumes 12% rate on $45,000 financed first year to satisfy problems predicted by the cash flow statement.

Rent: $800 per month for 1993 and 1994 and $1800 per month subsequently based on researched values ($19 per square foot) and adjusted for annual 7% increases.

Telephone: Estimates as a positive linear function of sales from an initial seed of $3000 for the first year of local and long distance service for four telephone lines (one for a facsimile machine).

Travel and expenses: Assumes six trade shows per year per person, $250 per person per trip, and 18 total one-day conferences at $150 each.

Training: Assumes 10 total sessions at $200 each per year.

Equipment: Toner cartridges, ribbons, repair; increases as we have more equipment and with greater age of the equipment.

Auto maintenance and gas: Increases with frequency of sales calls and expansion of geographical area (based on sales forecast and contact tree), and the age of the automobile(s).

Office setup: Assumes initial purchase of three desks and chairs, filing cabinets, window security. Gradual purchases of "comfort items" are allowed thereafter as profits increase.

Legal incorporation fees: Based on Pennsylvania fees for incorporation. Legal expenses are associated primarily with bad debt and are an increasing function of sales.

Depreciation: Straight-line method used on purchased equipment considering their variety of useful lives.

Bad debt expense: Estimated as 12% of sales for the first year and declining by 1% per year to a long run value of 8% as our collection methods improve.

Direct-mail expense: Considers the pattern of direct-mail advertising planned in the marketing strategy, costs of mailed packets, and postage (including planned increases).

Sales calls: Non-car transportation (for example, public transportation, taxis), estimated from the number of projected clients in dense urban areas.

Color brochures: Prices for the services of the "Color Q" company. Increases planned for inflation, increasing mailings of information about CBS, and the periodic design of new brochures.

Photography: Quoted rates from private photographer. Used for creation of new brochures periodically.

Market research: Fees for using the Wharton on-line Dun and Bradstreet system and quoted rates for the Computer Intelligence Corporation mailing lists.

Business lunches: Increase with activity; sales function used as a template after first estimating the total volume of needed lunches.

Mail: Nondirect advertising (administrative). Estimated as a function of sales (activity) and considers the postage rates.

Office supplies: Larger initial outlay for permanent items, subsequent budget increases with company activity.

Retirement of short term debt: The $45,000 borrowed initially is retired in three $15,000 payments in each of the final three months of 1993.

Taxation: CBS is an S-corporation, keeping all taxes at the personal income level—thus it is not reflected on CBS financial statements.

Dividends: Yearly and quarterly evaluations will be made as to how the retained earnings will be either distributed to the principals as dividends or re-invested into company expansion or improvements. The dividends will be distributed yearly as estimated on the income statement. This is a flexible policy that might change in terms of timing and allocation.

B. Pro forma cash flow analysis 1993–1997

Exhibit 5 contains pro forma cash flow statements for 1993–1997. The assumptions and substantiations are as follows:

Revenues: Projected as previously described.

Operating and marketing expenses: Derived from income statement.

Depreciation: Added back to cash flow because it is merely a paper transaction.

Change in accounts receivable: Projected under the assumption that two thirds of sales will be continually carried as receivables with 45 day turnover. Receivable write-offs for bad debts are also a part of the calculation.

Change in accounts payable: Assumes that most administrative expenses will be operating under 2% net 30 terms from suppliers, and that these expenses will make up the bulk of accounts payable.

Prepaid expenses: The health and life insurance policies of John Doe will be prepaid yearly, and adjusted monthly as they are depleted.

Purchases of fixed assets: Reflects projected purchases of two Macintosh computer systems, one IBM microcomputer system, a laser printer, software packages, a photocopy machine, a facsimile machine, and a scanner during the first year. Three systems are added each subsequent year to keep up with technology, as well as subsequent purchases of software and software updates.

Short-term debt: Due to projected cash shortfalls without debt, it is deemed necessary to incur $45,000 of short-term debt during the first year to meet start up costs. It is projected that through principals' currently high credit ratings, an interest rate of 12% will be secured.

Capital stock: 100 shares issued at $1 par. (John Doe: 51%, Stanley Doe: 25%, Jane Doe: 10%, Harry Doe: 5%, treasury stock: 9%).

C. Pro forma balance sheets 1993–1997

Exhibit 6 contains pro forma balance sheets for 1993–1997. Most assumptions behind the balance sheet are implicit in the income statements and cash flow statements, and have already been discussed. These statements give a view of how the company will appear at various instances in time over the next five years, on a cumulative basis.

D. Break-even analysis

Considering what effect a shortfall in sales will have on profitability, a break even analysis is presented for the first year in FIG. 5-8.

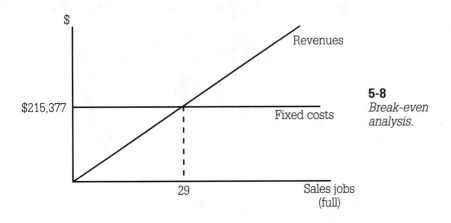

5-8
Break-even
analysis.

The minimum number of desktop publishing consulting jobs that must be completed to cover fixed costs is 29. (This number is adjusted upward to 32 jobs if bad debt allowances are made.) Because the conservatively projected number of jobs during the first year is 91, covering fixed costs seems a reasonable task.

E. Conclusions

The first year of operations will be flexible. CBS will only purchase equipment as it is needed, stalling for time until systems are completed and the collection of fees becomes a regular and stable activity. The central financial goal of the company is to cut costs whenever possible, but never to sacrifice the future of the business by forgoing necessities.

Exhibits 4 through 7 are shown as FIG. 5-9 through FIG. 5-12.

Exhibits

5-9 Exhibit 4—Pro forma income statement

	Jan-93	Feb-93	Mar-93	Apr-93	May-93	Jun-93	Jul-93	Aug-93	Sep-93	Oct-93	Nov-93	Dec-93
Revenues	14308	20308	26308	32308	38308	41308	47308	50308	56308	62308	68308	74308
Operating expenses												
Salaries												
John Doe	2084	2084	2084	2084	2084	2084	2084	2084	2084	2084	2084	2084
Stanley Doe	2084	2084	2084	2084	2084	2084	2084	2084	2084	2084	2084	2084
Jane Doe	1667	1667	1667	1667	1667	1667	1667	1667	1667	1667	1667	1667
Harry Doe	0	0	0	0	0	0	0	0	0	0	0	0
Consultant 1	916	1053	1189	1324	1460	1596	1732	1867	2003	2139	2274	2410
Consultant 2	0	1053	1189	1324	1460	1596	1664	1732	1867	2003	2139	2274
Consultant 3	0	0	1053	1189	1324	1460	1596	1732	1867	2003	2139	2274
Consultant 4	0	0	0	0	0	0	0	0	0	0	0	0
Consultant 5	0	0	0	0	0	0	0	0	0	0	0	0
Consultant 6	0	0	0	0	0	0	0	0	0	0	0	0
Secretary	1000	1000	1000	1000	1000	1000	1000	1000	1000	1000	1000	1000
Benefits	250	250	250	250	250	250	250	250	250	250	250	250
Life insurance, principal	417	417	417	417	417	417	417	417	417	417	417	417
Health insurance, principal	83	83	83	83	83	83	83	83	83	83	83	83
Interest expense	281	281	281	281	281	281	281	281	281	281	281	281
Rent	800	800	800	800	800	800	800	800	800	800	800	800
Phone	190	200	210	220	230	240	260	270	280	290	300	310
Travel & expenses	600	600	600	600	600	600	600	600	600	600	600	600
Training	167	167	167	167	167	167	167	167	167	167	167	167
Equipment maintenance	0	0	17	17	17	17	17	17	17	17	17	17
Auto maintenance & gas	124	154	184	214	244	274	334	364	394	424	454	484
Office setup/maintenance	450	150	50	25	25	25	25	25	25	25	25	25
Legal/incorporation fees	300	155	155	155	155	155	155	155	155	155	155	155
Depreciation expense	333	333	333	333	333	333	333	333	333	333	333	333
Bad debt expense	1717	2437	3157	3877	4597	4957	5677	6037	6757	7477	8197	8917
Total operating expenses:	13463	14968	16969	18111	19279	20086	21225	21964	23131	24298	25466	26633

Marketing expenses											
Advertising (direct mail)	1462	1462	0	0	0	0	0	0	0	0	0	0
Sales calls (transportation)	29	41	53	66	78	84	96	102	114	127	139	151
Color brochures	3110	0	0	0	0	0	0	0	0	0	0	0
Photography	250	0	0	0	0	0	0	0	0	0	0	0
Market research (D & B)	100	100	0	0	0	0	0	0	0	0	0	0
Market research (CIC)	500	0	0	0	0	0	0	0	0	0	0	0
Business lunches w/clients	378	536	695	853	1012	1091	1249	1328	1487	1645	1804	1962
Total marketing expenses:	5828	2139	748	919	1089	1175	1345	1431	1601	1772	1942	2113
Administrative expenses												
Mail	49	70	90	111	131	142	162	173	193	214	234	255
Office supplies	300	64	64	64	64	64	64	64	64	64	64	64
Miscellaneous	25	25	25	25	25	25	25	25	25	25	25	25
Administrative total:	374	158	179	200	220	230	251	261	282	303	323	344
Total expenses	19666	17265	17896	19230	20588	21491	22821	23656	25014	26373	27731	29089
Income before extraordinary items	-5358	3043	8412	13078	17720	19817	24487	26652	31294	35935	40577	45219
Short-term debt retired	0	0	0	0	0	0	0	0	0	15000	15000	15000
Net income	**-5358**	**3043**	**8412**	**13078**	**17720**	**19817**	**24487**	**26652**	**31294**	**20935**	**25577**	**30219**

5-10   Exhibit 5—Pro forma cash flow statements

	Jan-93	Feb-93	Mar-93	Apr-93	May-93	Jun-93	Jul-93	Aug-93	Sep-93	Oct-93	Nov-93	Dec-93
Cash flow (operations)												
+Net sales revenues	14308	20308	26308	32308	38308	41308	47308	50308	56308	62308	68308	74308
-Operating expenses	13463	14968	16969	18111	19279	20086	21225	21964	23131	24298	25466	26633
-Selling and marketing expenses	5828	2639	1248	1419	1589	1675	1845	1931	2101	2272	2442	2613
+Depreciation addback	333	333	333	333	333	333	333	333	333	333	333	333
-Δ A/R	9543	4002	4002	4002	4002	2001	4002	2001	4002	4002	4002	4002
+Δ A/P	260	260	260	260	260	260	260	260	260	260	260	260
-Δ Prepaid expenses	0	0	0	0	0	0	0	0	0	0	0	0
+Δ Other liabilities	0	0	0	0	0	0	0	0	0	0	0	0
Cash flow from operations	-13933	-707	4682	9370	14032	18140	20830	25006	27667	32329	36992	41654
Cash flow (investing)												
-Δ Fixed assets	12050	10000	10000	0	0	1000	0	0	0	0	0	0
Cash flow from investing	-12050	-10000	-10000	0	0	-1000	0	0	0	0	0	0
Cash flow (financing)												
+Short term debt incurred	45000	0	0	0	0	0	0	0	0	0	0	0
+Long term debt incurred	0	0	0	0	0	0	0	0	0	0	0	0
-Retirement of ST debt	0	0	0	0	0	0	0	0	0	15000	15000	15000
+Δ Capital stock par	0	0	0	0	0	0	0	0	0	0	0	0
Cash flow from financing	45000	0	0	0	0	0	0	0	0	-15000	-15000	-15000
Dividends issued	0	0	0	0	0	0	0	0	0	0	0	0
Net cash flow	**19017**	**-10707**	**-5318**	**9370**	**14032**	**17140**	**20830**	**25006**	**27667**	**17329**	**21992**	**26654**

5-11 Exhibit 6—Pro forma balance sheet

	31-Jan-93	28-Feb-93	31-Mar-93	30-Apr-93	31-May-93	30-Jun-93	31-Jul-93	31-Aug-93	30-Sep-93	31-Oct-93	30-Nov-93	31-Dec-93
Assets												
Cash	19017	8309	2992	12361	26393	43533	64363	89369	117036	134366	156357	183011
Accounts receivable	9543	13545	17547	21549	25551	27552	31554	33555	37557	41559	45561	49563
Prepaid expenses	5500	5000	4500	4000	3500	3000	2500	2000	1500	1000	500	0
Total current assets	34060	27355	25539	38411	55944	74586	98917	125424	156594	177425	202919	233075
Fixed assets	12050	22050	32050	32050	32050	33050	33050	33050	33050	33050	33050	33050
Accumulated depreciation	333	666	999	1333	1666	1999	2333	2666	2999	3333	3666	4000
Total noncurrent assets	11717	21384	31051	30717	30384	31051	30717	30384	30051	29717	29384	29050
Other assets	0	0	0	0	0	0	0	0	0	0	0	0
Total assets	45777	48739	56590	69128	86328	105637	129634	155808	186645	207142	232303	262125
Liabilities												
Accounts payable	374	158	179	200	220	230	251	261	282	303	323	344
Short-term debt	45000	45000	45000	45000	45000	45000	45000	45000	45000	30000	15000	0
Accrued liabilities	0	0	0	0	0	0	0	0	0	0	0	0
Other liabilities	0	0	0	0	0	0	0	0	0	0	0	0
Total current liabilities	45374	45158	45179	45200	45220	45230	45251	45261	45282	30303	15323	344
Long-term debt	0	0	0	0	0	0	0	0	0	0	0	0
Total noncurrent liabilities	0	0	0	0	0	0	0	0	0	0	0	0
Total Liabilities	45374	45158	45179	45200	45220	45230	45251	45261	45282	30303	15323	344
Shareholders' equity												
Common stock (par)	100	100	100	100	100	100	100	100	100	100	100	100
Paid in capital	0	0	0	0	0	0	0	0	0	0	0	0
Retained earnings	303	3480	11311	23828	41008	60306	84283	110447	141263	176740	216879	261681
Total stockholders' equity	403	3580	11411	23928	41108	60406	84383	110547	141363	176840	216979	261781
Total liabilities & SH equity	**45777**	**48739**	**56590**	**69128**	**86328**	**105637**	**129634**	**155808**	**186645**	**207142**	**232303**	**262125**

The implementation of desktop publishing systems has great potential to reduce publishing costs. In general, the amount of interaction between the publisher and printer decreases significantly upon adoption of a computer-based system. The publishing processes under a non-computer-based system versus a computer-based system are as follows:

Non-computer-based publishing

1) Manuscript received from author either on a disc or as a hard copy.
2) Source document word processed into publishing companies' convention, usually by typing in directly and sometimes by loading in directly from E mail or disk when formats match.
3) Document is copy edited; type specs or codes are added
4) Coded work sent to typesetter for production of preliminary proofs of only the textual meat of the documents (*galleys*).
5) Galleys returned to publisher from typesetter for approval and correction (any changes are billed to the publisher), the galleys are used to construct *mechanicals* by physically positioning galleys on a layout board and affixing with hot wax. Graphics and photographs are also positioned at this time.
6) Photographs are taken to produce *page-proof negatives*, which must be approved by the publisher before being used for final productions by the printer. Any further changes at this point require another costly cycle of this process.
7) The printer produces *blue lines*, which represent the document as it will appear in its final published form. The document is then ready for production.

Computer-based publishing processes

1) Manuscript received from author either on a disk, or as a hard copy.
2) Source document word processed, usually by typing in directly and sometimes by loading in directly from E mail or disk when formats match.
3) After editing, text transferred electronically to desktop publishing system. Graphics are created on the computer, merged with the text and layout done on the screen. Photographs are electronically scanned, sized, retouched, and merged into the document.
4) Computer files given to printer on disk from which blue lines are printed. The document is then ready for production.

Under the computer-based system, layout can be achieved much more easily than without the system. The main advantage is the increased flexibility and control in making changes at any time during the process on the computer screen rather than working through the non-computer-based process multiple times. In addition to saving time and production costs, the publication is allowed to incorporate information received up until immediately prior to publication, making the publication directly more valuable to its readers and indirectly more valuable to its advertisers. The estimated breakdown of cost savings is presented below for a biweekly publication of 35 pages, a typical size for publishers who can use desktop publishing*:

Saved costs	# Occurrences/issue	Unit savings	Item savings
Layout labor hrs:	(35 pages) × (45 min/pg) ×	$25/hr	= $ 937.50
Typesetting labor hrs:	(35 pages) × (1 hr/pg) ×	$20/hr	= $ 1000.00
Revisions after process:	3 times/issue ×	$70/time	= $ 210.00
		Total savings/issue	= $ 2147.50
		Total savings/month	= **$4295.00**

Average costs of a CBS designed and implemented system (excluding hardware, which is treated as a long-term capital asset of the publishing company):

Item	Unit cost		# Units		Total item cost
Software	$ 500	×	1	=	$ 500
Hardware	$10,000	×	1	=	$ 10,000
Consulting (design, implementation)	$ 60	×	70	=	$ 4200
Training	$ 50	×	50	=	$ 2500
Follow-up work	$ 60	×	10	=	$ 600
			Total charges	=	**$17,800**

Considering that it will take about one month before the publisher is completely converted and comfortable with the new system, it will take (conservatively) about five months before the system has paid for itself and has begun to generate positive value for the publisher. This considers only quantitative aspects.

Payback period = 5 months

* Data regarding costs to be saved by the publisher are based on average numbers of hours required for typesetters and graphic layout workers and their average respective wages. Other data is similarly estimated in average terms with the understanding that there will be some variance. All data is estimated by an Assistant Editor for the monthly publication *SIAM News* (Society for Industrial and Applied Mathematics, Philadelphia, Pa.)

6 Marketing your company

You can use guerilla marketing techniques in many ways to get greater exposure for your company. Here are some ideas:

- Put your company description on business cards and stationery
- Get free public relations
- Get paid to write articles about your company
- Learn how to piggyback paying exhibitors at trade shows (gratis)
- Get your suppliers to pay for your advertising

Guerilla marketing techniques

In your marketing campaign, you need to leverage all of the resources available to you: people, funds, and technology. Spend the correct amount of time planning a campaign with the right people. Spend as little on the campaign as possible. And take advantage of all technology to convey the best image. If you follow this advice, you'll run a successful guerilla marketing campaign. You can't help but win!

The basic requirements of a guerilla marketing campaign are commitment, investment, and consistency. You must be committed to the campaign that you undertake. You can't go half way into it. You must decide how much you want to invest. Then you have to make that investment. And, the entire campaign must be tied together. If it is not consistent, you will be sending off different messages to the people you are trying to reach.

In order to get people to purchase your product or service, you must be credible and convey confidence. How then can you promote this message of credibility to your present and potential clients?

The first component of your guerilla marketing campaign is established by the name you choose for your company. Different names convey different things—Joe's Software Development Company does not have the same connotation as The Software Development Company. Both names convey that the company provides software development. The word *Joe* versus *The* gives a completely different meaning to the company. Joe's Software Development Company sounds as if Joe is the one and only person in the company who develops software. The name makes you think that the company is located in one room (maybe even in Joe's house). The Software Development Company sounds as if it is truly the only company that develops good software. The name of the company also makes it sound as if it is a very substantial company—in a large, green-glassed building with hundreds of employees. What's in a name? A lot!

Once you've chosen the name of your company, you want to get that name in front of every possible person who could need your product or service. You can convey it using a host of guerilla marketing techniques.

Direct-mail marketing

Direct-mail marketing is a rifle shot approach to marketing. Identify those in your target market who want your product or service. Get a list of all those in it and hit them directly with a mail campaign. You have no clutter in this approach. You know that all of the people who you approach are potentially interested in what you are trying to sell.

Make sure that the presentation you give in the direct-mail piece conveys the image that you want to build. If you use a photocopied mail piece you will convey one type of image. If you use a multimedia diskette-based presentation, you give a completely different impression. It is amazing what computer applications now let you do for creating desktop presentations. They can be done very cost effectively.

Another element of a floppy diskette-based presentation is that you are differentiating your company through the use of this medium. Differentiation is key to successful penetration of the information bombardment that everyone encounters. I still pop floppy diskettes into my computer system (and check for viruses, of course) almost the minute I receive them in the mail. It is like getting a package that you want to open.

One way to reach an identified market using direct mail is to purchase mailing lists. There are two general sources of mailing lists.

One source is mailing list companies, which are solely in the business of selling mailing lists. Frequently, these companies don't own the mailing lists but lease them from other companies to resell to people like you.

Another source is magazines that sell their subscriber list. Magazine advertising might be too expensive for you. Or you might decide that you only want to reach a very specific portion of the magazine subscriber base. You might decide to purchase only a specific part of the magazine's mailing list and mail to it.

When you "purchase" a mailing list, you generally rent it, frequently on a one-time basis. Rental of lists is done by the name or by the thousand of names. You can expect to pay from a fraction of a penny to several dollars a name, depending upon the value of the list. You will either receive the list on magnetic media (floppy diskette or magnetic tape) or on labels suitable for mailing.

Companies that rent their mailing list often put *dummy* names in them to ensure that you are only mailing to the list once. Remember this! If you mail to a one-time list twice, you will at the very least be asked to pay for another rental of the list. You could find yourself in serious breach of a contract.

The message behind direct mail is simple. Target your market well. Get a good list. Gear your message to your market. And, deliver that message in a fashion that lets you catch your market's attention.

Convey your business statistics

In direct mail, as in all other guerilla marketing techniques, make sure that you convey all of the vital statistics of your business. The vital statistics are your business name, address, and telephone number and a facsimile number (if you don't have one, find a facsimile service whose number you can use). Vital statistics also include a message about what your business does (for example, Macintosh database software development or word processing service). Believe it or not, I have seen companies that sent out direct mail with no address or telephone number on it. How can you expect someone to get in touch with you, let alone do business, if they don't know where to find you?

Business cards

Look at the sample business cards in FIG. 6-1. Titles on business cards can be a tricky part of a guerilla marketing campaign. They can make it difficult for you to jump into other roles. I actually don't put a title on my corporate cards so I can launch into a sales role. Then I claim that I have to speak with someone else to make a final decision on a sales-related issue. I couldn't as easily do these dances if my title, President, were on my business cards.

In the same fashion, though, a card with a title of president on it can command a certain amount of respect. You might choose to carry two sets of

6-1 Sample business cards

Jane Doe
Doe, Smith & Jones
117 Main Street
Boulder, Colorado
(303) 999-6700

What does Jane Doe's company do? Does she work for a law firm, a consulting firm, or an accounting firm, or what?

Harry Feldman
Chief Software Designer
The Software Development Company
117 Main Street
Boulder, Colorado
(303) 999-6700
Fax: (303) 999-3300

*Macintosh software
development specialists*

This business card tells us not only what The Software Development Company does (through both its name and the description at the bottom of the card) but it also tells us what Harry Feldman does for the firm.

cards, one with and one without a title. Think about titles before you use them.

Stationery

Stationery is another weapon for your marketing guerilla warfare. Just as in the business card example, if you place your vital statistics on the stationery along with a description of your business, you will reinforce the image message of your company.

Invoices

Invoices are one of the most unexpected places to do marketing. A thank-you message printed on the invoice can be invaluable to reinforce an image.

Invoices are a place to put additional sales information. For example, if you sell floppy diskette formatting and you have a special for the month of January, imprint that on the invoice. True, the invoice might end up in an accounts receivable department of a company, but it might pass through the hands of either the end user of your product or service or the purchasing agent who could potentially place more orders with you.

Thank you notes

How many times do you get thank you letters when you pay someone's invoice? Probably not often. Well, people are very appreciative of the time it took you to write a separate thank you note just for paying the bill, especially because so few firms do it. It is another chance for you to reinforce your image.

Press releases

Press releases do several things. First, a press release can give you credibility in the eyes of the people who receive it. After all, doesn't a company have to be doing things of note to send out a press release? Do things of note happen because you're sending out a press release? Now, you're catching on! Secondly, press releases help differentiate you from all of the other mail that companies receive. Third, you can even get the information that you have printed on the press release published in newspapers and magazines. This builds credibility and might even get you business. Finally, when you send press releases to firms other than members of the press, it implies that you are sending them hot news about the company. They also feel that they are included on a special list, which can build loyalty.

If you are fortunate to get your press releases published, you can make reprints of articles where they appeared. Use these articles for further guerilla marketing. These articles are less expensive yet more credible than advertising.

The only problem with press releases is that you are never quite sure when they will hit the press. Therefore, you can't base solid results on these releases. A couple of things can aid this case:

- Telephone those editors to whom you have sent releases. Ask them if they received the release. Ask them if you can give them any further information for an article that they might write. When they hang up on you, don't be discouraged. They get a lot of these telephone calls.
- Keep on sending releases. The message will sink in after a while. You might be surprised that after several months, an editor might even call you.

What do you write all of these press releases about? Be creative! Yet also newsworthy. Remember to put the most important information, succinctly, at the top of your press release. Follow on with the *filler*, and end with some vital statistics about your company. A sample release is shown in FIG. 6-2.

The Software Development Company
117 Main Street
Boulder, Colorado
(303) 999-6700
Fax: (302) 999-3300

Macintosh software development specialists

Press Release
For Immediate Release

20 January 1994
For further information contact:
Mark Fiorvanti

The Software Development Company releases product to enable Macintoshes to translate between Japanese, English, and Russian, concurrently.

Tokyo, Japan—Harry Feldman, Chief Software Designer, announced that a product that enables Macintoshes to translate between Japanese, English, and Russian, concurrently, MacTranslate, has been released by The Software Development Company.

MacTranslate is operated with the simple push of a button. The user designates the language from which it is to translate (the source) and the language into which it is to translate (the target) and the rest of the process is automatic. MacTranslate contains the equivalent of a 100,000 word English dictionary and is touted as the most complete translation program on the market today. The product requires the Macintoshes to have one Kanji keyboard and one U.S. version keyboard. MacTranslate will run on any Macintosh.

MacTranslate has been developed by Dr. Feldman and a team of his esteemed colleagues over the last three and one half years. Based on the burgeoning demand for information in all three of these languages, The Software Development Company undertook this project.

The Software Development Company specializes in developing software for the Macintosh. Other products it has developed included MacSpeak (voice digitizer for the Macintosh), MacMail (a complex mail management program for the Macintosh), and MacTalk (a program that teaches young children how to speak properly). Headquartered in the old general store of Boulder, Colorado, the company employs 100 people and is privately held.

###

6-2   *Sample press release.*

Articles in the press Articles that you write can boost a guerilla marketing campaign, add credibility to your company, and even pay you for the publicity. Once articles are published, they can be reprinted for future use. I had a monthly column in a computer publication. It afforded me credibility and paid some of the bills. Did it generate business? Not always. People mentioned it and it was a credibility generator.

Serve on boards Association with other companies in the industry can give you perspective on your own firm but also be used as a marketing vehicle. Does it add credibility? You bet! Directorships, advisorships, and associations all do.

Seminars Did you know that you can give seminars? You get your company's name out and can get paid for presenting the seminar. If you are risk seeking, you can give seminars and charge for them. If you don't have experience in this area, you might take a big risk with an uncertain return. Find a company that might be interested in having you give a seminar to their employees. I still remember the second year my company was in business. Our business was computer format conversions, and a Bell Operating Company asked me to give a seminar to its employees on the topic. It paid $500 per hour for me to do so. Had my firm tried to establish a seminar with that Bell Operating Company, it probably would not have been able to do so. But through the Bell Operating Company's sponsorship, we attained credibility and made money. The guerilla marketing program continued.

Once you understand how to give seminars, you might want to put on the whole works. This is really a business unto itself. You might do well to hire a firm that has professional experience in giving seminars. Include the expense as a part of your guerilla marketing campaign.

Trade shows If you can get business through trade shows, you might want to include them as a part of the campaign. If you run a business in the Macintosh world, go to Macintosh-based rather than general computer shows. If you run a business that develops engineering software, you better attend shows that focus on engineering software. Remember, target your audience.

You can leverage your company at trade shows by being a part of someone else's booth. If you have a product or service that is particularly interesting to another exhibitor (especially if they are a larger company than you), that exhibitor might ask you to stand in the booth with them. If you have a software product that is particularly interesting to a hardware vendor on whose platform it runs, you might ask that hardware vendor to show your product at the trade show.

Often these *piggyback* arrangements will cost you nothing. You might even be able to get a copy of the list of attendees of the show so that you can do subsequent follow-up (either by telephone or by mail). You should be able to get a copy of the business cards collected during the show. Follow-up on the potential leads after the show.

It makes sense to qualify leads while you are at a show. Try and write down the areas of interest of those inquiring at your booth. You will better know what to talk about and even how hot the lead might be.

Magazine and newspaper advertising can take real dollars. If you are going to do it, spend very wisely. First, research the demographic profile of the market that reads the publications where you will advertise. Study the demographic profile of the publication and match it to your target market profile. If you are not going to be able to cost effectively reach your target market, don't waste your money! If 10% of the people who read the publication are in your target market profile, you have to assess what the cost of this reach will be.

Magazine or newspaper advertising

Reach *Reach* is the number of relevant people who you will hit through advertising. Assume a magazine has a subscription level of 30,000 people. You are only interested in 10% of them (or 3000). You have to look at advertising costs based on this 3000 number. If advertising costs $1000 per page, your cost per reach is $0.33. If it costs you $0.44 to mail a letter to someone ($0.29 postage, $0.02 for the envelope, $0.05 for the stationery, $0.08 for the labor), this vehicle is probably worthwhile. If the advertising costs $10,000 per page, you now pay $3.30 to reach people. Is this amount worth it? Only you can decide. The types of calculations shown are the ones that are generally used to substantiate reach.

Frequency *Frequency* is the number of times that an advertisement is taken out and potentially seen. In advertising, there is something called the *aggregative effect of advertising*. The aggregative effect means that awareness (of your company, product, or service) builds over time. As you repeat your advertisement, it will not only be seen by more people but will have a chance to sink in more.

One way to reduce the cost of advertising is to participate in what is called *co-op* or *cooperative* advertising. Co-op advertising is advertising that is paid for by more than one company on a cooperative basis. If you represent a large company, they will often include you as the local supplier in one of their advertisements. Some companies allocate co-op funds for use by the cooperating company in any fashion they see fit. The company only needs to include the name of the company that is paying for the advertising. Co-op funds are often attached to a certain level of sales. For example, if you sell $50,000 of a company's products or services, they might give you $2000 in co-op advertising funds. If you sell $100,000, the company might give you $5000 in cooperative advertising funds. Co-op advertising works only if you represent a company's product or service line that offers this participation.

If you make the decision to purchase magazine or newspaper advertising, with or without cooperative advertising funds, consider the relevancy of the readership profile, reach, and frequency of the advertisement.

Christmas cards
When you send Christmas cards to your clients (or potential clients), it is a simple way to keep your name in front of them.

Giveaways
There is a whole industry centered around giveaways or novelties. In fact, one of the businesses outlined in this book is a novelty-creation business. Giveaways are intended to be items that are kept around to reinforce the awareness component of your guerilla marketing campaign. Novelty creation can be expensive. It might or might not directly correlate to business. Be sure you understand why you're making this investment. Determine your objectives of a novelty-based component of a guerilla marketing campaign.

Newsletters
Newsletters can reinforce your image. One problem with newsletters is the effort of getting them out. You might decide to publish one about events relating to your business. Unless you assign the task to someone in the firm, and give her or him the proper resources to put it together, you might not get the product you want. Firms very often start out planning to publish a newsletter every quarter. The annual issue shows up two months late. Somehow the newsletter is pushed off as a forgotten priority. Unlike other marketing activities, you don't necessarily see the effect of a newsletter immediately unless you include some type of offer in it whose feedback you can monitor. Give a lot of thought to this vehicle before you decide to try it.

Telemarketing
Telemarketing is one of the most effective methods in guerilla marketing. You can get directly to the person you are looking for. You can directly solicit the person. The image you portray is completely under your control. You don't need to worry about the expensive brochure that you can't afford to produce. The playing field is level. You and everyone else using this vehicle has the same delivery mechanism—an audible voice.

Many of the Bell Operating Companies have done extensive studies to show the cost effectiveness of this channel. You save time on the road by not visiting people. If you don't make contact with someone on the telephone within seconds, you can move on to the next potential lead.

There are even computer-based systems that can do telemarketing with recorded messages to help get responses to make sales.

Canvassing
Canvassing is a technique that was made famous by Xerox and Fuller Brush. Door-to-door solicitation always seems to find someone who will listen to you, especially in government offices where workers are not commonly

greeted by outside guests. Although you can waste a lot of time, it can be a vehicle with a positive return.

Brochures

Brochures convey a message about your business. They are something that you can leave around for people to have available as a reference. They are particularly good as a leave-behind item when you canvass or are involved in a solicited sales call. Brochures can vary greatly in price from pennies a copy to hundreds of dollars per brochure.

The key point in a brochure is to get your message across clearly. Although brevity can be good, it can also indicate a lack of depth. And, although length can point to depth of organization, central points can get lost if you have too much information. Get your message across clearly. You will reap the rewards. Remember the size of your budget and plan accordingly.

On-line networks

Just like the telemarketing vehicle, on-line networks can create a level playing field for all involved. Because so many on-line networks are text-based, pictures or drawings can't easily be sent over them. Thus, words are all that can come from anyone. You are now on the same playing field as the company that has a $1 million advertising budget.

How does an on-line network work? Well, you can sign on to a network and send mail to users. A form of direct mail? Yes. You can go into a part of the network called a *forum* and post a message on a bulletin board. On-line networks such as CompuServe have forums on astronomy, aviation, coins, desktop publishing, education, and investment, to name a few. Pick your forum and go for it!

One on-line mail message that my firm mailed over one network (at a cost of $25) yielded a return of about $20,000 in sales. How is that?

On-line networks are not as cluttered as other media. The cost and return on that investment can be quite significant.

Facsimiles

Facsimiles are another medium for guerilla marketing. The price of faxing information is the price of a telephone call plus the message composition cost that is behind it. Call companies and get their facsimile numbers (or look in facsimile directories). You still need to know to whom you are sending your message.

With the proliferation of direct faxing or junk fax, this vehicle is one that must be used carefully. For companies whose facsimile numbers are listed in public directories, junk fax is the norm rather than the exception. Many of these faxes never get beyond the mail room. You could be wasting your money if you idly send faxes.

So what should you do? Make contact with an individual (at a firm) and then follow up with a facsimile transmission. The advantage to this medium is obviously speed. To a certain extent, the playing field is level because of the output quality from standard facsimile machines—remember that photographs do not fax well. So why include them in a facsimile?

Fax is another interesting way to cut down on the cost of getting your message across.

Yellow pages

If you have a retail-oriented business, yellow pages can be a good vehicle for you to use in guerilla marketing. Both the Bell Operating Company yellow pages and the Donnelly Directory solicit advertising from companies. Bell Operating Company yellow pages generally renew once or twice a year. Donnelly Directory advertising has a special feature that allows you to telephone a number and hear more about a company's special offers.

Personal letters

Personal letters can be a part of a direct-mail campaign. As long as your letterhead presents the image that you want to convey, guerilla marketing with personal letters can be cost effective. The key is to mail to qualified leads.

These are the specifics of a guerilla marketing campaign. Looking more broadly, you should understand the work of marketing to see where it fits.

What is marketing?

Simply stated, *marketing* relates to those activities that move a product or service from its initial source to its destination.

Marketing activities relate to the product (or service), place (the distribution channel), price, and promotion. The product or the service is the goods or service that you want to get to market. The place is the distribution channel that is used to get it to market. The price is the value that the market places on the product or service. Promotion is the way that the market actually finds out about it.

These marketing activities are contrasted to sales activities. Sales activities relate solely to the acquisition of short-term revenue. Sales are made based on a certain trust or confidence that develops as a result of both selling and marketing activities.

Once you've identified the product or service that you want to get to the consumer, you then have to figure out who is the consumer or the user. This information will better tell you how you market your product or service (the distribution channel that you use), the pricing that you will attach to it, and the promotional vehicles that you will use.

Your market is simply those individuals or firms who could potentially purchase what you sell. It seems as if this concept is so simple. Many people err in defining just who is in their market.

What is the difference between a market and a target market? A market is the potential group of individuals or businesses with whom you might do business. A target market is the group of individuals or businesses with whom you can do business. The operative differences in these definitions are the words *might* and *can*. A potential market is one that you might potentially reach. A target market is one that you can reach.

For example, assume you run the computer installation department of a ComputerLand. You are located in New Orleans. You charge $75 an hour to install computer systems. Historically, you do 99% of your business in the central business district in New Orleans. Today, you get a request from a company in Maine to install a computer system for them. You tell them your rate of $75 per hour. They say that the rate is acceptable. You then realize that you can't absorb the price of a round-trip plane or train ticket plus lodging in Maine. Then, what do you do about the travel time? Do you bill for it? Because people's offices in New Orleans were only five minutes away from yours, you have not charged for travel. Yet now, because you have to travel to Maine, you have to add $700 for round trip plane fare, $50 a day for lodging, and $25 a day for food. You estimate the work to take two days. Associated costs are $775. You realize that your travel time could be billable time in New Orleans. Therefore, you decide to add the 10 hours travel time at $75 an hour. Now you've added $1525 to the normal expenditures of the job. When you tell the potential client that you have to add this amount to the price, the client decides to find someone locally to install the computer equipment. So what is the point? The company in Maine was in your market. Due to geographic issues and economic constraints, they were not in your target market.

Your target market is the market that can be served by you in a fashion in which you can deliver a reasonable service or product at a rate that the market will pay.

Target markets can be defined at many levels: industry segments, geographic segments, corporate size, contract size, product or service attributes, or demographic profile. The target market differentiation is called *market segmentation*. In essence, you segment the market in a fashion that is consistent with other operational elements of the business. You define the market segment based on what is operationally, technically, or financially achievable.

Explore various segmentation strategies that you can use in a computer-based business.

Who is your market?

Markets versus target markets

Target markets

Industry segmentation

Industry segmentation is targeting by a specific industry. If you choose to sell your product or service to accountants, bankers, or lawyers, you segment on these three industries. Industry segmentation can be advantageous, especially because different segments might have different requirements, and different levels of profitability.

It might be easier to operationally perform contracts in some industry segments. This will help you focus on those segments where you can keep your costs down and raise your profits.

Geographic segmentation

Geographic segmentation is serving only a limited geographic scope. The concept is illustrated by the example of the computer installer. In order to make it financially worthwhile, the installer could only serve the New Orleans marketplace.

Corporate size

Corporate size is another vehicle by which you can segment. You might find that smaller firms don't have an in-house desktop publishing department. Yet they might want desktop publishing capability. You might find out that firms of less than ten employees might not be able to pay the fees for desktop publishing that you might want to charge. You might also discover that firms that are more than 100 employees are large enough to afford their own desktop publishing staff. Therefore, you might decide to segment on customers that have more than ten but less than one hundred employees.

Similarly, you might be able to segment corporations on revenues. You might determine that corporations that have revenues of less than $500,000 a year cannot afford to pay for your desktop publishing services. You might also learn that corporations whose revenues are greater than $30 million can afford their own in-house desktop publishing department. As a result of these findings, you might segment your market based on firms that do more than $500,000 per year in business but less than $30 million.

Contract size

Contract size or value is another way in which you can segment your market. Generally, contract size is the basis of an operational constraint. You can only handle contracts of a certain size because you don't have enough employees to be able to deal with any larger size. Or, based on the size of your organization, your overhead might be so great that you are not able to accept contracts of a certain small size.

For example, assume that you run PC Concepts, a training company. A contract possibility comes through the door to do all of Smith Kline's word processing training. You look at the contract proposal due date. It is due two days from now. You look at the contract commencement date. It is two weeks from now. The initial training required is to run 10 two-day classes, concurrently, for the first five weeks. You have two people who are capable of performing the training. You need eight more people. Can you find these people, train them yourself, and ensure the quality of presentation needed in the next two weeks? Probably not, unless you have a series of subcontract employees who can jump in at a moment's notice to perform the training. Because you don't happen to have these contract employees, you find yourself in a dilemma. You can't bid on this contract because you don't have the resources to do so.

Product or service attributes

Product or service attributes are also a vehicle for segmentation. Clients might require that certain parameters be met for the product or service. The result is that you might or might not be able to meet the parameters and provide a product or service to the company.

Demographic profile

Your product or service can cater to people of different demographic profiles. *Demographic profiles* are the commonly held stereotypical attributes in the population. These attributes might be age, sex, race, economic strata, education, and religion. An example of segmentation by age is Nintendo software. Very often these games are targeted to a young audience. An example of sex segmentation is football-based software games. They are generally targeted more to a male than a female audience. Software that has a certain racial or cultural orientation is the educational software specifically targeted to a black audience. Economic strata segmentation is found in money management software.

Programs that specialize in the sciences are an example of a product with a specific educational target market segment. A chemical equation software package is targeted to people who are educated in chemistry.

All of these vehicles for segmentation give you a reason to develop a defined target market. After all, if you know exactly who to target, you should have much better success at selling your product.

Place

Once you know to whom you are selling your product or service, you can determine the best channels to make it available.

There is a chain of potential parties who can be a part of a distribution channel shown in FIG. 6-3.

Traditionally, a manufacturer was a company that actually created the product that would be passed on to other components of the distribution channel. Today, as the economy has changed to be a more service-oriented economy, the definition of manufacturer has been changed to include service-based companies that are the origin of a service.

The wholesaler or distributor facilitates the sale of the product or service created by the manufacturer to the next level, the retailer. The wholesaler or distributor will frequently make a commitment to buy (or sell) a certain quantity of a manufacturer's product in return for a substantial discount off

Manufacturer

Distributor/wholesaler

Retailer

End purchaser

End user

6-3 *Potential components of a distribution channel.*

the retail selling price of the product or service. At one level, the wholesaler or distributor runs interference for the manufacturer with the retailer to whom it sells the product or service. The mere presence of a wholesaler or distributor can keep the selling and marketing costs of the manufacturer lower than what they would be if the wholesaler or distributor were not present. The wholesaler or manufacturer can help push the product to the next level, the retailer.

The retailer sells the product or service to the end purchaser. The retailer doesn't move the same amount of products or services as does the wholesaler. The margins that the retailer receives on selling the product will probably be greater than that of the wholesaler. The retailer can very often help push the product to the end purchaser.

The end purchaser might or might not be the end user. In the case of large corporate and government purchasers, there are purchasing agents who do nothing but shop around for the best deal on a product or service. They make purchases as a result of their research. Often, purchasing departments are given their direction by the end user who tells them where they might make specific purchases.

The distribution channel can be simple or complex. It might include some or all of the various levels that are outlined above. The process can take on a life established by norms created by manufacturers. Some of the variations on distribution channels that might be created are shown in FIG. 6-4.

6-4
Various distribution channels in the computer industry.

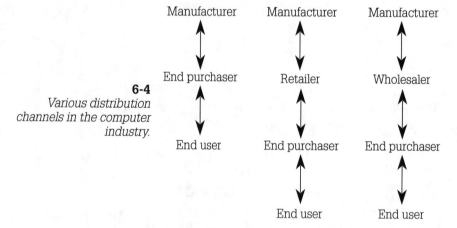

These channels are not all of the possibilities. They do show you that there are many types of distribution channels.

The conversion service division of my corporation was originally structured with the distribution channel seen in FIG. 6-5.

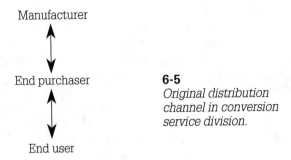

6-5
Original distribution channel in conversion service division.

Percentage of end user selling price:
Manufacturer: 100%

In order to extend the product life cycle of the division and increase price thresholds, another dimension is added to the distribution channel—the retailer—to try to keep prices higher (see FIG. 6-6).

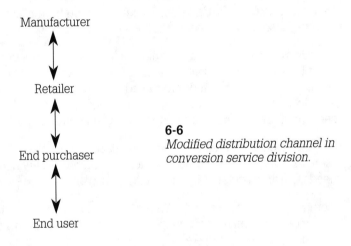

6-6
Modified distribution channel in conversion service division.

Percentages of end user selling price:
Manufacturer: 50%
Retailer: 50%

The dollar value of the transaction was such that the retailer was not inclined to participate in the channel.

Therefore, as you see from this example, you can take different directions in the way you distribute your product or service. Various distribution channels will have an impact on sales volume, margins in each element of the distribution channel, and ultimately, the selling price.

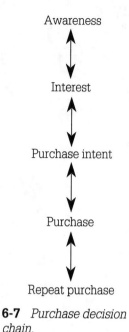

Awareness

Interest

Purchase intent

Purchase

Repeat purchase

6-7 *Purchase decision chain.*

Product or service distribution is extremely important. You can't forget those who you are ultimately trying to sell, your specifically identified target market. You must have gone through a successful definition of your target market to get to this point. Target market definition is key. Your target market for your product or service might be one group of people. It is entirely possible that other people might be involved in the sales process. They might either become the target market or the people who influence the purchase decision. It is important for you to understand the decision process in order to understand how you should approach the market.

For example, many of the children's toy companies (such as Mattel) will target all of their advertising to those who influence the purchase decision: the child. The child becomes enamored with the product. The child pesters his or her parents to buy it. Many companies with children's products will not target children at all. They focus on the true purchaser: the parent. These are companies that might market products that are not as appealing to children as they are to adults. Children's medicine is an example. The key is to focus your promotion in an area where you can get the greatest push or pull effect to get to the purchase decision. To help understand this comment, refer to the purchase decision chain in FIG. 6-7.

For customers to even consider purchasing your product or service, they must be aware that it exists. The first step is to create this awareness. Awareness can be created through advertising and promotion. It all finally evolves to a word-of-mouth level-of-awareness creation. A secretary might see a good deal on computer paper. She then conveys it to her boss.

Once awareness is created, interest must be stimulated. Often in society, there might be absolutely no need for a product or a service. Demand or a need is ofttimes created by the selling party.

Actually, as the selling party in a transaction, you want to create a situation where demand for your product or service (purchase intent) becomes strong. You then just need to make the party aware of your product or service. Hopefully, they will progress from purchase intent to purchase of the product or service.

Different products and services have different levels of ease in taking a potential purchaser through the purchase decision chain. You should evaluate your product or service to see how it fares on this attribute.

Additionally, different products and services are more or less conducive to the last link of this chain—the repeat purchase. You should consider how repeatable your product or service is. In the conversion service division of my company, we would move information from one computer system to another. It wouldn't be until the purchaser decided to move again, to another new computer system, that she or he would make a repeat purchase.

Why is repeat purchase an important attribute to your product or service? Quite simply, isn't it easier to take someone who has already purchased your product or service to the next step, the repeat purchase? The alternative is to start all the way at the beginning of the cycle and:

1. Create awareness
2. Create interest
3. Create purchase intent and then, finally, yet again
4. Accomplish a purchase

Businesses with repeat purchase capability generally are those businesses that commonly offer products or services that tend to be *commodity based*. A *commodity-based* product or service is one that is in abundant supply. It has little differentiation from other products or services in its product or service category.

In the computer industry, some commodity-based products are computer supplies businesses such as floppy diskettes, computer paper, toner cartridges, and facsimile paper. No matter how the manufacturers of these products try to differentiate themselves, there are few distinctions that can easily be made. Consequently, price is frequently used as a point of differentiation. Quality is truly the point of differentiation that manufacturers would like to use as their comparative advantage. More often than not, the consumer ignores quality. He or she feels that it is a minor point of differentiation and uses price as the exclusive point of differentiation. Price is used as an attribute when there is an abundance of supply of the product and it seems to be the only thing left on which to differentiate.

Commodity-based services include facsimile and photocopying services (such as Kinko's). There are so many places that you can go to have a photocopy made or a facsimile sent that you see an abundant supply of services between which you can't seemingly differentiate.

Viewing the facsimile service, you could differentiate on product quality. Yet, a fax is a fax. The only attribute on which you can differentiate is price. But what about convenience? Kinko's facsimile service is located one block away from you. They charge you $0.10 per facsimile page less than the facsimile service located right down the hall. Will you pay the $0.10 per facsimile page more? What is your time worth? What is the attribute of convenience worth?

Now, assume Kinko's is 10 blocks away. They pick up and deliver for the same price as the service located right down the hall from you. Now a new dimension—time—is added to the equation. Because Kinko's is located ten blocks away, it should take them longer to pick up your facsimile than for you to walk down the hall. Therefore, time, which translates into convenience, actually does play a role in this service. So is it a pure commodity-based service? Almost.

A photocopying service can be a commodity-based service as well. Given that the photocopying service provides solely black-and-white photocopying on standard-weight photocopying paper, convenience is about the only factor on which it can differentiate.

Now assume the photocopying service adds color photocopying. Now, there is a point of differentiation. Not all photocopying services offer this. Color becomes a comparative advantage. Convenience might now diminish in importance if the photocopying company right down the hall from you doesn't offer color photocopying but the service three blocks away does. You might now choose to go three blocks for the service.

You also become less price sensitive in seeking out the service because you are looking for a certain quality (or attribute): color photocopying. The differentiation might lead to less of a repeat business. Sometimes when a product or a service becomes specialized (less like a commodity), the need also becomes more specialized. This more specialized need might translate into less use and, in turn, a less predictable repeat purchase behavior.

Specialization doesn't always lead to less repeat purchases. The color photocopying service might have as many who need to constantly make color photocopies reproduced as black and white.

There is a value to product or service differentiation. Through differentiation from your competitors, you create a reason for people to purchase your product or service. Yet, through differentiation, you lower the mass-market appeal for it. There is a relation between the commodity-like nature of a product and price as shown in FIG. 6-8.

There also seems to be a relationship between the commodity-like nature of a product or service and repeat purchase possibilities as shown in FIG. 6-9.

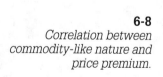

6-8
Correlation between commodity-like nature and price premium.

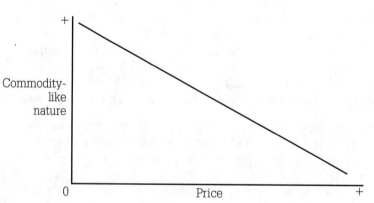

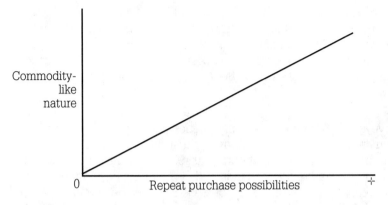

Commodity-like nature

0   Repeat purchase possibilities   +

6-9
Correlation between commodity-like nature and repeat purchase possibilities.

The ideal scenario is to differentiate your product to command a premium price, and yet create a situation where you have a high amount of repeat purchase behavior.

Consider where your product or service fits on the scale of product differentiation, repeat purchase behavior and price. Consider ways in which you can restructure it to more fully optimize these attributes.

One element that plays into this equation is the market opportunity. If your product or service is serving a $500,000 market, worldwide, you might not have as many competitive forces than if the market were in a $4 billion market. In the $500,000 market, you might be able to better differentiate your product or service. You can optimize price along with repeat purchase behavior because the market is so small. In the $4 billion dollar market, you might be forced to deal with products or services that are extremely commodity-based that enable you little differentiation and premium pricing. The market is so large that many competitors feel that even if they capture a small share of the market, they might have a good-size operation. Even in markets of this size, you still might find ways to differentiate so that you can preserve premium pricing. The key, though, is to understand the market.

Determining market size

There are a host of ways to determine the size of a target-market segment. Many people guess. Although this method seems as if it is quite easy, it is also quite inaccurate.

Trade associations

Trade associations often track activity that occurs in the markets that they encompass. Some trade associations track information only about global market trends, but others track information on a very targeted basis. In trying to figure out a market size, these trade associations can steer you in the direction of the information, even if they don't track it themselves.

You can find trade associations through a variety of vehicles. The first is to look within trade publications. Trade associations are very often listed there.

Secondly, if you know people who are active within a market, they will often know what the trade associations are. Finally, you can ask either your local, regional, or national Chamber of Commerce for the names of trade associations. If a Chamber of Commerce doesn't have the name of the trade association, you can go to the United States Department of Commerce or one of its branch offices.

Market surveys

Market surveys are another source of information about overall markets or market segments. Primary market research is first-hand information you gather from the market by asking it questions. Secondary market research is research that has been previously conducted. It might not be completely relevant to you, but it might give you a perspective on some part of the market.

Industry-research firms

Industry-research firms can be sources of information about market size. They might even specialize in the market for which you want information. Good sources of industry-research firms are trade publications, colleges, and the yellow pages, if you live in a large enough metropolitan area.

Based on another product or service

If you have a new product or service, it is frequently difficult to get any information about the market and its size. There might be no competitors or history of the market. Thus, one way to get information about the market is to look at products or services that might depend upon it or those products or services that the market might depend on. For example, assume you develop a new revolutionary voice recognition software that runs on an IBM PC (or compatible) computer system. You might not be able to tell what the market is for this new product. You can, though, extrapolate market size based on the size of the IBM PC (or compatible) computer market.

Add size of competition

Another way to determine market size is to look at the number of competitors in a given market. Then add up their total sales volume. Assume there are ten competitors in the market. Five of the competitors do $50,000 in sales each year. The remaining five, $25,000 in sales each year. In aggregate, all of the competitors do $375,000 in sales. This is the market size.

Market segment growth

In order to determine how much any market segment has grown, you need to have market size information over some desired term. You look at the change in aggregate market size from one year to the next. You can then determine how the market has grown.

Market growth rate

Present market growth relates to the growth from the previous to the present year. How has the market changed in size over the past year? The amount (in real dollars, units, or as a percentage of aggregate size) is the present market growth rate.

Market research is conducted to better understand the market. It can help determine market size, growth, and attributes.

Elements of market research vary considerably, depending on the type of business. Attributes that merit market research do so because of an interest in knowing more about them. In computer service businesses, areas of research include service offerings. If the company is a word processing service bureau, what kinds of work do customers request? What kind of accuracy and turnaround are required? What type of pricing will the potential client pay? If a product-based business (for example, educational software development), what is the expectation for educational content? To what ages should the software appeal? For which type of computer operating system should the software be written? And, for which type of computer hardware should it be written?

There are primarily two types of market research that help give you a better knowledge of the market: *primary* and *secondary* market research.

Primary market research is research that is done directly by you or another individual (or firm) to evoke information directly from the market. There are many vehicles to use in doing primary market research. Each vehicle has its place.

Focus groups   *Focus groups* are small groups (generally six to eight people) brought together to discuss their feelings about a certain topic. The focus group is led by a moderator. The moderator's sole purpose is to serve as a catalyst to the flow of conversation. The moderator is there to guide the group to cover all of the topical areas that the group sponsoring the focus group wants to cover. A good focus group moderator will be able to ask one question in the beginning of a focus group session that will stimulate conversation on the topical area. She or he will then be able to direct the conversation by merely looking at certain people within the group.

The goal of focus groups is to get a general, preliminary, and nonstatistical sense for what people are thinking in a certain area. Focus groups are frequently recorded on audio or video tape. After the session is finished, they are played back to glean market information from the reactions of the people within the group. The focus group is by no means a statistically significant sample, though. As a result, to get more scientifically accurate information, other market research techniques might be in order.

Questionnaires   Once a focus group has been completed (or even if it has not been completed), a set of questions can be developed to give you further insight about the market. A questionnaire serves to get a broader view of the market than does a very limited (in number of people responding) perspective gleaned from a focus group.

Market research

Primary market research

One of the most effective questionnaires that I developed was done for a potential high-end luxury railroad service that was going to run between Philadelphia and New York City. Even though the questionnaire isn't directly involved in the computer industry, it is an example of information gathering that includes the ability to solicit sales at the same time. The questionnaire is shown in FIG. 6-10.

6-10 Railroad market research questionnaire

1. How many months each year do you intend to buy monthly commuter railroad tickets? (circle one)

   1   2   3   4   5   6   7   8   9   10   11   12

2. What train station do you most frequently depart *from* in the morning?

   _____ Philadelphia, 30th Street
   _____ North Philadelphia
   _____ Trenton
   _____ Princeton
   _____ Other_____

3. What train station do you travel *to* in the morning?

   _____ Princeton
   _____ Newark
   _____ New York
   _____ Other_____

4. Which trains do you most frequently take in the morning?

   1 = Most frequent   2 = Sometimes   3 = Seldom   4 = Never
   (Answer all that apply)

Philadelphia	____ 5:45 A.M.	____ 6:20 A.M.	____ 6:50 A.M.	____ 7:00 A.M.
North Phila.	____ 5:55 A.M.	____ 6:30 A.M.	____ 7:00 A.M.	____ 7:10 A.M.
Trenton	____ 6:20 A.M.	____ 6:58 A.M.		____ 7:41 A.M.
Princeton	____ 6:32 A.M.	____ 7:10 A.M.		____ 7:53 A.M.

   Other_____

5. Which trains do you most frequently take in the evening?

   1 = Most frequent   2 = Sometimes   3 = Seldom   4 = Never
   (Answer all that apply)

New York	____4:48 P.M.	____5:00 P.M.	____5:06 P.M.	____5:18 P.M.	____5:38 P.M.
Newark	____5:02 P.M.	____5:12 P.M.	____5:19 P.M.	____5:34 P.M.	____5:55 P.M.

New York____6:00 P.M.   ____6:05 P.M.   ____6:30 P.M.   ____7:00 P.M.   ____7:05 P.M.
Newark ____6:12 P.M.   ____6:23 P.M.   ____6:43 P.M.   ____7:12 P.M.   ____7:20 P.M.

            Other_____

6. If you could ride in a railroad car to and from work that:

    1) Guaranteed you a seat,
    2) Offered breakfast in the morning and snacks/drinks in the evening,
    3) Offered cellular telephone service,
    4) Had "Mahogany paneling and oriental carpets," and,
    5) Had a shoe shine service,
    would you pay $500/month for this service   (Circle one)   Y   N

    a. If you could have breakfast on the railcar, what would you eat at least
       twice a week? (Check all that apply)

       _____ Bagel   _____ Coffee   _____ Grapefruit juice
       _____ Muffin   _____ Tea   _____ Pancakes
       _____ Toast   _____ Milk   _____ Waffles
       _____ Eggs   _____ Orange juice _____ French toast
       _____ Sausage   _____ Apple juice   _____ Other_____
       _____ Bacon   _____ Tomato juice
       _____ Danish

    b. What would you drink at least twice a week in the evening?

       _____

    c. What snack/light dinner items would you eat in the evening?

       _____

    d. How often would you use a cellular telephone?

       _____Not at all
       _____Less than 1 hour/week
       _____1–2 hours/week
       _____2–3 hours/week
       _____3–4 hours/week
       _____4–5 hours/week
       _____More

    e. How often would you get your shoes shined for:

                     1/week   2/week   3/week
       $1.50/shine   _____   _____   _____
       $2.00/shine   _____   _____   _____

6-10 *Continued.*

f. If this railcar could run on only one train in the morning, which one would you like to see it run on? _____

g. If this railcar could run on only one train in the evening, which one would you like to see it run on? _____

h. Comments_____

_____

_____

If you are interested in receiving more information about a service of this kind, please give us the following information:

Name _____

Street address _____

City _____ State _____ Zip _____

Telephone _____

The first question in this survey asks how many months each year the respondent intends to buy a monthly commuter ticket. The purpose of this question is to determine if the respondent is a regular commuter. If the respondent answers on the low end of the scale (0–3), you know that she or he is not a regular commuter. If the answer is 11/12, you know that this respondent is a fairly serious commuter.

Question 2 and 3 answers help you determine where you should start and stop picking up passengers in this "private rail car." Actually, the answers to 2 and 3 are strictly correlated to question 1. It lets us tell the locations from where most people commute.

Questions 4 and 5 are intended to let us know on which trains we should place this private railroad car. The responses to questions 1, 2, and 4 are correlated along with 1, 3, and 5 so that we could determine the optimal train.

Question 6 is the first place where the notion of this high-end luxury train car service is introduced. The price that you see on this questionnaire was varied throughout the 1000 surveys that were distributed. Some respondents got surveys that asked if they'd ride this car for $250, $300, $350, $400, $450, and

$500 per month. The answer to this question let us determine what price sensitivity existed in the potential ridership. When we correlated these answers to questions 2 and 3, we could tell what commuting locations would bear what fares.

Questions 6a through 6c let us plan our morning and evening menu. We only used responses from those people who answered that they were commuters (in question 1) and would pay over certain price points for their fare (question 6).

Question 6d lets us determine the frequency with which riders will use cellular telephone service.

Question 6e gets at the interest in a shoe-shine service aboard the train. The question is worded in such a way that it determines not only price sensitivity issues but also usage.

Questions 6f and 6g are what is called *cross-checks* on questions 2 and 3. Were the answers that the respondents gave in 6f the same as for question 2? Were the answers that the respondents gave in 6g the same as for question 3? If the answers in the correlated questions don't match, you question the validity of the responses and don't use them in your survey results.

Question 6h solicits further information from the respondent in what is called an open-ended fashion. We let the respondent make comments in any fashion desired. Until this point in the survey, the respondent had to answer the questions in the manner that we specified.

The last question asks for name, address, city, state, zip code, and telephone number, if the respondent is interested in receiving more information. The result of the surveys with this section completed is a qualified list of people who are interested in riding a high-end luxury train car while commuting. The market research took us through the awareness and interest stages for all of the people who answered this question. We now stand ready to get them from the purchase intent to purchase dimensions in the marketing chain. Pretty effective!

The net result of this survey is that I knew exactly how to run this high-end luxury train service. I knew what services to offer: food, telephone, and shoe shine. I also knew how much to charge for the service, where to pick up and discharge passengers, and, best of all, who to solicit for the service.

The goal of any market research questionnaire is to get the most accurate and thorough responses from the largest group of people necessary to give you statistically significant information. Different techniques will yield different response rates and varying levels of accuracy of information. Based upon what you want to find out and from how many people you want to find it, you will use varying market research techniques.

In-person surveys   In-person surveys are where questions are asked and responses are given to the surveyor. The reason personal interviews are conducted relates somewhat to the underlying reasons that focus groups are given: open-ended responses are desired, sometimes due to complexity of subject matter. The only issue with both the focus group and the in-person surveys is the openness and honesty factors. When people are asked to respond directly to someone's face, they might not be as open as they might otherwise be. Additionally, these in-person surveys cost a lot in both time and money. Appointments have to be set up and travel time must be taken into account between surveys. My wife traveled all over South America and Europe implementing an in-person survey for a large money center bank. The cost and time involved was immense. Yet the survey was very complex in nature and needed someone face to face with the respondent to try and get the best and most complete answers possible.

Telephone surveys   Telephone surveys involve calling people on the telephone and asking them questions. The questions might either be open- or closed-ended (you can either ask a person a question and let them respond openly or you can ask them a question that has a set of specific responses). There is a certain level of anonymity that can be achieved with a telephone survey. Telephone surveys can also be disturbing to people because they don't know to whom they are talking. This factor, combined with the excessive use of this technique in the United States, has led many people to either be distrustful of the technique or not enjoy completing surveys in this fashion. Telephone surveys are a less expensive vehicle to use, though, than in-person surveys. The response rate might be fairly high because the surveyor can push the respondent to respond, just as in in-person questionnaires.

Mail questionnaires   Mail questionnaires are generally sent through the mail to people for response. Again, questions might be either open- or closed-ended questions. The sentiment behind mail questionnaires is that anonymity is better preserved, especially if you don't solicit a person's name. If this is the case, responses will be more valid, honest, and open than other techniques. One good vehicle to deal with the anonymity issue is to have a place reserved for the person's name and other vital statistics at the end of the questionnaire. By using this technique, you can get the individual to fill out the entire survey. Then, at the end, she or he can make a choice to either fill or not fill out that section of the questionnaire. Response rates for mail questionnaires tend to be lower than that of other techniques because people have to make an effort to return the questionnaire. Self-addressed and stamped envelopes can help facilitate the response rate. *Guilt* money also helps. *Guilt* money is money included in the questionnaire as an incentive for people to fill them out and return them.

There are all types of variations on these survey techniques. In fact, the high-end luxury rail survey used a variation on a mail questionnaire. I got permission from Amtrak to pass out these questionnaires on board certain targeted trains (which we thought might be candidates for the service). Questionnaires were laid on the seats of the train car. People filled them out. Part way into the journey, I had one person walk around and collect the surveys. Many of the people felt the survey was being conducted by Amtrak. Because these people were basically captive while sitting in the train waiting to get to their destination, they filled out and returned the surveys. Of the 1000 surveys that were passed out on different commuter trains, 770 were completed. This 77% response rate is extremely high. Additionally, the last page had 88 respondents who stated they would ride this train car and wanted further information. They provided their name, address, and telephone number. The high-end luxury rail car could only hold 40 people. So, with the survey results in hand, it looked as if the car was filled to capacity twice. There were some political risks to the business and, as a result, it never got off the ground. The message here is that you can use market research to get all sorts of information that can help you run your business. And the expense doesn't have to be prohibitive. The entire cost of the survey outlined for the railroad was less than $300. The result of the survey is that it double-booked a high-end luxury rail car.

Understanding your competition

Assume you've read the last portion of this chapter. You've even implemented some type of market research in order to better understand the needs of the market to whom you are selling. There is another component to the market—competition. Unless you know your competition and can react to any and all moves that they might make, you might find yourself surprised by them.

The first step to understand your competition is to identify them. There are two types of competitors—*direct* and *indirect* competitors.

Direct competition

Direct competition is competition that competes directly with you. They offer the same product or service that you offer. Direct competition competes not only in the area of service or product but in the same marketplace. For example, assume I run a facsimile service in Wilmington that sends and receives facsimiles for clients in Wilmington. You run a facsimile service that operates in Los Angeles. We offer the same service but are so far away from one another that we are not direct competitors (we are not in the same marketplace). Someone in Wilmington would not walk down the street to Los Angeles to deal with your service over mine. If I run a facsimile service in Atlanta, my direct competitor is another facsimile service that operates in Atlanta.

In this example, direct competition is bound by a geographic restriction. Yet this restriction is not always the case. A diskette format-conversion service can have clients throughout the country (or the world). Therefore a diskette format-conversion service that operates in California is direct competition to a diskette format conversion service in Long Island, New York.

Indirect competition

Indirect competition is simply competition that doesn't compete with you directly. To follow through with the facsimile example, indirect competition to the facsimile service would be people's private use of their own facsimile machines. They (the facsimile machines) are an alternative to the facsimile service. Options that are alternatives, although they might not be identical, are considered to be indirect competition.

One of the first things that you should do is identify your direct and indirect competitors. Once you've identified them, you should get detailed information about their businesses. Remember the old cliché that knowledge is power. The more you know about both your direct and indirect competitors, the more you will be able to anticipate their moves and your moves against them.

A good way to get information about your competition is to ask them direct questions. If your competition doesn't know you, you can ask them questions yourself. If they know you, then you might need someone else to ask them questions.

The best way to get information from your competition is to pose as a potential customer or client. Then ask questions. If you are concerned about blowing your cover, you might want to ask them questions over the telephone. That way, you will be more relaxed as you try to get information. If you want to assess the entire operation, though, you might choose to visit the company. In so doing, you will be able to see who works for the company, how many people work for it, how busy they appear to be (a barometer of workflow), the image that the company conveys, and other impressions that you can pick up only through a visit.

Assume you wanted to learn about your potential word processing service bureau competitors. Ask questions of each competitor like:

What type of services do you offer?   Get them to either give or send you a brochure. The brochure should reveal a lot about how the business operates, including what it considers to be important. By analyzing the brochure, you will be able to tell how the principals of the company think.

How much do you charge for your services?   Ask them about a specific service or product, or they might think that you are just fishing for information. You might even focus on one service or product that you are particularly interested in offering to your potential clients.

What hours can work be brought to you?   This question helps you determine your own hours of operation. It also indicates the workload of the competition. For example, if they are a word processing service bureau that operates from 9:00 A.M. to 5:00 P.M., what does that say about them in relation to their competition whose hours are 24 hours a day? Is the 24 hour a day competitor serving the needs of the market? Or is that competitor so busy that it needs to operate 24 hours each day? If the business is located next to a college campus, the reason that it might be open 24 hours a day is to serve the needs of the student population. If the business is located in a suburban office park and is open 24 hours a day, it might be open due to market demand.

What type of quality control do you use?   This question will give you insight about their quality control methods. If you like what you see, you might even want to take some of their ideas and expand upon them. If you don't like what you see, you might discover how you can create a competitive advantage over the competition.

How long have you been in business?   The question might give you some indicator about the staying power of the firm.

Do you have any other locations? If so, where?   If they have other locations, you might be able to glean how they are doing through this fact alone. Much to the contrary of what most people think, when you open new locations in businesses it can frequently be a cash drain on the business. If they open up new locations, and quite frequently, it could mean that they either have:

- An investor with deep pockets
- A very profitable operation that is funding this expansion
- An operation that might be teetering as a result of expansion

Scope out all of these possibilities. You will get a better perspective on the financial health of the company.

Ask for customer references   Companies never give you poor customer references. They frequently give you their best customers as a reference. If you ask for three customer references from each of your ten competitors, you now also have a leads list of 30 potential customers. Why? Because these customers, even though they might be your competitors' best customers, might still be able to be swayed in your direction. You have to offer them even more than your competitors. When you call these references—and do call them—make sure you assess what they like and don't like about your competitor. See what you can do to better address those areas where your competitors are falling down on the job.

These questions are just a start. Depending upon the nature of your specific business, your questions will vary. Don't sound as if you are reciting a script when you ask questions of your competitors. If you do, they will begin to suspect something.

Armed with all of this competitive information, factor it into your own product or service planning. See what you can take from the competitors to improve your product or service and what you can do to create comparative advantages over your competition.

Once you've assessed the market and your competition, you must then figure out your comparative advantages over the competition. These are the unique selling points of your product or service. Quite simply, it is the reason or reasons why people would want to buy your product or service over a competitive one. Hopefully your comparative advantages will be in the areas of product or service attributes (for example, you can send a higher-quality facsimile faster and less expensively than your competition). These are three attributes—quality, speed, and price—that can very often play into comparative advantages over competition. In commodity-based markets, where product or service attributes seem to become irrelevant, price comes through as the only attribute that matters in a competitive situation.

Price Price is an important attribute in marketing of a product or service. You can use a host of techniques to set it. Pricing can be done using cost-plus, market-based, competitive-based, or perceived-value techniques.

Cost-plus pricing *Cost-plus* pricing is done in a very straightforward manner. All of the direct costs of the product or service are tallied. Then, once you know this cost, add some percent to it to arrive at the selling price of the product or service. For example, you might come up with the cost of a product as $1. If you use cost-plus pricing, and add 5% to the cost, the selling price will be $1.05. This type of pricing technique is very popular in contracts with local, state, and federal government agencies.

Market-based versus competitive-based pricing *Market-based* pricing is often considered to be the same as *competitive-based* pricing. There is a difference. To do competitive-based pricing, you look at direct and indirect competitors' prices. You arrive upon a price for your product or service based upon what the competition is charging. Market-based pricing is like competitive-based pricing. It also takes into account what the market might pay for a product or service. In the case of a new product or service, it is based upon forecasting techniques where you extrapolate from existing products or services to guess what you might be able to charge for new ones.

An example of competitive-based pricing techniques might be seen in a data-entry service. There are five competitors in the market. Each charges $1.75 per 1000 keystrokes for identical services. If you choose to charge $1.75 per 1000 keystrokes, you are using competitive-based pricing techniques.

Perceived-value pricing *Perceived-value* pricing is one of my favorite pricing techniques. It involves figuring out what the market perceives the value of a product or service to be. You then charge that optimal amount of money. Perceived-value pricing was used a lot for the early silicon chips. Initially, a lot of the development costs were layered into chip prices. Once that development had been expensed (through the volume of chips sold), the price was left at the grossed-up price. Even though the cost to manufacture a chip fell to pennies a chip, they were still sold for hundreds of dollars per chip. When competition entered the picture and charged less, pricing had to be shifted to competitive pricing techniques.

In the service sector in the computer industry, perceived-value pricing takes hold with hourly consulting rates. Why is it that one computer expert can bill at $70 per hour ($560 per day), and another with the same expertise (or maybe even less), is billing $3500 per day? The answer is simply perceived value. The person who bills $3500 per day has created a greater perceived value to his service than has the person who bills at $560 per day.

Pricing is extremely important. It impacts upon the revenues that you can reap from your business. The person who bills $560 per day, in the example above, can bill a maximum of $140,000 per year (assuming five days per week, 50 weeks a year are billable). The person who bills $3500 per day can bill a maximum of $875,000 (assuming five days per week, 50 weeks a year are billable). Should you take pricing seriously? You bet!

In summary, product (or service), place (distribution channel), price and promotion all go into the creation of a successful marketing campaign. Always be aware of the comparative advantages that you have in the marketplace. Ensure that you define your marketplace and research it. Adequately understand not only to whom you are selling but the profile of your competition so that you can take advantage of that knowledge. Above all, plan your guerilla marketing campaign well and understand how to leverage your time and dollars to get the most out of one of the most important elements of running your business—marketing.

7 Running your company

Several important steps are required to set up and run a PC-based company. The three central areas you need to cover are business setup, team formation, and running the business. Those steps that are concerned with business setup are:

- Name your company
- Register your company's name
- Choose the appropriate business structure
- Plan for all the needed resources

Those that are concerned with your employees and work teams are:

- Form the team—get the right people involved at the right time
- Shape your corporate culture with each employee you hire
- Write proper job descriptions for the business needs
- Create employee incentives by understanding what motivates employees
- Create sensible compensation programs

Considerations for running the business are:

- Learn how to prioritize
- Manage your time
- Manage people
- Manage funds
- Manage technology
- Know when and how to train people

This chapter addresses elements necessary to set up the business. Various business structural forms (for example, sole proprietorship, partnership, and corporation) are discussed from a functional as well as a marketing perspective. What do you tell the world if you are The Information Corporation versus John Smith & Associates? Why should you reserve several business names for your company to use? How do you go about reserving names for the company?

Team formation is particularly important if you are in a high-growth area like the computer industry. Who do you put on the team and when? What should their personalities be like? What skills should they have? How do you compensate them? With cash? With equity? How much equity? How do you define roles within the firm once the team is in place? What do you do about overlapping skills? These questions and more are discussed in depth in this chapter. The questions are critical to computer business success—valuable team members can make or break a computer company.

Managing the business is equally important. Have you ever made payroll? Why worry about cash flow? Do you really know what is involved? How do you manage programmers, especially concerning deadlines? How do you manage and provide incentive for support personnel? How do you train new employees? What kind of a corporate culture do you create for the firm—a California or New York culture? What does the corporate culture do for employees' morale and productivity? How do you decide to give up responsibility and delegate tasks? What do you do to best help people to grow within your firm so they meet goals and objectives?

Naming the business The first thing most people do when they set up a company is to name it. The company's name has a tremendous impact on how your company is perceived. Many people brainstorm with their friends and family to see what name sounds good. The process is a difficult one. It is fascinating to see how some people arrive at the names of their firm. A firm once known for its dedicated word processors was so aggravated by all of the companies that ran around using acronyms for names that they decided to create a parody on it. They named their company NBI, which stood for *Nothing But Initials*. One of WordPerfect's founders became so frustrated by their inability to arrive at a name that as he sat at a railroad crossing and watched a freight train pass by, he saw the initials SSI on the side of a train car. And that's how SSI International named itself. As the company grew and its main product, WordPerfect, became more well known, the firm changed its name to WordPerfect, Inc.

Some companies use computer programs that randomly generate names. Exxon was a name generated by a computer to replace the old Esso corporate name.

The name of your company does convey an image of the firm. Joe's Bar and Grill, Inc., sounds like a small bar and grill. Don's Pizza sounds like a

Setting up the business

proprietorship. Karen & Dave's Company sounds like a small partnership, but who knows what it does? At least you know that Joe's Bar and Grill is a bar and grill and that Don's Pizza sells pizza.

Many companies opt to tell you what they do through their names. This technique is a guerilla marketing technique. If you choose to do something else in your business, though, your name might constrain you.

If you start your company and call yourself Karen & Dave's Programming Company, what happens when you want to start to sell computers? Does this name convey that you sell computers? No, it doesn't. So do you change your name?

Name changes can be harmful to your company's health. When people begin to learn about your company, you begin to build awareness in the people of your products or services. When you change your name, you might have to re-reach all of the people you have previously reached in order to make them aware yet again of your company's existence. Be careful.

Some names convey a very specific business while others give the impression of a general business category. For example, The Word Processing Service Bureau gives the impression of a company that is a word processing service bureau and nothing more—a very specific business. General Electric or General Motors are names that imply that they deal with things that relate to electricity and things that have to do with motors.

When *general* is used as an adjective, it gives the impression of a very large firm. *International*, if used as an adjective also implies a large firm. International Machines, International Business Machines, International Graphics, and International Computers all sound as if they are huge companies. The proper choice of an adjective can convey the impression of a large firm, even if the firm is tiny.

You need to decide, before you choose your name, what type of image you desire to convey to the world. Do you want to appear large or small, specific or general?

Registering the name There might be a problem even after you have spent hours, days, or weeks to arrive at the best possible name for your business—someone might already be using that name. There are complex laws, which vary from state to state, regarding the use of corporate names. It is important to check with the state in which you will register that name before you become completely wed to it. With corporation names, most all states will only let one company register that name for use. Before you incorporate, you can call the Secretary of State's office and reserve a name (or several names) for your potential use. Even if you incorporate in a state other than your own, you can reserve names to ensure that they will be available for you.

Multiple name registration is common to make sure that companies don't attempt to use a name that you use because of an acronym that is created from your name. The best-known example is IBM's registration of not only IBM but International Business Machines.

Business form   Once you have chosen the name of the business, you have to decide the appropriate structure for the business.
Businesses can take on one of three basic forms—corporations, proprietorships, and partnerships.

Corporations   Corporations are an entity unto themselves. They have a perpetual life, or at least until their existence is terminated. Ownership of a corporation is through a share of it called *equity*. Equity is either in the form of common or preferred ownership.

The corporation is owned by stockholders (owners of equity). Corporate liabilities do not pass through to the owners of the equity; that is, unless the corporate veil is *pierced. Piercing the corporate veil* means that the corporate structure is ignored and the stockholders are found to be liable. This action takes place when there is an extremely close tie between the corporation and the shareholders, often when there is only one shareholder. The shareholder, in this instance, is the corporation. And the corporation is the shareholder. Unless the corporation is a subchapter S corporation, the corporation has its own tax liability. If the corporation is a subchapter S corporation, the tax liability passes through to the shareholders. The corporation doesn't pay any taxes.

If you form a corporation, you are required to incorporate. This incorporation is done in one of the fifty states. The corporation is *capitalized* (a certain amount of money is put into it) by the shareholders in order for it to be formed. Certain registration issues need to be followed to be a corporation in the state in which it is incorporating. The shareholders need to adopt a certain set of bylaws and have periodic meetings. The meetings can be pro forma meetings, which are held solely to satisfy the requirements of the state.

States also have certain requirements for corporate names. Generally, the corporation is required to include one of certain terms in its name. For example, the terms, *Inc., Co., Incorporated*, and *Ltd.* are acceptable suffixes to the corporate name to show that the firm really is a corporation.

Proprietorships   Proprietorships (or sole proprietorships) are companies that are owned by one person. They have a limited life, and their life correlates to the life of the proprietor. All of the liabilities of the proprietorship fall on the shoulders of the person who is the proprietor. If the business is sued, the proprietor is sued. If the business owes taxes, it is the proprietor who owes taxes.

State governments require that proprietorships be registered with the government, generally only for tax purposes. There are no naming conventions that are applied to sole proprietorships except that they cannot use the suffixes that are required by corporations.

Partnerships   Partnerships are a group of two or more people or corporations who own an interest in an entity used to do business. Partnerships will very often be established for a specific purpose. For example, a partnership might be set up to invest in real estate. A partnership might be set up by a venture capitalist to invest in growing computer companies. In these types of partnerships, there is often something called a *general partner*. The general partner is the individual or corporation set up to manage the partnership. As a result, the general partner also has most of the liability for all events in which the partnership is involved. The other partners, who frequently only have a financial interest in the partnership, are called *limited partners*. The term *limited* implies that their liability is limited as well as are their power to run the affairs of the partnership.

If you get involved in a partnership, it will probably be with another individual who wants to help run your computer-based business. You will each agree to invest a certain amount of money and share responsibilities to run the company (partnership) in a specific manner. You will share in the responsibilities and liabilities of the company, including the liabilities for tax payment.

Partnerships also must be registered with the state for tax purposes. There are no naming conventions that characterize partners except for the suffix of *partnership* or *partners* in the name (for example, Emily Rose David Partnership).

Just as a name might convey a certain meaning to the outside world, the use of a business form can convey a specific message. Proprietorships, generally through their names, indicate a small firm. Partnerships' names speak also. Jenkins & Associates, Capital Partners, and The David Partnership all seem to convey a marketing image of a small, tightly knit group. Names can convey many images from large to small, general to specific. None of these names, though, might convey the real size of the firm. A partnership might have assets of billions of dollars wherein a corporation with a large sounding name might be worth virtually nothing. The name you choose can help you achieve the size that you might want to build. If you choose a name that sounds as if the firm is immense, it might more easily become large. Perceptions can actually create the desired effect.

You've now chosen your company's name and form. What next? You need to understand just what resources you will need to run the firm. People, funds, and technology, the three resources of the firm, all must be layered into the firm and its growth. These resources will always be in great demand. There never will be enough of them. The most important resource you need to decide upon are the people you need to successfully run the firm.

How and when do you decide to give up responsibility to do everything, admit that you must assemble a team, and delegate tasks to them?

Hopefully it won't be when you are pulled in so many directions that you can't manage everything anymore. If you are in that position, you now need to consider hiring people to do things for you. You now must look towards the management of the firm instead of just the doing element of it. This decision is really the first step in team formation.

Getting the right people involved in the company and at the right time is actually the key component that separates success and failure. In order to determine who you need to layer into the firm and when, you need to look at all of the major milestones that you face in the firm. Hopefully these milestones will follow some logical path if you've planned properly. Along with their path, you will be able to decide what people skills you need to execute them.

You now face a rent versus buy decision. Do you hire these skills on a full-time basis or do you acquire them on some sort of a contract basis? It really depends on how long you will need the skills and whether or not you are able to afford putting these skills on your payroll. The second factor is most frequently the more important one. Within any company, you never seem to have the funds to be able to afford the people who you really want to hire when you really want to hire them. What do you do? You can take one of four courses of action:

- Contract for their services or equivalent services
- Forgo another expenditure and hire them now
- Hire no one, struggle without their skill set, and jeopardize the company
- Hire someone who has a less valuable set of skills and settle for less

Each one of these options presents different end results. You will be able to shape a firm in the manner in which you choose based on how you make each one of these decisions. When you contract for services, you get what you need when you need it. The drawback to this approach—you will end up spending at a rate that is much greater than what you might expect to pay for these equivalent services from an employee. Yet you are probably getting more expertise from those from whom you are contracting. Therefore, the total cost of the project is probably less with contracting.

As an example, you might hire an employee and pay an annual salary of $30,000. Or, you might hire a consultant for three months to accomplish the same task that it will take the employee one year to accomplish. You might pay the consultant $15,000 for those three months. The hourly or daily rate that you pay the consultant is four times that of an employee. Yet the task is actually accomplished sooner.

Another benefit is that you have to worry about having a permanent employee after the project is complete. While this freedom might be beneficial (from the lack of a financial commitment to the individual), you might want the individual to assist you after the term of the contract. Because this individual was hired on a contract basis, he or she has had to seek a contract after yours ran out and might no longer be available. In this example, you have a reduced cost, your liability is reduced, but you don't have the same level of commitment from the individual that you have from an employee.

If you forgo another expenditure and hire the employee now, you prioritize your expenditures. This prioritization might be perfectly acceptable. It really depends what you forsake so that you can make this expenditure. If you give up something that is more critical to the organization than this employee might be, then you are not making a wise decision. If you are not, then it is probably a sensible decision.

Another option is to hire no one. If you choose this option, you can put the entire firm at risk, especially if the individual's skill set is critical to the success of the organization. The analogy is attempting to open a doctor's office without the doctor. Lack of a doctor could jeopardize the whole operation. In fact, it is quite doubtful that you will be able to attract anyone to your doctor's office without the doctor.

When you hire someone for less money, it conjures up the example that many attorneys like to cite. Assume you have to research a case on computer fraud. The expert on computer fraud, an attorney, bills at $750 per hour. The attorney has prosecuted 85% of all computer fraud cases in the country and is extremely familiar with the other 15%. In sum, this attorney is truly familiar with all of the cases in the computer fraud body of law. Conversely, you find an attorney who has no familiarity with computer fraud issues but claims to be able to learn about them quickly. This attorney will only charge you $75 per hour. After 20 hours of research on your specific issue ($1500), the attorney returns to you and tells you that he or she can't solve the problem. Faced with no other alternative, you go to the attorney who is the expert on computer fraud and ask that attorney to address the issue. After 12 minutes of study, he or she gives you an answer that is complete and thoroughly substantiated. The fee is $150. Which is the better deal?

The lesson is simple. On the surface, one service or one potential employee might look less expensive than another. Yet it is entirely possible that you might have a situation like the one outlined here where it is actually less expensive to buy the higher-priced talent. If you don't believe that you can afford this talent, you might want to restrict the amount of time you let it spend on a certain issue or project. Set dollar limits with which you are able to cope satisfactorily.

To form the appropriate team at the appropriate time is particularly important if you are in a high-growth area like the computer industry. If you do finally decide to hire people, who do you put on the team? Obviously, you add those people whose skills are critical to the survival and growth of the company. You add those whose skills and talents can't be entrusted to a subcontractor because it is presumed that the subcontractor might not be as loyal as the employee.

When do you hire people? When they are needed for the success of the organization. If you don't hire them, you could jeopardize the company's success. It is better to have market demand drive the hiring of personnel. Sometimes, in anticipation of market demand, you have to layer in people even before you perceive the demand to be there. In high-growth computer companies, where you need the people in order to deal with expected demand, it is tough to justify hiring decisions too early. After all, overstaffing can create so much overhead that the company will not be able to survive carrying that level of fixed costs.

What do you do if your product demand is great, but you don't have the sales to justify the technical support people you need to help you make sales? A company that my firm deals with was in this position. There were four employees of this firm. One individual was in sales, another wrote the one and only software program that the firm sold, another was in technical support, and one who claimed to run the company. My firm found three potential clients for this company's product. The first firm wanted to better understand the product to see how their data would fit into it. The firm who developed the product attempted to find time to get the data into its product for two months. How did our client react? Not very well. The one person who wrote the software was the bottleneck. No one else knew how to modify the software. So not only did our Fortune 500 client wait but so did many other customers. Did people begin to look elsewhere for solutions? Yes. Should the company that developed the software hire another programmer to deal with the many software code modifications that are necessary? Absolutely. Yet they didn't have the revenues to justify the expense. So how do they get the revenues? By having another programmer. But how do they pay the programmer? By having the revenues. Quite a vicious circle.

What do you do in a situation like this one? Drive everything to the near breakpoint. Then, hire the individual to program, hopefully as just enough funding is being generated from the cash flow. Or find an outside funding source to help you hire those people who you so desperately need. Or go find a corporate partner who might be able to share a programmer with you.

The key point is that you very often need people before you can afford to hire them. Understand how to push the envelope by putting off hiring decisions until you absolutely can bear it no more. Learn this skill and you'll learn how to perform a delicate balancing act. The best way is to understand when the need will be present. Just as a conductor of an orchestra knows when to ready the string section for its performance, so the entrepreneur knows to ready the process for hiring needs that will arise. Judgement, more than anything, gives you the signs that the time has come. This judgement can only be learned through the guidance of someone who has experienced this situation before or through the experience that you have gained through this experience. There is no other substitute.

There are signs that give you the knowledge that your organization is at or near its breaking point, a time to hire more employees. The first sign is you and your employees. Is everyone working 18 hours a day? Does everyone feel as if they have so much to do that there is no way that they will ever get it done? Do people walk around talking about how stressed out they feel? Do mood shifts occur so that people are somewhat unpredictable in their behavior? Does everyone seem to be wearing more than one hat? Do customers or resellers of the product or service that you sell complain about delivery time? About delivery quality? Is quality really suffering? If you can answer yes to one or more of these questions, over more than one week, you might be in a situation where it is time to hire more people talent to help run and build the company.

Make sure that you hire the right people. One of the situations outlined in the last paragraph could exist within your company. You might have more than enough warm bodies to be able to deal with all of the problems of the business. Your problem might be that you might have the wrong bodies. In the previous example of the company that needed another programmer, assume that it actually had the software programmer, the company president, and three clerical people. While the organization might need five people, these five skill sets are not necessarily the correct ones. In fact, they are somewhat correct and somewhat incorrect. If the company had five people—a president, salesperson, technical support person, and two programmers—it might have the correct combination. Yet the firm that would include three clerical personnel would not be the correct configuration.

The result of the incorrect individuals in the firm can be stress, unpredictable behavior, and long hours. But these problems show up only with those employees who truly have the needed skills within the organization. The other employees might not work much at all. These employees are labeled as slack resources. They don't function at optimal levels and can disrupt everyone. Other individuals in the company begin to resent the slack resources. They feel that these people don't carry their weight. These people might do everything that they possibly can. Yet their skill sets limit them as to what they can do. These people might want to work as hard as the others but due to their own limitations, they might not be able to do sales, the technical support, or the programming.

Organizations can deal with slack resources in a host of ways. They can get upset and tell the slack resources to work harder. They can attempt to change the ways in which slack resources work. Or they can realize what is happening and treat the slack resources appropriately.

The first reaction—to get upset and tell the slack resources to work harder—is the most natural reaction. There are a couple of issues here. Slack resources are not necessarily lazy but lack work that they can perform. The other resources in the organization might work so hard on other tasks that they have not offloaded the appropriate tasks to the people who have become slack resources. What is the person who is the slack resource to do? Is it her or his fault that other people do what they normally do? No. So the resources that work at overcapacity should realize that planning is necessary to involve those resources that are now slackened. And if they don't plan accordingly, then there might be no way to involve the slackened resource. Probably one of the best examples of this situation is the individual who works on a project through the night. At 3:00 A.M. he or she needs a secretary to type a twenty-page document that is due at 9:00 A.M. at a client's office. Because the secretary is not there just waiting to type the document, the individual has two options—call the secretary to come in and type the document or to type the document. (My typing skills are what they are because I have been in this situation and realized that the second option is the better option.) If you choose the second option, you feel that you are now not only doing your job but also your secretary's job. And as you type away, you begin to wonder why you even have the secretary on payroll in the first place. And somehow you forget that it is 3:00 in the morning. Is this right when you could have planned to have the typing ready at 3:00 the previous afternoon? No, its not. Most often, though, when you are overworked and overstressed, you forget about the two most important elements of running a business that is short on resources—prioritization and time management. Unless prioritization and time management occur by the resources that are overburdened, the slack resources will just remain slackened.

The second reaction is an attempt to change the ways in which slack resources work. People within the organization who are overworked might realize that there are holes in the skill set in the organization that must be filled. They try to plug these holes with the resources that are available. This scenario might be doomed before it even starts.

Return to the example where the organization is in need of one sales person, one technical support person, and one programmer. It now has these three clerical people who are perceived as the slack resources. The need for the sales person, technical support person, and programmer are all recognized by all of the five people within the company. You decide to use the five people who are now present in the organization to fill these roles. One clerical person is to serve as the sales person. Another clerical person will focus on technical support. The other will become a programmer. All these responsibilities are added to any that they now have. Now what happens, you ask? Any number of scenarios might develop. You might get extremely lucky and all of the clerical people might be trainable in each one of these areas. Even better, they might all be able to pick everything up naturally. The complete opposite might occur—they are all unable to perform any of these functions. Or you might land in some middle ground where one or two of them are able to pick up some of what is needed.

The key to dealing with this realignment of resources is the level of expectations that you have. Everyone in the company can agree to give these new duties a try. If they don't work out and no one is penalized, then life might be in line with expectations. In reality, though, whenever this sort of thing happens there are expectations that might be unrealistic. Because each one of these individuals has an additional role, if they can't cut the mustard, they are no longer contributing to the company. It is amazing how expectations do change even when people say that they won't change.

In a smaller firm where resources are in short supply, resources might be shifted and they might not succeed at the reassigned task. So does this lack of success mean that these people are not valuable to the company? In a lot of growing firms the quick answer is yes. The perception is that these people failed at their responsibility. How can you say that if a person was hired to be a secretary and performed secretarial tasks quite well? Yet when the job responsibilities were coupled with those of programming, the person couldn't program? The answer is too often, quite easily. The programmer position is perceived to be more necessary to the company than the clerical position. What the people really want to do is get rid of the clerical person, until needed again. They want to hire a programmer now and then rehire the clerical person when the need arises. These situations can be quite ugly. In fact, there is a $200 million computer software company that operates in the banking industry whose founder boasts that the only original employee left within the firm is himself. He claims the needs of the organization have changed such that people needed to be replaced along the way. In my opinion, he suffered from the clerical-to-programmer retooling syndrome.

There are ways around what can become excessive turnover. The best way is to truly monitor the organization's personnel needs through excellent planning. Don't always purchase an employee on a permanent basis. Rent one on a consulting or temporary basis if you perceive the needs for their skills to be only a short period of time. Personnel needs of a fast-growing organization change rapidly. Understand this issue. Its delicate management is a key to success. With my own firm, I see technology-based needs changing so rapidly that I would much rather rent (on a subcontract basis) skills that I can count on than purchase them, especially if there is an uncertain future demand for them. By way of example, when my firm was asked to link a telephone system (PBX) to a voice-mail system (DVX), I reasoned that the person who was most familiar with the various systems could solve problems well and rapidly. Who was brought in to solve the problem? One of the chief designers of one of the largest private telephone networks in the country. Could I afford to hire this person? If my firm had other jobs in this area, absolutely. Yet because other work was uncertain, the best way to deal with the situation was on a subcontract basis. No other significant opportunities have presented themselves since then, and it appears that rental was much better than a purchase decision.

This rent versus buy decision is appropriate as almost a daily exercise in some high-technology firms. When it is properly executed, a minimum number of slack resources will be hired in the first place. If slack resources are in place, frequently while the resources might be slack today, tomorrow, they might not be. This sensible treatment is really the only way for survival and growth in the computer industry.

There are many firms in the computer industry that grow and become ridden with people who become slack resources as the marketplace changes. These firms are faced with retooling or firing dilemmas. Often, neither of these things happen and the companies end up carrying slack resources. They become a drain on the profitability of the firm. As market conditions change and the organization wishes to pursue new technology-based opportunities, it might realize that it can't turn on a dime. It doesn't have the people in place to react to these market opportunities. It will then start renting the resources. It will hire contractors or consultants that serve to make its personnel even more slackened. With short product life cycles in the computer industry, these issues can become even more exacerbated.

So you've gone through the rent versus buy decision on employees and figured out how and when you really do need them. You realize that the process must be very well thought out. It also must be constantly monitored. You know that you will buy some employees at certain times. Now it is time to deal with the specific issues that relate to the employee.

What should their personalities be like? They should mesh with you and the other team members. You should all be able to work together. If you can't get along as a team, you will constantly be worrying about personality issues rather than business issues.

Goodness of personality fit is accomplished through both scientific and nonscientific means. It is hard to tell which means is more accurate. Scientific measures are the personality tests that are given to prospective employees. There are organizations that specialize in designing, implementing, and scoring these examinations. These examinations can show where an employee's interests and strengths lie and what personality traits an employee might have. Some companies even develop personality profiles to find employees. If you match this profile, then you will fit into the organization. These profiles will be different for different jobs within the firm.

Although some individuals and firms believe that these personality tests are a panacea, others question their validity.

Especially in a computer-based business, where personalities might be a little different (that is, the stereotypical programmer), you might want to open up your horizons to more qualitative judgements on worker personalities. A computer programmer's personality might be a complete misfit with every other team member in your organization. Yet the programmer might be the world's absolute best programmer. As a result, you might figure out a way to enable this person to work in the organization without creating problems.

You might have to be creative to structure a working relationship with those who have skills your organization might need. In fact, when you call attention to a misfit's status, it can help them fit into the organization. Statements such as "He's the guy who only eats Chinese food and rides a bicycle to work" differentiate the person from the rest of the people within the company. If presented properly, the employee will actually feel special. You can build entire suborganizations within a company with this special feeling.

Corporate culture

The personalities of the firm shape something called the *corporate culture*. As the lead entrepreneur, you influence the type of people who are attracted to the company by the sort of culture that you build. Likes will begin to attract likes. Dislikes will repel. So, the organization will evolve. This corporate culture, if strong enough, will begin to shape personalities of members of the firm.

In the computer industry, Apple Computer, Inc. is known as a flexible and creative, relaxed firm whose employees all work very hard. Apple enables employees to work in their homes. Employees can work flexible hours as long as they get the job done. Based on the computers the firm produces, you can see the level of creativity that is embodied in the corporate culture. The human interface that comes from the systems are creative and fun. The firm is extremely relaxed culturally. Employees commonly show up to work in casual attire. Even the chief executive officer is often seen in a polo shirt addressing large audiences. Apple, especially in its early days, was thought to be a cult. Employees, customers, developers, and resellers all hoped to be members of the cult. The mores of the cult became known. As Apple has grown and changed, the cult-like appearance kept many corporate users from using their systems.

Until recently, IBM has had a completely different corporate culture from Apple Computer, Inc. Although Apple will hire people from almost any walk of life at any time in their career, IBM tends to hire people straight out of college. The company then shapes their personalities to fit into the IBM corporate culture. IBM feels that people who have just graduated from college are much more malleable than are people who have gained experience. The IBM stereotype is an individual who is very professional and businesslike, oriented towards dealing with the major corporations of the world. That individual follows a set of strict guidelines established by IBM. This stereotype is typically less malleable than the one found in the Apple Computer corporate culture.

Neither one of these corporate cultural descriptions is complete or necessarily fair. Many believe that certain, if not all, of these dimensions are relevant in the respective corporate cultures. These cultures developed over time and have been based on the views of the many individuals who have worked for the firm.

You can establish your own corporate culture. You can create the personality profile of the firm, or you can just let it evolve. The evolution is subject to your personality. The personality profile involves many different dimensions that you can consider—outside interests, business style (relaxed or traditional), sense of humor, and (most important), skills. Personality profiles and corporate cultures will evolve around these parameters. You too can consider these dimensions when you add to your team. As a direct result, your corporate culture will evolve.

What kind of a corporate culture do you create for the firm? A California or New York culture? Corporate cultures can be different not only in different types of firms but in different geographic locations. A California corporate culture might be laid back and relaxed, and a New York culture might be more always on-the-go. Where you locate your company might actually have a tremendous impact upon the corporate culture that is built. You might want to consider this dimension heavily before you settle in one place.

What does the corporate culture do to people's morale and productivity? Everything. The corporate culture shapes morale. If the corporate culture is upbeat and positive, it will be reflected in the personalities of the people who work for the firm. If the culture is negative, this element will come through. Common sense tells you that a positive culture will aid productivity. A negative one will detract from it.

What skills should your employees have? Based on your specific organizational needs, all of your employees should have some fundamental technical skill. This skill might be typing, or it might be software programming. You should include someone on your team because they have functional technical skills. In a smaller organization, you might require them to have more functional or technical skills than in a larger firm. To the degree that each employee will need to deal with people, she or he should have people skills. Even your programmers need to interact with people. To the extent that employees must interact, they must have people skills.

Write job descriptions. This job description should actually be a part of your planning process. Keep it simple yet ensure that it is thorough. Figure 7-1 shows a sample job description.

Programmer

The programmer should be able to program in the C programming language. He or she should be versatile enough to learn Pascal if needed. Must be able to interact with systems analysts to translate what they have developed as needs into a working program. Must be able to write efficient code as set forth by the judgement of the chief programmer. Experience should include having written some financial-management software. Relevant education should include an undergraduate degree in computer science. Salary range: $25,000–$30,000 per year.

Skill set measures

	Low	Moderate	High
Technical skill: Programming			X
People skill: Interaction		X	
Financial skill	X		

This job description is a bit novel. Job descriptions generally include only the first component of the one found in the illustration; an actual description of the job, the required experience, education, and salary. Although the traditional job description is commonly accepted, this format makes you determine the resources—technical, people, and financial—that you require. These scales will slide over time. Job descriptions change as the organizational needs change. Keep an eye on both the job descriptions and the sliding scale found here. You will be better able to anticipate the people needs of your organization—the skills that you have in-house and those that you will need to acquire (through either renting or purchasing people). You might become so wrapped up in running your company that you feel that spending time on people needs of the company is a low priority. The people of your company are the most important part of your firm, especially in a service-based organization. Their importance cannot be emphasized enough.

Employee incentives

You want to compensate employees in a fashion that not only makes them happy today but provides them incentives in the future. Different things provide incentives for different people. Understand the hot buttons of your employees.

What motivates employees and how should incentives be built? There are a host of things that motivate people. A list of some of them follows.

Opportunity   Opportunity is most often thought of as potential or hope. If people believe that they have potential for something to happen, they often look forward and work towards that potential. You find potential in most of the items in the rest of the list found here.

Money   People like the opportunity to make money. Often, when a new firm is established, people will join it not for the money that they make today (because this might be less than what they might be able to make elsewhere). They will join it for the potential money that they might make in the future as the firm grows and as they grow within it. Use money as an incentive very carefully. Expectations must be aligned with reality, or the individual whose incentives are based on money will be disappointed. If you idly promise an employee that she or he will earn $15,000 more each year, and the revenues of the firm don't permit you to do so, the expectations will not be met. The employee will become dissatisfied and will probably leave the firm. If you tie the growth of a monetary incentive to something over which the employee has control, the employee can only be disappointed if he or she doesn't perform. Provide the salesperson incentive in a percentage of the sales that person makes. If performance is not good, the salesperson can only be disappointed with her or his own performance.

Monetary incentive systems are extremely difficult to figure out. You have to look at what you can afford to pay and what you must pay to be competitive. Creatively layer in a dimension that gives the individual as much control over his or her compensation as possible. Compensation should be tied directly to an individual's performance.

Responsibility   Many people are motivated by responsibility. Everybody wants to feel as if what they do matters. They want to be an important part of the organization. They want to feel responsible for something. How often have you heard the expression that someone has a responsible job. Have you ever thought what that means? Doesn't it really mean the person is responsible for something that is important to the organization?

Make everyone in your organization feel as if they are responsible for something that is very important. Many organizations instill this sense of responsibility through titles they give employees. *Chief of Sanitation Engineering* sounds a lot more responsible than the *trash person*. You have to be careful with titles; they can get out of hand.

Some organizations believe that titles are completely unimportant. This decision is one that shapes the corporate culture. If you don't avail yourself of titles, figure out a system that somehow recognizes responsibility. Monetary incentives, numbers of people someone manages, and budget management all relate to levels of responsibility.

Recognition   People always find incentive in recognition. Recognize a job well done. Recognize a specific accomplishment. Employee of the month programs recognize someone who has done a good job. Financial bonuses are vehicles of recognition. Title changes (for example, from vice president to senior vice president) are vehicles of recognition. Awards given to specific employees are recognition. Fringe benefits given for a job done well are recognition vehicles.

People feel good as a result of recognition.

Intellectual curiosity   Some folks are so intellectually curious that giving them the proper tools to pursue their intellectual curiosity can motivate them to perform at heightened levels. There are programmers who go wild when they are given the latest computer to tinker with. They might create wonderful new programs that take advantage of a new piece of software, firmware, or hardware, just to see what they can possibly do with the technology. Their intellectual curiosity might work to your advantage—they not only train themselves on this technology but they might create something that has benefit to the company.

Accomplishment   Everyone understands a sense of accomplishment. When an author writes a book, she or he feels a great sense of accomplishment when it's complete. You can feel a tremendous sense of accomplishment when you complete a task.

If you understand this, you can structure projects so that people gain a sense of accomplishment upon their completion.

Power   Power is the ability to control. If you want power to control your own life, independence is key. If you want power to control other people's lives, there is a whole different issue. There are certain individuals who are motivated by control of other people's lives. You might be one of those people. This creates a restrictive nature to those whose lives are being controlled. Either they will rebel against it (quit) or submit to it. Be careful. Understand fully the ramification of what you've done.

Assistance in growth of an organization   There are many people who like to feel as if they can contribute to the growth of an organization. Building something is a tremendous motivator. Many entrepreneurs are motivated to build a company. Employees also can be very motivated to build. Yet they might not want to bear the risk of the entire entrepreneurial pursuit. If people have the feeling that they can contribute to the growth of a company, that is enough for them.

What do you do to best help the people grow within your firm so they meet goals and objectives? If you provide the right incentive to the right people with the correct tools at the appropriate time, you can accomplish much to motivate an employee. As a byproduct, you can realize goals that you set for the company.

How do you decide on the appropriate compensation structure? Early in the growth of an organization, you can ask people. Ask them first what motivates them and consequently structure a compensation plan around those things. When you create this structure, be sure that you consider the precedents you set for the future. These precedents are set for everyone in the company.

When you set up a compensation structure, realize that you've created a path for the future. This framework must deal with events as they unfurl in the corporation. If you aren't careful, you might give away the ship. There is one software company that recruited a salesperson early on to set up a distribution channel east of the Mississippi. The company gave this individual three percent of the gross receipts of the product sales he generated. This unnamed word processing package became one of the hottest on the market. The individual retired. I don't think that the company has ever done another deal like this one again. They had given away the ship but they perceived that it was necessary in order to motivate this person to perform. Probably the classic story is McDonald's. Ray Kroc had so little money that he offered his secretary equity in the firm in lieu of salary. She took the equity and retired a millionaire.

So how do you compensate employees? With cash? How much cash? With equity? How much equity? And when?

There are no magic formulas for compensation. The general theory is that cash is less expensive than equity. With equity comes longer-term value to the equity holder. Yet, with equity comes a longer-term cost to the company. There is a reduced short-term cost to equity, which is why so many firms will opt to give it to employees. Certainly Ray Kroc made this decision. Over time, when you give up ownership, you give up potential returns from the economic success of the corporation. If you create a team that is inclined to perform based on the potential financial return that they might reap, you might elevate the chances of economic success of the firm.

Who you compensate with equity and who you compensate with cash are important decisions. Generally, employees whose skills are readily obtainable in the marketplace are those who you should compensate with cash only. Those employees whose skills are not readily obtainable are those who you might want to compensate with both cash and equity.

When you structure a cash-plus-equity compensation, even if it is for only one employee, it makes much sense to have some type of a waiting period after which the employee is eligible to purchase stock. The reason? The employee might not work out. If you've given the person equity in your firm before you have time to make this determination, you might have someone who has equity that you don't want to. This might still develop if you have a lag period before you give equity to the employee. As a result, it makes infinite sense for you to have some buy-back provision in the equity that you offer to your employees. If you terminate their employment, you should automatically be able to buy back their equity at a specified price. This price might change over time (increase or decrease) and correlate to the value of the firm. You should also spell out how you'll calculate the value of the business.

If you choose to offer an employee stock options, it makes sense to go to a financial planner or an attorney who deals strictly with these matters. He or she can tell you the pros and cons of all types of employee stock ownership plans. Remember that whatever you do, you set a precedent. Many of these plans require that you include certain categories of employees in the plans. A professional who deals with these matters will know how the law reads and how you should handle it.

You've now got your compensation structure in place and are primed for the growth of the company. How do you deal with the changing roles that take place within your team as the company grows? What do you do about overlapping skills?

If you look at a computer company where change is the watchword, roles are often redefined rather quickly. If you start out with two people—one as the president/sales person and the other as the programmer, what happens when your company grows to $1 million in sales per year? You now need a chief operating officer. You feel that the programmer should really report to that officer. But the programmer is one of the founders and feels that the chief operating officer should report to him.

There's a conflict in this situation that is quite common. People need to be layered in above the founders. Or as the company grows, people need to be layered in above existing employees. An example is the salesperson who does a tremendous job selling but in no way is management material. She or he can't manage his way out of a paper bag. Based on increased consumer demand, you need to hire another salesperson. You decide to hire a salesperson/sales manager. The old salesperson now reports to the sales manager and no longer the company president. Does a conflict arise? Inevitably.

So how do you deal with changing roles as the company grows? There are two good ways to cope with this dynamic situation—communication and flexibility. Communicate what happens in the company when it is happening. Even better, communicate with people before things happen. Involve them in the decision making process. They might then become the ones to realize or even suggest that changing people's roles in the organization is the best thing to do.

Flexibility is the second important element needed to deal with organizational shifts in personnel. If people understand what is going on, they are more likely to be flexible as change is needed. If they don't understand or are inflexible, they might create an impasse to the change that needs to occur for the benefit of the company.

Both of these elements must be present for success. Even with them, there is no guarantee. Tact and grace must be exercised with all concerned. Egos of founders and early entrants into companies can become extremely large yet fragile. If they feel at all put upon, their egos can become bruised, and that creates problems for the organization.

Another source of potential problems is if the founders themselves have overlapping skills. This situation is resolvable only under two conditions—1) one of the founders has skills beyond the overlapping skills and wants to flex those muscles or 2) the company grows so rapidly that both of the skill sets of the founders can be used. In the first instance, both of the founders have sales skills. One of them also has management skills. If the one that has management skills wishes to manage, the company is in good shape. The second instance arises when both of the founders might have sales abilities in a brokerage business. The sales growth is so great that they both can sell and not collide with one another. In this instance, you might need to hire a manager to run the company while both founders continue to sell.

If there is a conflict with overlapping skills in situations other than those outlined, they are generally not resolvable. These situations lead to breakups of corporations or partnerships. Beware of overlapping skills before you enter into a partnership or a corporation with people who have similar skill sets. Make sure you really know what they want to do and what their real agenda might be.

Managing the business

Now that you have the proper team in place and you understand when to hire and how to provide incentives, how do you manage the business? You must manage all of the resources of the firm—people, funds, and technology. The key elements necessary to deal with management of a computer-based firm are prioritization and time management.

You must know how to prioritize. When you are faced with five tasks, which one do you do first, the easiest one or the most complicated one? The task that will take the shortest or longest amount of time? How about the one that is the most important? How do you determine what is most important? Is it based on who screams the loudest? Who pays you the most? Is it based on which one is the most complicated? The answer might be any one of the above. You have to sit down with the business plan that you have devised. Assess which tasks are most important in order to achieve your short- and long-term goals. These goals and objectives will then determine how you establish your priorities.

In addition to the goals and objectives of your business plan, there will be external factors that determine how you prioritize what you do when. If your star employee walks into your office and says he or she is quitting, do you drop everything and deal with the situation? Or do you say, "I'm sorry, you'll have to wait your turn in the queue of priorities." I drop everything. You probably will too.

Some people are so busy dealing with these external factors that they never seem to begin to address their own list of priorities. When this type of situation arises, you need to reassess how you can accomplish those things that you want to do. Maybe you don't need to take the sales calls of every person who calls you. Maybe you can have someone else in your organization deal with those calls so you can do something else.

Setting priorities is interrelated to time management. You have to manage your time the way you want or people and their priorities will constantly shift you around. Sit down in the evening and rank those things that you want to get accomplished the next day. Rank them in priority order. Even if you have only one item on your priority list, it can be affected by at least ten other external factors.

When you run a computer-based company that is constantly changing, you need to reprioritize frequently. You should map out a realistic schedule of what you want to accomplish in a given day. Prioritize those tasks and then attempt to accomplish them. If you don't get through each one of these tasks on a given day, reprioritize for tomorrow. Move those tasks that you didn't finish today to tomorrow and give them the highest priority, unless something more important takes precedence. An easy task? Not hardly. Yet the better you can establish priorities and manage time, the better you will run your business.

Management of priorities and time extend to management of people, funds, and technology.

Managing people

This book cannot begin to attempt to explain adequately how people might be managed. In people management, you can somehow get them to do what you want them to do. Management is generally thought to be a positive issue. At times, it can require negative means to get people to do what you want them to do. Management is accomplished when you understand what motivates an individual. You can push those buttons that get a person to accomplish what is set forth as the goals of the company.

Management requires an understanding of human nature. In order to motivate people to do something, you must be able to understand them. Good managers are often those who are trained in human psychology because they understand motivation elements of the human spirit. Perceptivity is the single most important skill in people management. When you can perceive how people will react, you can evoke the sort of response that you want to achieve.

If you can't manage people because people skills are not one of your best skills, find someone that can. People are your most important asset and must be treated as such. If you ignore their needs, they will ignore your needs. The organization will suffer.

You need to know how to manage funds, especially cash. When a business starts out or is young, it might not be able to establish credit with suppliers or banks. The business might be required to pay for everything as it buys it. The business might be on a cash-on-delivery basis and need as much cash as it does business. Actually, the more a business grows, the more cash it will need to pay for more supplies and employees. Yet, the customers to whom you sell your computer products or services might not pay you as you deliver. So, as you do more business, your cash position gets worse, unless you are able to establish credit to purchase supplies or a line of credit to meet your short-term payment needs such as payroll. Figure 7-2 shows how increased business can actually negatively affect the business if it doesn't have available credit.

Managing funds

7-2 Increased business versus cash flow

	Month 1	Month 2	Month 3
Booked revenues	$1000		
Cash outlay for components of revenue	$ 750		
Billed revenue		$1000	
Cash collection			$1000

In the example in the illustration, notice that you have a real cash outlay of $750 in month 1, which is not collected until month 3. You have to come up with that $750 in month 1 in order to support the sale. If you are unable to come up with the $750, you will not be able to fund the product or service creation needed to bill and collect the revenues. One solution is to collect money up-front so that you will have money to pay the cash outlay as you need it. This solution is tremendous, if you can achieve it. The problem is that many firms will not pay any money up front, no matter what the reason. You must find a way to have the cash available. You have to look at all cash sources available to you.

Cash-flow management is one of the most important elements of running a business. If you don't have the cash to pay your payroll, do you know what happens? The first time you don't have the cash, your employees might be tolerant. The second time, they will probably be a little more nervous. Beyond that, they will probably look for new jobs.

Payroll is the single most important expenditure that you have to make. Also, you must pay your payroll taxes. If you don't pay the payroll taxes of the federal, state, and local governments, you can be held personally liable for them even if it is your company's responsibility to pay them.

In addition to payroll and payroll taxes, there are probably some key suppliers who you will have to find cash to pay. Finding cash for these sources might mean that you forgo paying yourself. Welcome to the world of entrepreneurship. Welcome to the world of cash management. Very early on in your business life, it should be ingrained in you that cash flow is the most important element to provide life to a company. It is the blood that runs through the veins to ensure that the life is present.

Cash flow must remain positive or you will dig yourself into a hole. What is a positive cash flow? *Positive cash flow* is a flow of more money into the company than goes out of it. It is determined by the actual billings and expenditures of the company first. If your actual billings are less than your expenditures, you are not making a profit. In turn, the cash flowing into the company will be less than that flowing out of the company. If there is no source to bridge the gap between the cash flowing out of the company and that flowing into it, the company will not have enough cash for operations. It will be forced to go out of business.

You want to be able to bill more than you spend. Therefore, you generate more incoming cash than cash flowing out. There is a saying that happiness comes from a positive cash flow. It has a lot of validity.

As mentioned, making payroll is your most important payment. Fred Smith, Chairman and Founder of Federal Express, didn't have enough money to make his payroll. He gambled what he had in Las Vegas and won enough to pay payroll. What would have happened had he lost? You are always best off if you have an established reserve and don't ever have to get this low. Believe me, worrying about payroll can keep you up at night. Until you've done it, you'll never understand the feeling. After you've done it, you'll realize that you will lead your life in time frames based on your pay periods. Will I have the cash for the payroll on the 15th of the month? How about the payroll at the end of the month? It is an endless cycle.

You can ensure that you have a positive cash flow by doing two things—ensure that you generate a profit and collect cash faster than it leaves the company. It takes constant effort to keep this balance tipped in the direction of a positive cash flow. There are some ways to aid it along.

Always try to collect as much money up front as is possible. Call it a down payment, a deposit, or a retainer, but get as much as you possibly can. Give discounts off the entire purchase price if you can collect everything up front (my firm once got the United States Securities and Exchange Commission to pay everything up front for a 5% discount off of the purchase price).

If you can't collect money up front, try to collect it on delivery. Don't give people their product until they pay you. (My firm frequently sells software and hardware on a cash-on-delivery COD basis.) In this situation, you can closely correlate the time you need to pay for merchandise (if you are on a cash-on-delivery basis with your suppliers) to when you collect the money. That way, you don't have to carry the cash outlay for that long. It is no more difficult to deliver a service cash-on-delivery than a product. Your plumber and electrician do it to you, don't they?

If you need to bill the customer, politely hound the living daylights out of him or her to ensure that you are paid on time. One way to encourage timely payment is to offer discounts on the selling price if payment is made within 10 days. Commonly 2/10, net 30, are terms that can be extended to clients. The terms 2/10, net 30, means that the customer will receive a two percent discount if you receive payment within 10 days of the invoice. At day 30, you can send a written statement or begin the calls to the accounts payable department.

On the payment side, you want to be able to stretch them out to as many of your suppliers for as long as possible. If you have credit terms with your suppliers, you have a better opportunity to extend payment. If not, you might not be able to do so. Just as you try to collect money owed you, they will attempt to collect from firms that owe them money. Remember to maintain a delicate balance with payment extension. You want to be able to get supplies from suppliers when you need them. One trick is to have multiple suppliers of the same product or service. Make sure that you keep one of them on good terms at all times. You might even want to rotate who is kept on good terms at certain times of the year.

Always remember that however you play this game, your cash flow must remain positive. There are those who say that the three most important elements to running a business are cash flow, cash flow, and cash flow.

Managing technology

Technology management is a combination of funds and people management. For hardware, software, and firmware, the management decision is rather simple. Figure out what capabilities you will need—survey as completely as possible within the constraints of your time for all available hardware, software, and firmware. Perform a cost-benefit analysis on what you can possibly buy. Then, make your decision. Your decision is correct at the moment you make it. It is guaranteed to be wrong the following day. Why? Because technology changes so rapidly that you can only be right at that one time. Obviously, when you make the technology decision, try to anticipate trends within the market to ensure that your decision will be correct for more than one moment. Quite conceivably, it might not be correct the next moment. Recognize that you've given it as much time as you had to dedicate to the decision. You've made it. Hopefully you've hedged your bet through either borrowing or renting technology.

Part of your technology management might find you managing programmers. Unless you understand how to program, you might find yourself at a loss. There is one cardinal rule for success: manage a programmer as you would manage anyone else. Establish milestones and have the programmer agree to those milestones. Place time limits on each of the milestones. Enforce the completion of those deadlines by the programmer. Make the milestones small enough that, if a programmer is unable to complete any one milestone, you will be able to judge the capability (that is, whether or not the programmer is unable to complete the task). You can then find someone else to perform the task. If these milestones are small enough, you will not have lost any major time in completion of the project.

How do you judge if a programmer is capable if you can't program? For that matter, how do you judge if any individual or firm that has a technical bent is competent if you can't understand the technology? There are a host of vehicles. Some of them are:

- Find someone who understands the technology, whose judgement and intelligence you otherwise trust, and ask them to judge the capabilities for you.
- Ask the firm or the individual who is engaged in the technology development for at least three references. Call the references and see what they think. If they are satisfied, then proceed with caution.
- Ask to see some of the individual's or the firm's completed, operational work. If you like what you see, you are making headway.
- Finally, once you make a decision, do establish manageable milestones that permit you to judge progress. If you sense incompetence, change horses.

Training

Finally, in running a firm, you must consider the element of training. How do you train new employees? How do you train firms who do work for you? Develop a training program, a briefing about the firm, and some informational pieces that quickly bring people up the learning curve so that they can be productive. Rent a video camera. Film yourself giving background information about the firm or the project. Distribute it to new employees or contractors to quickly bring them to a level playing field. People can take these videos home with them and virtually train themselves independent of you or other people in the firm.

Videos also effectively train people on how to use computer hardware and software. Videos are a vehicle used by people who run the computer-based training companies described in this book. Videos are controllable. They let you know what the employees or contractors actually do know. In computer business management, more and more companies are acutely aware that technology changes require both initial and repeat training.

There are many dimensions to operation of a successful computer-based company. The essential elements are:

- Set forth good plans to run the firm
- Assemble the right team at the right points in time
- Remain flexible to deviate from your plans when necessary
- Understand and actually do the right things to manage all of the resources of the firm—people, funds and technology

8 Understanding your company's finances

Financial statements report the results of a company during a given period of operation. Frequently this period is one year. It can be for a shorter period, such as one or a few months.

There are different financial statements. They are:

- Income statement
- Balance sheet
- Cash flow statement

Reading financial statements

Financial statements appear to be very complicated if you aren't accustomed to them. With a few definitions, examples, and practice, you can easily become comfortable with using them.

Income statement

The *income statement* (also called the *profit and loss statement*) shows the amounts received and the costs incurred by the company from the sale of goods or services. Figure 8-1 contains a sample income statement.

Revenues

The first entry on the income statement is revenues. The most important item is the net sales, which is equal to the gross sales less any returns or allowances.

Sample computer company
statements of consolidated earnings
for the years ending December 31

	1993	1994
REVENUES	10,755,000	10,200,000
COSTS AND EXPENSES		
Cost of goods sold	8,200,000	7,792,000
GROSS PROFIT	2,555,000	2,408,000
General and administrative expenses (see schedule)	735,000	715,000
Selling expenses (see schedule)	900,000	835,000
TOTAL EXPENSES	1,635,000	1,550,000
EARNINGS BEFORE INCOME TAXES	920,000	858,000
PROVISIONS FOR INCOME TAXES	510,000	485,000
NET EARNINGS	410,000	373,000
EARNINGS PER SHARE	$1.54	$1.49

Sample computer company
schedule of general and administrative expenses
for the years ending December 31

	1993	1994
Secretaries' salaries	62,000	57,000
Managers' salaries	150,000	145,000
Depreciation	150,000	135,000
Office supplies	175,000	172,500
Repairs and maintenance	45,000	52,000
Professional fees	28,000	31,000
Utilities	125,000	122,500
TOTAL GENERAL AND ADMINISTRATIVE EXPENSES	735,000	715,000

Sample computer company
schedule of selling expenses
for the years ending December 31

	1993	1994
Sales staff salaries	210,000	205,000

Commissions	100,000	97,500
Automobile expenses	47,000	52,000
Travel and entertainment	150,500	125,000
Depreciation	150,000	135,000
Advertising	202,500	177,500
Telephone	40,000	43,500
TOTAL SELLING EXPENSES	900,000	835,000

Cost of sales is also called *cost of goods sold*. This item is the cost of the items that are purchased for resale. It is equal to the beginning inventory plus the purchases made during that period. It also includes any direct costs attributable to the purchases less the ending inventory on the last day of the period covered by the income statement. For a manufacturing company, the cost of sales will usually include all costs incurred in the manufacturing process to convert the raw materials to finished products. In addition to the purchase price of raw materials, these costs include the factory overhead costs such as rent and utilities, depreciation of related equipment, and the labor costs of the factory workers. The cost of sales or cost of goods sold is equal to:

Cost of sales

> \+ Beginning inventory
> \+ Purchases
> \+ Direct costs (freight, overhead)
> – Ending inventory
> _____
> = Cost of goods sold

Gross profit is equal to revenues less cost of sales. It shows the profit made on the product before deducting other expenses such as general and administrative or selling and taxes.

Gross profit

This expense includes the salaries for the sales staff, sales commissions, advertising, marketing, and sales promotion. A supplemental schedule might be provided that indicates a breakdown of the various items that make up the selling expenses.

Selling expense

The salaries and wages of the personnel who operate the company are classified as a general and administrative expense. This also includes the office rent and related supplies.

General & administrative expenses

In some cases, the next item on the income statement is generally the nonoperating income and expenses such as interest, dividends, and gains or losses from the sale of assets.

Net profit   The residual between the business revenues and expenses is labeled as *Net Profit or Loss Before Taxes* or *Earnings Before Income Taxes*. Then, federal and state income taxes are deducted. The tax expense is usually segregated into two categories:

- Taxes due based upon the income tax return
- Deferred taxes, which represent the difference between the taxes calculated from the income statement and the taxes calculated on the company's income tax return. It is common to list taxes separately and report the company's income both before and after taxes.

After adding any capital contributions such as the sale of stock or deducting distributions such as dividends or the corporation's purchase of its own stock (*treasury stock*), the company's net income will be added, or its net loss subtracted, from retained earnings from the beginning of the period. The retained earnings are discussed in the section on the balance sheet.

For a partnership or proprietorship, the net income is added to beginning capital. Deductions are made for any distributions to the partners or proprietor in a manner similar to a deduction made for dividends paid to shareholders in a corporation.

Balance sheet   The balance sheet lists the company's assets, liabilities and equity on a given date. The balance sheet provides a snapshot of the financial position at a given point in time. It is helpful to look at a balance sheet for both the beginning and end of the reported period. In contrast, the income statement reports the results of the company's operations over a period of time. The income statement provides the revenues and the expenses and the difference—which is the profit or loss—of the company.

Figure 8-2 shows the relationship of the balance sheet and the income statement.

The balance sheet reflects the basic accounting equation of assets less liabilities equals equity.

$$\begin{array}{r} \text{Assets} \\ \underline{-\text{ Liabilities}} \\ =\text{Equity} \end{array}$$

The balance sheet can also be explained as a T account where the left side is equal to the right side (see FIG. 8-3).

The three major categories of the balance sheet (see FIG. 8-4) are:

Assets   *Assets* are economic resources that are owned by the company. They are expected to provide a future benefit to operations. Some examples of assets that are frequently on the balance sheet are cash, investments,

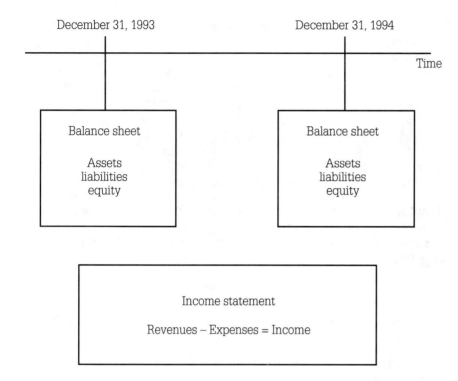

8-2
The relationship of the balance sheet and the income statement.

accounts receivable, land, buildings and equipment. There are other assets, such as rights, claims, options and, in some cases, goodwill, that are not always listed on the balance sheet.

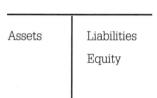

8-3 *The balance sheet as a T account.*

Liabilities   *Liabilities* are obligations that are owed by the company to others. Liabilities are typically incurred to operate the business. Some examples of liabilities include accounts payable, notes payable, mortgages payable, and taxes payable. Accounts payable are the unsecured amounts the business owes to its suppliers and vendors for goods and services. If a liability has a legal note, bond, or mortgage, it is referred to as a note payable, bond payable, or mortgage payable.

Equity   A business *equity* is the net resources invested by the owner. The equity is also equal to the assets minus the liabilities. Equity is what is left over after the assets of the business are used to satisfy all of its obligations or liabilities.

On the balance sheet, the assets are generally listed in order of their liquidity. *Liquidity* is the ease to convert an asset to cash. Therefore, cash is listed first. The first group of assets is usually the current assets. They generally include the following:

Assets

Cash   Cash includes the company's balances in checking, savings, and money market accounts.

Marketable securities   These items include any temporary investments that can be easily and quickly converted to cash. Marketable securities are usually publicly traded securities.

Accounts receivable   This asset represents the monies owed to the company by its customers. The total or gross accounts receivable are reduced by an amount representing the estimated amounts that will not be collected. This is referred to as an allowance for doubtful accounts. It is calculated based on the past collection performance of the company and its customers. If the accounts receivable are reduced by an allowance for doubtful accounts it is referred to as *Accounts Receivable, Net.*

Inventory   *Inventory* is the goods owned by the company that are being held for resale in the normal course of business. The inventories can be valued based upon a variety of methods, or accounting assumptions including first-in, first-out (FIFO); last-in, first-out (LIFO); weighted average; and specific identification.

8-4 Sample balance sheet

Sample computer company balance sheet as of December 31

	1993	1994
ASSETS		
Current assets		
Cash	460,000	300,000
Marketable securities	600,000	580,000
Accounts receivable	1,500,000	1,250,000
Inventories	595,000	675,000
Total current assets	3,155,000	2,805,000
Other assets		
Loans receivable—shareholder	100,000	125,000
Notes receivable	325,000	300,000
Prepayments and deferred charges	100,000	90,000
Total other assets	525,000	515,000
Fixed assets		
Land	450,000	450,000
Building	3,800,000	3,600,000
Machinery	950,000	850,000
Office equipment	100,000	95,000
Total fixed assets	5,300,000	4,995,000
Less: Accumulated depreciation	−1,800,000	−1,500,000
Net fixed assets	3,500,000	3,495,000
TOTAL ASSETS	7.180.000	6.815.000

LIABILITIES

Current liabilities

Accounts payable	435,000	345,000
Notes payable (current portion)	850,000	1,025,000
Accrued expenses payable	450,000	435,000
Federal income taxes payable	510,000	485,000
Total current liabilities	2,245,000	2,290,000

Long term liabilities

Notes payable (net of current portion)	3,200,000	3,000,000
Total long-term liabilities	3,200,000	3,000,000
TOTAL LIABILITIES	5,445,000	5,290,000

STOCKHOLDERS' EQUITY

Capital stock

Preferred stock	800,000	800,000
Common stock	210,000	200,000
Retained earnings	725,000	525,000
TOTAL STOCKHOLDERS' EQUITY	1,735,000	1,525,000
TOTAL LIABILITIES AND STOCKHOLDERS' EQUITY	7,180,000	6,815,000

For purposes of illustrating the different methods of valuing inventories assume that the company made the purchases seen in FIG. 8-5.

With the first-in, first-out (FIFO) method, it is assumed that the first goods acquired were the first to be sold. The balance remain in inventory. In this example, the cost of the 60 units sold is $57.00. The ending inventory is $44.00.

The cost of goods sold is computed as follows:

30 at $1.00 per unit from the 1st purchase = $30.00
30 at $0.90 per unit from the 2nd purchase = 27.00

Total $57.00

The ending inventory (see FIG. 8-6) is computed as follows:

10 at $0.90 per unit from the 2nd purchase = $ 9.00
10 at $1.10 per unit from the 3rd purchase = 11.00
20 at $1.20 per unit from the 4th purchase = 24.00

Total $44.00

8-5 Purchases made by a company

Date	Number of units	Unit price	Total price
January	30	$1.00	$ 30.00
April	40	$0.90	$ 36.00
September	10	$1.10	$ 11.00
December	20	$1.20	$ 24.00
Total	100		$101.00

It will also be assumed that of the 100 units purchased, 60 were sold and 40 remained at the end of the year.

With the last-in, first-out (LIFO) method, it is assumed the last goods acquired were the first to be sold. Conversely, the older goods acquired remain in inventory. Based on the preceding example, the cost of the 60 units sold is $62.00. The value of the ending inventory is $39.00.

8-6 Computation of ending inventory (FIFO method)

Date	Number	$/unit	Total
January	30	$1.00	$ 30.00
April	40	$0.90	$ 36.00
September	10	$1.10	$ 11.00
December	20	$1.20	$ 24.00
Total	100		$101.00
Items sold	60		
Items remaining	40		

The cost of goods sold is computed as follows:

20 at $1.20 per unit from the 4th purchase = $24.00
10 at $1.10 per unit from the 3rd purchase = 11.00
30 at $0.90 per unit from the 2nd purchase = 27.00

Total $62.00

The ending inventory (see FIG. 8-7) is computed as follows:

30 at $1.00 per unit from the 1st purchase = $30.00
10 at $0.90 per unit from the 2nd purchase =   9.00

Total $39.00

LIFO increases the cost of goods sold. It reduces the company's income during times of rising prices. The lower income decreases the tax liability in the current period. During inflationary periods, this method causes the value of ending inventory, as listed on the balance sheet, to be below the replacement value. As a result, it is prudent to determine the method used to value the inventory. There could be a significant difference between the replacement value and the reported amount.

8-7 Computation of ending inventory (LIFO method)

Date	Number	$/unit	Total
January	30	$ 1.00	$ 30.00
April	40	$ 0.90	$ 36.00
September	10	$ 1.10	$ 11.00
December	20	$ 1.20	$ 24.00
Total	100		$101.00
Items sold	60		
Items remaining	40		

With the *weighted average* method, the price for each individual unit is calculated based on the average cost of the total units purchased. This is determined by dividing the total purchase price of all units purchased by the number of units purchased. The average cost per unit is then multiplied by the number of units sold to determine the cost of goods sold. It is multiplied by the number of units remaining to calculate ending inventory.

In the preceding example, the cost per unit is $1.01 ($101.00/100). Thus the cost of goods sold equals $60.60 ($1.01 × 60). The ending inventory equals $40.40 ($1.01 × 40).

Figure 8-8 illustrates the different cost of goods sold and ending inventory values that were calculated utilizing the previous example under the FIFO, LIFO, and weighted average methods of valuing inventory.

8-8 Comparison of FIFO, LIFO, and weighted average methods

Inventory method	Cost of goods sold	Ending inventory
FIFO	$57.00	$44.00
LIFO	62.00	39.00
Weighted average	60.60	40.40

As the figure shows, the choice of an inventory method can affect both the company's income, through the cost of goods sold, and the company's total assets, via the ending inventory.

With the *specific identification* method, the business specifically identifies the cost of the items sold. The specific items on hand are included in the company's inventory. This method can be used only where it is practical to identify each item that is sold or is on hand at a point in time. Businesses that sell a relatively small number of high priced and easily identifiable goods can use this method.

Other current assets   Some examples of other current assets include prepayments. They are future subscriptions, memberships, or rents that have been paid for use in the future.

The balance sheet generally includes a category for fixed assets, which frequently includes building, land, and equipment.

Building, land, & equipment   These items are listed on the balance sheet at their original cost. Even if land and buildings that were previously purchased are worth many times their original purchase price, they are listed at their original cost. The only departure occurs when the value of the asset has decreased. In that case, the asset is listed at the lower of cost or market. During times of rising real estate values, the balance sheet could significantly understate a company's true net worth.

Depreciation   *Depreciation* is the using up of a physical asset over time.

The historical cost of the buildings, equipment, and other fixed assets, except land, are reduced on the balance sheet by the accumulated depreciation. The total accumulated depreciation is generally listed separately from the cost of the assets on the balance sheet. Accumulated depreciation represents the sum total of all prior depreciation on the asset. In sum, depreciation represents the expensing of a company's cost of its fixed assets over the projected life of the item.

There are methods of accounting for depreciation that permit an asset to be depreciated more heavily in the initial years following the purchase. If a company seeks to reduce its income and maximize its tax deductions these methods are frequently advantageous.

Generally the only fixed asset that is not depreciated is land. However, the cost of a natural resource that can include timber, coal or oil is expensed in a manner similar to depreciation. The expensing of natural resources is referred to as amortization. The depreciation deducted each year is listed on the income statement, under the appropriate expense category.

There are four basic depreciation methods that are most frequently used:

- Straight line—nonaccelerated
- Units of production—nonaccelerated
- Sum of the years digits—accelerated
- Declining balance—accelerated

Straight line   This method provides for the depreciation expense to be spread equally over the estimated useful life of the asset. The depreciation expense is equal to the cost of fixed asset less its estimated salvage value (the dollar value of an asset at the end of its depreciated life) divided by the estimated useful life, or

$$\frac{\text{Cost} - \text{Salvage value}}{\text{Useful life}}$$

Units of production   *Units of production* calculates depreciation based upon the usage during each particular period. Under this method, the depreciation cost per unit of production is first calculated. Then it is multiplied by the units produced or used during a particular period. The result equals the expense for that period. This calculation is illustrated as follows:

$$\frac{\text{Cost} - \text{Salvage value}}{\text{Estimated units of production}} \times \frac{\text{Number of units used or}}{\text{produced during particular period}}$$

Sum of the years digits   With the *sum of the years digits* method, a fraction is applied to the cost of the asset less its estimated salvage value. The numerator of this fraction is equal to the number of years of remaining useful life of the asset. The denominator, which remains constant, is the sum of all of the year's digits. So the depreciation under this method can be illustrated as follows:

$$\frac{\text{Total life} - \text{Years in use} \times (\text{Cost} - \text{salvage})}{\text{Sum of the years digits}}$$

For example, if an asset has a five-year life, the sum of years digits equals 15 (5 + 4 + 3 + 2 + 1 = 15). The fraction applied in the first year is $\frac{5}{15}$, in the second $\frac{4}{15}$, in the third $\frac{3}{15}$, in the fourth $\frac{2}{15}$, and in the fifth $\frac{1}{15}$.

A simple way to determine the denominator for a given number of years, where *N* equals the number of years of expected service, is as follows. *SYD* means *sum of the years digits*.

$$\frac{N \times N + 1)}{2} = SYD$$

Declining balance   With the *declining balance method*, a uniform multiple is applied to the fraction computed by the straight-line method. The result is multiplied by the total cost of the asset. The most common multiples are 200%, 175%, or 150% of the straight-line percentage. The double declining balance or 200% declining balance method is illustrated as follows:

$$2.00 \times \text{Straight-line percentage} \times (\text{Cost} - \text{Prior years depreciation})$$

The 150% declining balance method is illustrated as follows:

$$1.50 \times \text{Straight-line percentage} \times (\text{Cost} - \text{Prior years depreciation})$$

Regardless of the depreciation method used, an asset can never be depreciated below its salvage value. If the total depreciation in one year would result in this, the depreciation is reduced to keep the adjusted basis (cost less depreciation) from falling below the salvage value.

Intangible assets   *Intangible assets* will only be listed on the balance sheet if they have been acquired in a transaction. They are recorded in the company's books at cost. Some examples of these assets include goodwill, trademarks, or copyrights. For example, if the company buys another business, a portion of the purchase price might be allocated to goodwill. This amount is listed in the *Intangible Assets* section of the balance sheet.

Deferred charges & prepaid assets   *Deferred charges and prepaid assets* include amounts that were paid for services to be rendered beyond the one-year accounting period. Unlike current assets, these assets are for items purchased beyond a one year horizon.

Other assets   This broad category can include a wide variety of assets such as investments that are not expected to be converted into cash within the current accounting cycle of one year or less.

Liabilities

The next major section of the balance sheet consists of liabilities. They are divided into the following major categories:

Current liabilities   *Current liabilities* are amounts owed that arise in the ordinary course of the company's business. They include amounts owed for the purchase of materials, goods and services. Other current liabilities include payables such as wages and salaries due to employees (wages and salaries payable), tax liabilities (taxes payable), and liabilities for dividends declared and scheduled to be paid in the current year (dividends payable). Each of these items is generally listed separately in the current liability section of the balance sheet.

Long-term liabilities   *Long-term liabilities* are debts that mature more than one year after the date of the balance sheet. The current portion of long-term debt is due within one year and should be deducted from the amount listed in the long-term liability section of the balance sheet. It should be listed separately in the current liabilities section. Long-term debt can include notes payable, mortgages payable, bonds payable, and loans due stockholders or officers.

Contingent liabilities   *Contingent liabilities* do not have a set value yet. They might develop as obligations of the business. Contingent liabilities can include:

- Obligations where the amount owed has not yet been determined. One example is income tax assessments resulting from pending audits.
- Amounts owed arising from damages from pending law suits for personal injury or product liability.
- Reserves recognized that originate from a guarantee or warranty of the company.
- Liabilities that will only become debts of the company if the primary debtor fails to pay the obligation.

Frequently, if the amount of a contingent liability involves a considerable degree of uncertainty, the classification is listed in the balance sheet without an amount. A note to the financial statement explains the item in further detail.

Deferred income taxes   *Deferred income taxes* represent the difference between the actual income tax liability based on the tax return and the liability based on the company's income from its financial statement. For example, variations on the tax return and financial statement can be caused if different depreciation methods are utilized on the tax return and financial statement. This can give rise to deferred income taxes.

Equity

A business *equity* can also be referred to as its *surplus*, or in some cases *capital*. Equity is the difference between the assets of a company and its liabilities. The accounting terms used in this section differ based upon the legal form of the company—corporation, partnership or proprietorship.

Corporation   The equity section of a corporation's balance sheet is generally divided into the following categories:

Common stock   If the stock has a par value (set value at issue) the amount listed next to the heading reflects the number of shares multiplied by the par value of the stock. If the common stock has no par value, the amount listed next to the description represents the price for which the company sold stock.

Paid in capital   *Paid in capital* only exists if there is a par value. It represents the difference between the total price at which the corporation sold the stock and the total of the par value.

Other classes of common or preferred stock   The amount of shares authorized, issued, and outstanding is also provided. In addition, if the shares have special rights such as conversion privileges or cumulative dividends it is generally noted in this section of the balance sheet.

Retained earnings   *Retained earnings* is the residual amount on the company's balance sheet. The retained earnings also equal the sum of the company's prior earnings, less the sum of all of its prior losses and dividends.

Treasury stock   *Treasury stock* is stock that the corporation issued but repurchased. The shares that are repurchased are a deduction from the capital or equity account. They are generally listed, depending on the circumstances, at either purchase cost or the par value.

Partnership   The equity section of a partnership financial statement merely contains the total partners' capital. The partnership's capital account is equal to the following:

> Capital account beginning of the year
> \+ Partnership income during the year
> \+ Capital contributions made during the year
> − Capital withdrawals made during the year
> = Capital account end of the year

Capital contributions represent additional funds or assets contributed to the partnership by the partners. Capital withdrawals or drawings represent funds or assets paid to the individual partners during the year. In many cases, a partnership does not pay its partners a salary. Their drawings represent their sole distributions from the company. A salary is a deductible expense of the partnership, a withdrawal is not an expense. A partner can receive both a salary and drawings from the partnership.

In some cases, the balance sheet or a supplemental schedule to the balance sheet contains a breakdown of each individual partners' capital account including the beginning balances, additions, distributions, share of income and ending balances for the individual partners.

Proprietorship   The equity section of a proprietorship's balance sheet is the same as a partnership except that the capital is referred to as *proprietor's capital* and *proprietor's drawings*.

Cash flow statement

The *cash flow statement* reports the changes in the financial position of a business by presenting the sources and application of cash during the period. The cash flow statement classifies cash receipts and cash payments into three categories: operations, investing, and financing activities.

This statement explains the change during the period of cash and cash equivalents.

Cash equivalents include money market funds, commercial paper, short-term United States Treasury obligations as well as cash in the bank.

Operating activities generally involve the production and delivery of goods and services.

Cash inflows from operating activities include cash received from:

- The sale of goods and services as well as from the collection of customer notes that arose from sales
- Interest and dividends received from other companies' debt and equity instruments
- Other transactions that are not included in investing or financing activities

Some examples of other transactions are proceeds from a lawsuit and insurance settlements that do not relate to financing or investing activities.

Cash outflows from operations include cash paid to:

- Acquire goods for manufacture or resale as well as payments to suppliers and employees for goods and services
- Governments for taxes, duties, fines and fees
- Lenders and creditors for interest
- Other transactions that are not investing or financing activities such as lawsuits, refunds to customers and charitable contributions

Investing activities involve the making and collection of loans. They include the acquisition and disposition of debt, equity and assets held for or used in the production of the company's goods and services.

Cash inflows from investing activities include cash received from the:

- Collection or the sale of loans made by the business or of debt instruments of other businesses
- Sales of other enterprises' equity instruments
- Returns of investments in other enterprises' equity investments
- Sales of the company's fixed or productive assets such as equipment and facilities

Cash outflows from investing activities include cash paid to:

- Acquire loans made by the business or to acquire existing debt instruments
- Acquire other enterprises' equity instruments
- Purchase fixed or productive assets

Financing activities involve the activities by the business to raise or repay its own debt or equity capital.

Cash inflows from financing activities include cash received from:

- Issuing stock
- Issuing bonds, mortgages, notes, and other loans

Cash outflows from financing activities include cash expended to pay:

- Dividends or distributions to owners
- Repurchase of the business' stock
- Principal payments on loans or other borrowings

Figure 8-9 shows a sample cash flow statement.

Analysis of financial statement ratios

When you review a financial statement, certain information has varying importance, depending on your purpose for reviewing it. For example, a purchaser might be more interested in the growth in the company's sales and income. A lender might be more interested in the ability of the company to repay, in the short term, its loan obligations.

There are a variety of ratios and comparisons that are used to review a company's financial statements. Generally the ratios are grouped into four categories:

- Liquidity ratios
- Leverage ratios
- Activity ratios
- Profitability ratios

Liquidity ratios

Liquidity ratios measure the company's ability to meet its current obligations.

Working capital is the excess of current assets over current liabilities. It is a measure of the company's ability to meet its current obligations.

Working capital = Current assets − Current liabilities

In addition to determining the amount of working capital, use the *current ratio* to analyze the relationship of the current assets to current liabilities as follows:

$$\frac{\text{Current assets}}{\text{Current liabilities}}$$

The *quick ratio*, also referred to as the *acid test*, compares the total current assets that are easily and quickly converted into cash with the current liabilities. The quick ratio represents the current assets less inventory divided by current liabilities.

$$\frac{\text{Current assets} - \text{Inventory}}{\text{Current liabilities}}$$

Leverage ratios

The *leverage ratios* determine the portion of the company's capital that has been contributed by its owners versus the funds provided through debt, by creditors. Creditors are concerned with the amount of funds owners have invested in the business as opposed to how much they've raised by borrowings. If the owners have invested only a small portion of the business' capital, their risk is minimal as compared to the creditors' risk.

8-9   Sample statement of cash flows

Sample computer company
statement of cash flows
for the year ending December 31, 1993

OPERATING ACTIVITIES

Net income	410,000	
Adjustments to reconcile net income		
to net cash provided by operations		
depreciation	300,000	
Changes in assets and liabilities		
Accounts receivable	−250,000	
Accounts payable	90,000	
Purchase of marketable securities	−20,000	
Inventory	−80,000	
Increase taxes payable	25,000	
Accrued expenses	15,000	
NET CASH FROM OPERATING ACTIVITIES		490,000
INVESTING ACTIVITIES		
Purchases of property and equipment	−305,000	
NET CASH FROM INVESTING ACTIVITIES		−305,000
FINANCING ACTIVITIES		
Increase in borrowings	200,000	
Payments of debt	−175,000	
Proceeds from issuance of stock	10,000	
Repayment of shareholder loan	25,000	
Dividends paid	−60,000	
Increase in note receivable	−25,000	
NET CASH FROM FINANCING ACTIVITIES		−25,000
NET INCREASE (DECREASE) IN CASH		160,000
Cash at beginning of year		300,000
CASH AT END OF YEAR		460,000

The *debt-to-asset ratio* (also called the *debt ratio*) compares how much of the total business funds were provided by creditors. Owners prefer a high ratio because raising money through the sale of equity might cause a relinquishment of some control. A high debt ratio can serve to propel earnings during boom periods and can cause severe cash flow problems during periods of business down turns. This ratio equals:

$$\frac{\text{Total debt}}{\text{Total assets}}$$

The *debt-to-equity* ratio is similar to the debt ratio as it compares the company's liabilities to its equity.

$$\frac{\text{Total debt}}{\text{Equity}}$$

Another ratio is the *times-interest earned ratio*. It calculates the percentage of the company's income that is applied towards interest repayments.

$$\frac{\text{Earning before deducting tax and debt interest}}{\text{Debt interest}}$$

This ratio shows the percentage of the company's income needed to meet the interest obligations of its debt.

A similar ratio is the *interest-to-sales ratio*. It shows the percentage of the company's sales that are applied towards the payment of interest.

$$\frac{\text{Interest}}{\text{Sales}}$$

Creditors are extremely concerned with the two previous ratios because they show how much of the company's income or sales are needed to pay interest charges.

Activity ratios   The *activity ratios* illustrate the results of the corporation's operations and the utilization of its resources.

The *inventory turnover ratio* shows how frequently on average the company sells its inventory. This ratio is illustrated as follows:

$$\frac{\text{Cost of sales}}{\text{Average inventory}}$$

This ratio can help determine whether the company generally has an inventory that is either too large or too small. If the inventory is too large, additional costs such as warehousing, insurance and the lost interest revenue on the funds used to purchase the inventory will be incurred. In the opposite scenario—the inventory is too small—the business will constantly have to incur the costs of reordering. Moreover, sales will be lost because stock outages will cause customers to make purchases elsewhere instead of waiting for the goods to be shipped.

Profitability ratios   The *profitability ratios* show how profitable the company is in its operations.

The *return-on-equity* ratio compares the company's net profits with its equity, or capital.

$$\frac{\text{Net profits after taxes}}{\text{Equity}}$$

This ratio shows the yield that the company's investors are receiving on their investment.

The next ratio is referred to as the *return-on-sales ratio*. It compares the company's net operating income with its sales. Simply stated, this ratio shows the percentage of each sales dollar that the company receives becomes profit.

$$\frac{\text{Net profit after taxes}}{\text{Sales}}$$

9 How much money do you need?

This chapter deals with what is commonly referred to as the uses of capital. You want to figure out what is absolutely needed in the business and what is not. Run it mean and lean, but don't skimp on those expenses that are necessary. This chapter does not cover all the items that you can buy of those things you actually need to run your business.

How much money you need in your business is completely related to your goals and objectives. Typically, when you put together a business plan, you can identify various sources and uses of capital. How you use this money can reflect a whole corporate culture.

Needs   "On what do you need to spend money?" The key word in this question is the word *need*. Needs are both perceived and real. Sometimes there is a blurring of the lines. Perceived needs are those needs that you perceive yourself to have. They are not needs that are critical to survival. Real needs are those that relate to survival.

The best illustration of this point is found in a company called IRIS, a company that is no longer. I visited IRIS as they liquidated the assets of the company. I thought I might get a good buy on some of them. IRIS was initially capitalized with $13 million as a company that would provide global information on line. Initially, the target market was the insurance industry to allow insurers to better assess risks in underwriting. IRIS hired reporters to compile the information that was to be on line. These reporters hired from such papers as *Le Monde* (in Paris), *The Times* (in London), *The New York Times*, and *The Washington Post*. IRIS assembled a board of directors that had international acclaim.

Some thought the company's goal was to build this large, globally oriented database. (In fact, that is how the reward structure was established. If the database was built, senior managers would get additional bonuses.) Some thought the company's goal was to sell information and build a worldwide corporation that was financially sound. Others, myself included, thought much differently. After seeing what was left of the company in those final days, I thought that the goal of the company was to create the image, through its corporate culture, of one of the most successful corporations in the world.

This start-up company had its own kitchen. No big deal, you say? Well, what would you say if I told you that this kitchen was better equipped than most gourmet restaurants? And, I almost forgot, there was a staff chef on payroll to prepare the food for the day. I mustn't forget about the wine cellar that was a part of the kitchen and of course stocked with only the best of California and French wines. While I'm at it, would you like to hear about the bathrooms? They were built with a black onyx shower and one of those quiet-flush toilets that costs a fortune. Finally, all (and I mean all) the furniture was the most expensive on the market. Their office space was in one of the more expensive buildings in Crystal City, Virginia, right near Washington National airport, to facilitate all of the people that called on them.

Were these expenditures a good use of funds? They argued that they were because they impressed the right people to invest further in the organization. But where is that organization today? In fact, the organization burned through this $13 million in a little more than a year. Was that a good use of funds? Did it impress the right people? Evidently not.

As I walked the halls of the company, I asked about their customers. Who were they? The response that I received was that there were none. And there never had been any. I asked what their marketing plan targeted. I asked for an explanation of their selling strategy. I was told that none of these dimensions had been considered, yet. When were they going to consider these dimensions?

Understanding real needs

The underlying lesson in the example in the previous section, and the underlying lesson in this chapter is simple—understand your true and sensible priorities in order to run your business and achieve your goals and objectives. You need to assess what absolutely, positively needs to be spent and what doesn't. It is interesting how a person can become blinded by what is truly needed and what is perceived as being needed. Did IRIS need a gourmet chef? They perceived that they did. I doubt that they did need one, at least not at start up.

The best start up won't even have an office. Did you know that Nike started in a laundry room? Did you know that Apple Computer started in a garage? Initially, unless your business requires you to greet customers, try to use improvised office space. Can you operate your business out of a spare bedroom in your house? When you grow to the point where you don't have any more space at home, your spouse is threatening to leave you because you run a business in your house, or you have enough surplus cash flow on a consistent basis (more than four or five months), you will then want to consider office space.

Be careful when you decide what type of office space you actually need. Consider the location of the office. Is it near transportation arteries? Do you need to be near transportation arteries? Are there enough people in the locale of the office to be able to hire them as your company grows? You might find a wonderful office space near transportation arteries but with no one who has the skills you need to run your business. If you need programmers and there are none in the area, can you import them?

There are businesses that do import people from other areas. This comes with a cost—commuting cost (for the employee), potential constant threat of loss (if the employee decides not to move), and a real cost of moving the employee (if he or she decides to move nearer to the company.)

Be sure that you have a good read on all of the resources near your potential office location, including banks, post offices, the delivery services that serve the area (do UPS and Federal Express deliver to this area and how often?), restaurants (you and your employees have to eat), and office supply stores.

Factor the image of the office into your decision-making process. What type of an image do you want to convey—that of an old barn or a shiny new office building? Do you want to have your own building (even if it does have a relatively small area) or are you satisfied being a part of a larger space? How will your clients perceive you in this space? You mustn't only consider how you feel about this image today but how you might feel as you grow.

Allow for growth　Another very important factor to consider is growth. Can you get more space in this rental area if you should need it? What is the cost of moving? Will you have to pay some additional money to get out of one space and into another? If you are located in the same building (or even the same building complex), the landlord or owner will probably be more than happy to let you have additional space. Be sure that you negotiate this option early, even if you don't think you'll need it.

Probably the biggest issue you will confront is the rental expense that you will face. How much is it? Rent is generally calculated in larger office spaces by square-feet. For example, the rent might be quoted at $15 per square foot. This quote means that you will pay $15 per square foot per year. Divide by 12 for the monthly rate. Is the number a gross or a net number? A *gross rent* means that it includes everything—utilities, insurance, and taxes. If you find a lease that is called a *net lease*, it excludes utilities. If the lease is a *net-net lease*, it excludes utilities and insurance. If it is a *net-net-net lease*, it excludes utilities, insurance, and taxes. Don't be deceived. Rental agents might tell you that your rent is $10 per square foot. You might think that you have a good deal. If this $10 is on a net-net-net lease and the utilities average $3, the insurance averages $1, and taxes are $4, you have a lease that is equivalent to a grossed up lease of $18 per square foot.

Rental agents play other games, too. They might give you rental rebates in the form of "no rent for a certain period of time." Here again, don't be deceived. These rental agents must make up the rent somehow. It will be in the future rents that they charge you. For example, a rental agent might give you six months free rent if you sign a three-year lease or a year's free rent if you sign a five-year lease. In months 6 through 36 of the three-year lease, you must pay $20 per square foot. In months 13 through 60 of the five-year lease, $22 per square foot. Had you gotten no free rent in either case, you would have paid $15 per square foot throughout the term of both leases. Although constant rent throughout a term is not realistic (rent escalates annually, increasing with the consumer price index), the point is illustrative. As they say, you can pay me now or you pay me later. The free rent might be extremely attractive to you from a cash flow perspective. And that is exactly why it was developed as a technique. Remember, though, that you will eventually have to pay for this initial benefit. Free rent can be a vehicle to finance your business. In fact, in tough times, landlords will often agree to finance moving expenses to be able to rent their space.

Paying for leasehold improvements (improvements to the office space) is another way that rental agents will try and attract potential tenants. Remember, again, the adage that you can pay me now or pay me later. This expense will be absorbed as a part of the rent.

Allow for flexibility

When you decide on your office space, you must decide how much flexibility you want to build into your lease. My business has had three-year, one-year, monthly, and three-month leases, all based on different times and needs of the business. The term of the lease will affect the flexibility that you have in expanding and moving your business. Remember that fact before you rush to sign a five-year lease with the low rent.

Coupled with office space decisions are asset-acquisition decisions. Now that you have an office space, you need furniture. You need telephones. You need more computers. How do you get them? And what type do you acquire? Perceived need might come into this decision-making process. Don't replicate the IRIS scenario, but buy what is actually necessary and loan furniture to your company if possible. I have a friend who loaned her dining room table to her company so she wouldn't have to buy a conference room table. I've loaned furniture to my company as well.

Image will enter into this equation; it can't help doing so. Remember that cash is key. Don't spend the money if you don't need to spend it. Borrow furniture first. Rent or lease it second. And, if there are no other alternatives, buy it. Rent, lease, or buy what you believe to be the bare minimum on which you can get by. Go to second-hand stores and furniture auctions.

Borrow, rent, lease; then buy

With all assets you need for the business, it is wise to follow the borrow, rent, lease, buy sequences. Borrow the capability if you can. If you can't borrow it, rent it on a short-term basis (which can be extended if necessary). If you can't rent the asset, only then sign a longer-term lease on it. Finally, if there is no other way, buy it. This four-step sequence first saves cash. If you are successful at borrowing, you've got something that has no cash outlay. You also reduce your obligations to the assets through this procedure, which increases your flexibility (especially important if you don't know what the future will bring). When you borrow, if you don't need (or like) the underlying asset, you can return it with no obligation. At the other end of the spectrum, getting out of a purchase is more difficult. This cash outlay-obligation relationship is shown in FIG. 9-1.

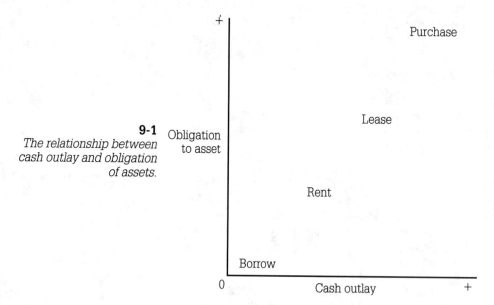

9-1
The relationship between cash outlay and obligation of assets.

This relationship can be expanded beyond just the assets of a business. It can be extended to the people and technological assets of your company.

If someone will work for free, you are in essence "borrowing them." You have little obligation to this person (except for all of the guilt that you've built up).

This person has little obligation to you. If you hire a temporary employee from a temporary agency, you "rent" them., although you have little obligation to this person (you can "return" them to the agency if you don't like them). The temporary employee should (although they might not) have a greater obligation to you than the borrowed employee. If you sign a one-year contract to retain someone to work for you, you "lease" them. They have a longer obligation to you and you to them (one year). If you hire someone, you've "bought" them. Although hardly ever the case anymore in today's transient society, the perception is that you have a long-term obligation to them and they to you.

If you borrow someone's computer program to make one calculation, you are obviously borrowing technology. There is no long-term obligation for either party. If you ask them to use the program for a short term and agree to rent it from them, obligations on both sides increase. A lease—assigning a longer term with more stringent financial terms—lengthens this obligation. A purchase of the computer program (although it is generally a lease) will leave you with the computer program for a long term basis.

Operating in the lower left-hand corner of FIG. 9-1 gives you more flexibility at a lower cost. The upper right-hand corner has the greatest obligation and cost associated with it. You should look at all resource use decisions in your business with this table in mind. It will serve as a methodology to decide how much money is needed for each element of your company and, in turn, your entire computer business.

10 Finding capital for your company

To understand where to get capital, first clarify the type of business that needs the capital and the forms of capital that are available to it. Is the business a corporation, sole proprietorship, or partnership? There are two general sources of capital for financing your business. These sources are debt and equity. In all three types of business structure, debt is called *debt*. Equity is called *equity* in a corporation, *owners equity* in a sole proprietorship, and *partnership capital* in a partnership.

Debt *Debt* is an obligation to repay a sum of money within a time period at a certain interest rate. Debt can be considered a loan. Loans have certain conditions or covenants. These conditions are the terms of the loan. Loan terms include:

- Interest rate. The interest rate is a percentage of the loan that is the fee for the loan. There are different types of interest but they are all based on the amount of money (the *principal*) loaned as well as the term of repayment.
    - *Simple interest*. Simple interest takes the loan amount (the principal) and multiplies it by a certain percentage, annually, to arrive at a simple interest rate over the course of the year. If you take out a loan of $1000 at a simple interest rate of 12%, your annual interest payments would be $120; your monthly interest would be $10.
    - *Compound interest*. Compound interest is calculated on the principal balance plus the interest. In other words, interest becomes principal, and then interest is recalculated on this amount.

~ *Term.* The term is the duration of the loan. Loan terms can be almost any length of time. Commonly they coincide with the life of the item for which the money is used. If you buy a computer whose useful life is five years, you might decide to take a loan on the computer with a term of five years. After all, it makes no sense to set up a loan for seven years when the computer will only last for five.

- Repayment terms. Repayment terms for a loan could fill a book. Some of the more important ones include interest-only loans and interest-plus-principal loans. *Interest-only* loans require you to pay the interest on a loan until the principal comes due. At the time the principal comes due, you pay it off in a *balloon payment*—one large payment. More commonly, you see a loan payment that involves repayment of interest plus principal concurrently.

- *Secured* versus *unsecured* loans. Whenever a loan is made, the lending source wants to be certain that it will be repaid. To determine whether or not to make a loan, often the lender will complete a credit assessment of the potential borrower. If the lender believes that the credit of the potential borrower is strong and that it will absolutely get repaid, it will not ask for any collateral to secure the repayment of the loan.

- *Collateral. Collateral* is an asset that can be translated into cash to repay a loan. Collateral is what is required in a secured loan. Collateral does not necessarily have to be 100% of the loan value. Collateral is often some type of security that the loan will be repaid. The security can come in the form of a personal signature or guarantee, if an individual's credit is good enough, or a deposit of funds or a real estate equity with the lender.

When you start your computer-based business, it will have no operating history. Therefore, it will not have credit needed to get a loan on its own unless you received a cash injection (capitalization), and these funds are the basis for security of a loan. As a consequence, debt sources that are available for your business are really only those available to you. You might borrow money yourself and then lend it to the business.

What debt sources can you use in your computer-based business in order to fund it?

Debt sources

Credit cards   How many credit card solicitations do you get weekly? If you have good credit, you might get one a week. You might find these solicitations to be an annoyance. Many people don't want to have an excessive number of credit cards or credit card debt. Yet if you start a computer-based business and you wonder where you might get money to pay for the things that you need, credit cards might be the solution.

When you evaluate credit cards as a source of debt financing, you should be concerned with the cost of money to you.

Prevailing interest rate   The prevailing interest rate is the rate of interest that you will be charged on the use of funds if you don't pay them back within a specified time period (generally one month). Because different financial institutions issue credit cards, they have the prerogative, within certain statutory limits, to charge whatever rate of interest they choose. Each state in the United States sets a limit on what interest may be charged on credit cards. These limits are called *statutory limits* and are ultimately the ceiling on the interest rate that the issuing financial institution can charge. Two states in the United States were quick to attract major credit card issuers to their states by offering them higher statutory ceilings on interest rates than other states. These states were South Dakota and Delaware. As a consequence, you might get a disproportionate share of credit card solicitations from these states. When you get the solicitation, check the interest rates they offer. Although the financial institution is excited to offer you a higher interest rate, over time you will not be so excited—the cost of financing will mount.

Credit limits   Beware of credit limits. Financial institutions will try to lure you into their fold by offering you a credit limit that is an attractive amount of money. Their intent is to have you accept their offer that gives you a $10,000 credit limit. Higher credit limits are often offered along with a higher prevailing interest rate.

Purchase prevailing rates of interest   Prevailing rates of interest are charged on purchases that you make with your credit card that you don't repay immediately. In the fine print of the credit card solicitation you've gotten, you will see the prevailing rate of interest that might be anywhere from 10 to 20%.

Cash-advance prevailing rates of interest   Cash advances are advances of cash that you can receive against your credit card credit limit. The cash-advance credit limit is only a portion of the entire credit limit. This credit limit has its own prevailing rate of interest that is always higher than that of the purchases' prevailing rate of interest.

Annual membership fees   A lot of financial institutions that offer credit cards try to convince you that their card is a good deal because they don't have an annual membership fee. Often, they might waive the annual membership fee for the first year you use the credit card. These low membership fees (or no membership fees) might be a way to get you to use a credit card. Low or no annual membership fees might also be in return for a higher prevailing rate of interest.

The lesson is twofold. First, credit cards might be an ideal way for you to finance your computer-based business. If you have a credit line available for both purchases and cash advances, you might be able to finance your entire business with credit cards. If you have a $10,000 line of credit—with a maximum cash advance limit of $2500, you could use $2000 to purchase a computer system that would leave you with $8000 left to run your business. For your absolute cash needs (to pay your telephone and electric bill), use the cash-advance portion. Use the remaining $5500 to make credit purchases (for example, if you can pay cash at the office supply store or pay with a credit card purchase, use the credit card). You can even use your cash-advance amount to pay the minimum amount payment when your bill comes due. You can use one credit card cash-advance to pay the minimum balance on another. Although this strategy is extremely attractive, it is one that can catch up to you. Be careful that you either have a way to repay the credit cards separate from your actual or potential business, or be sure that you see cash flowing from your business to pay down the balance on the credit cards.

If you do not have a method of repayment of the credit cards, you can easily get into a credit crunch where you build up more debt and dig yourself deeper into a hole. In order to avoid this situation, first set a limit on the amount of credit card debt that you feel makes sense for you to carry (and somehow repay).

Don't fall into the gambling trap of "just another dollar," where, if you invest another dollar, it is the one that will finally give you the positive return. Follow a business plan that you have hopefully developed using the methods set forth in this book. If you don't meet the projections in your financial statements, figure out why and limit what you will invest. Given your plan is sensible, you won't be way off base with the projections and you won't find yourself in a credit crunch. If you are wrong, recalculate and either set forth a new plan or cut the cord on the venture. These comments actually speak to any type of debt or equity investment but can be particularly relevant when you dig yourself into a hole with credit card debt.

Second, when you choose a financial institution's credit card, do so proactively, not reactively. Isn't it easier to answer a solicitation that comes in the mail than to go out and research where you can get the best prevailing rate of interest coupled with the highest line of credit? You bet it is. Research credit card offerings through consumer groups, local, regional, and national banks. Apply for those that you feel are the best bets (using the information contained in this section) and then make your own decision as to which cards you will or will not want. Return those credit cards that might be issued to you but you don't want. Include a letter stating that you are canceling the credit card. Keep a copy of the letter and send the letter to the issuing financial institution via certified mail, return receipt, so that you are sure it reaches them. Be proactive and make your own choices. Don't have the financial institutions choose for you. Their interests are the complete reverse of yours—they want to make as much money from you as possible. You want to spend as little money as possible.

Second mortgages   Second mortgages are also known as home-equity loans. If you own a house you have probably built up some equity in it (the asset base that you have in your home). You probably have a mortgage on your home. Depending upon when you purchased your home, how much money you gave as a down payment, and the rate at which the value of your home has increased, you have a certain amount of equity in your home. As an example, if you purchased your home one month ago for $100,000 and gave a down payment of $25,000 on your house, you have built up little equity beyond the $25,000 down payment. Your house has had no time to appreciate in value, nor have you had any time to pay down the amount that you owe on your mortgage. If you purchased your home ten years ago for $50,000 and your neighbors just sold their house (which is identical to yours) for $100,000, you have an increase of $50,000 in the equity value of your home. You purchased your home with a down payment of $20,000. You've paid $15,000 into the principal of your 30-year mortgage. Therefore, you have $85,000 in equity in your home.

No matter what the equity is in your home, there are institutions that will lend against it. In the first example, the equity was $25,000. In the second, $85,000. Generally lenders don't like to lend so that the total amount of mortgage on the house (first and second mortgages) is greater than 80% of the total market value of the house. So, in the first example, the second mortgage lender would lend you up to $5000. In the second example, the second mortgage lender would lend you up to $80,000. These are still loans. They are secured by the value of your home. They often require an amount of insurance that is the market value of the home. The house and insurance secure the loan, but you still need a method of repayment of the loan. Again, you hope to find this method of repayment out of the cash flow of the business.

Second mortgages or home-equity loans will often charge you points. *Points* are a way for the lender to make you think you are getting a lower interest rate than you are actually receiving. Points can also be called a *loan origination fee*. The financial institution that issues the home-equity loan receives initial points plus an ongoing interest rate. You must add both costs together to arrive at the total cost of the second mortgage. Choose the bank that will give you the lowest total cost. If you are confused about the cost of the loan, ask an accountant to show you how the costs are broken down.

With a home-equity loan, you borrow money personally and then either invest it in (as equity) or lend it to the business.

Borrow from your life insurance policy   As you pay premiums on any type of life insurance policy (except for a term policy), the cash value of the policy builds in value. This cash value, plus the *accrued* interest (that has built up on the cash value), is rightfully your money. You can lay claim to it before you die by borrowing against the cash value. There is a set interest rate when you borrow off a cash value of an insurance policy. This rate is established as a part of the policy itself. This amount is most always much less than the prevailing rates in the market. As a result, many people borrow off the policy. If there is an outstanding borrowed balance at death, this amount will be subtracted from the amount that is paid to the beneficiary of the policy.

A life insurance loan is quite an interesting vehicle. You pay the life insurance premium on the policy, but you might not be required to repay the amount you have borrowed from the policy. The premiums that you pay into the policy go to rebuild the cash value of the policy. Check the terms of your own policy before you attempt to use this vehicle. When you buy your insurance policy, determine whether the policy builds up its cash value. Some policies do not, and you can't borrow against them.

Borrow from a bank   You can always take out a personal loan from a commercial bank or a savings and loan association. The bank will evaluate you as a credit risk and determine whether or not it will make the loan. If it makes the loan, it will decide if the loan should be secured or unsecured. It will establish any additional terms of the loan.

Borrow from your credit union   If you have access to a credit union, you can borrow from it as you would from a bank. Each credit union has different parameters to make loans so you should check with your own to see what their terms and conditions are. Some credit unions ask you to repay a loan when you leave the company, although this is not generally the case. Some credit unions are more lenient in their terms and conditions than are other lenders. They might issue you a loan at a rate lower than market. They might also be more lenient in their credit checks and required collateral.

Borrow from your brokerage account   You borrow from a brokerage account in the following method. Assume you purchased stock for $2. Today, the market value of the stock is $100. If you were to sell the stock, you'd realize a $98 taxable gain on the stock. If you leave this stock in your brokerage account, it can serve as collateral for a loan. The loan is made on what is called a *margin account*. The loan can be made up to 50% of the market value of the account. So, with stock worth $100, you can borrow up to $50. If the equity in your account falls below 30% of the original market value, you will be asked to either put more money into the account to bring the equity value up to 30% (a *margin call*) or sell some of the equity to bring it to 30%. As an example, if you borrowed $50 on your $100 stock and its value were to drop below $80 ($30 equity), you would be asked to take one of the actions outlined above.

When you borrow this money, you pay an interest rate on it.

If you are fortunate enough to be able to use the reputation of your business, there are a host of ways to obtain loans. Many of the vehicles that are outlined below require an operating history of the firm. If you are creative and intelligent, you might be able to get loans from some of these sources from the start of your business.

Trade credit   Trade credit is extended to you by your present or potential suppliers. You want to buy computer diskettes for your computer diskette copying business. You order them from a diskette supplier. If the supplier lets you pay for them in thirty days, you have credit and a loan for thirty days. If you are good, you can order diskettes from your supplier, receive them, copy them, and send them to your customer cash on delivery (COD). You have use of this loaned money for three weeks before you need to pay for the diskettes. If you invest the money for three weeks, you can even make money.

Because it is common to pay commercial invoices in thirty days, you can use this time as an interest-free loan. If you want to build up a good credit rating, you probably want to pay your bills in 30 days. Yet, many businesses stretch out payments even longer to suppliers, especially if they know that they don't report your payment history to any credit bureaus such as TRW, CBA, or Dun & Bradstreet. If your supplier doesn't report payment history, you might want to stretch out your payment to them for 60, 90, even 120 days. In essence, you have an interest-free loan for this time.

There are drawbacks to this strategy. First, the supplier might not be too happy with you. The supplier might not want to do business with you as a result. Second, some suppliers attempt to collect interest on outstanding balances due to them. This interest is seldom paid. Even if you paid interest to them, you have a built-in loan source via your suppliers and the amount of trade credit they have afforded to you.

Suppliers might issue you lines of credit, which allow you to maintain an outstanding balance of a certain limit. When you reach this limit, they might ask you to pay off the entire balance. If you don't, they might send you merchandise only on a COD basis. There are no rules to this form of credit. What you negotiate is totally up to you.

Commercial banks   Commercial banks offer a variety of loans. Six are discussed here. They all seem to be more relevant to businesses with an operating history. But, you might be able to take advantage of them early on in your business life.

Line of credit   A *line of credit* is a loan amount that is established by a lending institution, usually a bank, from which you can borrow funds. As an example, you might get a line of credit with a bank for $10,000. You borrow $2000 off the line of credit. You only pay interest on the outstanding balance of the line of credit. So in this example, you will only pay interest on the $2000 that is outstanding. The line of credit is the maximum amount that you may borrow.

An interest rate is set on a line of credit. For the time that the loan is outstanding, you are responsible to pay either interest on the outstanding balance or interest and principal. Repayment terms are negotiated with each loan. Often, a lending institution wants to see you cleanse your line of credit to know that you have the ability to repay the loan. They will leave the loan outstanding for a period of 11 months, for example. In the twelfth month, they will want to see it repaid (a zero balance). Be sure that you know all of the terms on a line of credit because a cleansing of the line, such as this one, can catch you by surprise.

Lines of credit can be issued as secured or unsecured lines.

Accounts receivable financing   You need cash. You have $20,000 in accounts receivable that you know will eventually be paid. Yet, now you have no cash. Accounts receivable financing allows you to borrow money based on the outstanding balance of your accounts receivable. The commercial bank will analyze the type of accounts receivable that you have and will then let you know what amount is eligible for accounts receivable financing. Many banks exclude all service-based receivables from accounts receivable financing. The bank's concern is that a service-based receivable is not as secure as a product-based receivable. Companies might dispute the validity of a service-based receivable more than a product-based one. This Neanderthal reasoning hopefully will change. Banks will hopefully realize that service-based businesses are a growing sector of the economy.

Government receivables are tough to include in accounts receivable financing. Many banks are leery of the amount of time it takes to collect from government agencies and with good cause. My company waited for six months for the Internal Revenue Service to pay us! (Yet if you owe the IRS a penny, they are extremely quick to collect it.) The U.S. Army traditionally pays my firm within five to six months. We did get the Securities and Exchange Commission to pay up front, though collection varies from government agency to agency.

There is a prompt payment act that states that all Federal government agencies must pay within 30 days of proper receipt of an invoice. The way all agencies seem to get around this act is by interpretation of the terms *proper* and *receipt*. If an *i* is not dotted, the government agency will argue that the invoice is not properly received. Government agencies also claim that the correct person within the agency has not received it. With payments of this sort, you have to stay on top of things. Track every person through which every dollar must pass. Banks don't want to have to wait decades to receive money on accounts receivable financing. Therefore, they very often choose to exclude Federal government receivables as part of receivables financing.

If you have accounts receivable financing, a bank will set up a lock box (nothing more than a post office box) to which it will ask you to direct all your receivables. When money comes into the box, it is used to offset the amount outstanding on your accounts receivable line of credit.

Banks will loan anywhere from 60 to 80% of your eligible accounts receivable. They keep a close eye on your receivables. They might demand that they see monthly (or even more frequent) statements of outstanding accounts receivable.

Accounts receivable interest rates vary from bank to bank. They might be fixed or they might float with the *prime rate* (the rate at which the Federal Reserve will loan money to the biggest banks in the country).

Unsecured term loans   *Unsecured term loans* have no collateral requirements attached to them. They are set for a specific term with either a fixed or a floating interest rate. You either pay just interest or interest plus principal. Unsecured term loans are given to businesses with an operating history that is strong.

Chattel mortgages and equipment loans   This type of lending is also called *asset-based* lending. It is lending that uses buildings or equipment that the business owns as collateral for a loan. The security (or *chattel*) is insured through a security agreement that is filed with the state in which it was executed under the terms of the Uniform Commercial Code (UCC). The lien will show up as a UCC filing until the loan is completely satisfied. Very often these loans are term loans, whose term is correlated to the life of the underlying asset on which the loan is made. Interest rates and terms are highly variable with each lending institution.

Conditional sales contracts   If you purchase a large asset, often the company that sells it to you lets you buy it with only a down payment. They let you pay off the rest of the purchase over time. Interest might or might not be charged on the outstanding balance. When the balance is completely paid off, the sale will be officially consummated. This strategy has interesting tax consequences for both the buyer and the seller. To learn more about them, contact an accountant.

Plant improvement loans   *Plant improvement loans* are generally linked to a piece of property. They are another form of mortgage on a property. But, they might be tied to a specific use. Plant improvement loans most frequently have a fixed term with fixed or variable interest rates.

Commercial finance companies   Commercial finance companies operate somewhat like commercial banks. They commonly make loans that a bank might not accept. Because these loans might be riskier, they often require hard assets as collateral. Their interest rate is higher than those normally charged by a commercial bank. Commercial finance companies make loans similar to banks (accounts receivable and term loans), but interest rates might be anywhere from 2 to 6% higher.

Factors   *Factors* are companies who purchase accounts receivables from companies. The factor collects the receivable. Receivables are purchased at a discount of anywhere from 5 to 15% off the face value. In essence, if the receivable is worth $100, the factor would purchase it anywhere from $85 to $95. Many factors will give you an additional sum of money based on the time that it takes them to collect the receivable. For example, if it takes them 30 days to collect the receivable, they might give you another 2% of the receivable value. If it takes them between 31 and 60 days to collect the receivable, you might receive only an additional 1%. If it takes them more than 60 days, you might receive nothing more. If the factor is unable to collect the money at all, the factor takes the loss on the receivable. As a consequence, factors often carefully choose the receivables that they will purchase.

Factors frequently refuse to accept government receivables for the same reason that they might not qualify for accounts receivable financing—collection time can take forever.

The interest rate that factors extract might be considered to be usurious. A discount of even 10% appears to be a 10% interest rate. Not so! If it takes the factor three months to collect, it has in essence charged you 10% interest over a three-month term. Annualized, the interest rate would be equivalent to 40%. Factors hope that companies will not look at the situation in this way. Any way you slice it, factors are quite an expensive means of financing.

Leasing companies   *Leasing companies* are companies that finance assets. They purchase an asset that you want to use, hold title to it, and let you use it for a certain period of time (the lease term) in return for your payment of a monthly lease. At the end of the lease term, depending upon the structure of the lease, you can either purchase the asset for some predetermined price or return it to the leasing company.

There are several advantages of leasing to you, the *lessee* (the person or company that leases the asset):

- You don't have to allocate funds for an entire asset purchase at one point in time.
- The entire lease payment is deductible as a business expense (as opposed to a loan where only the interest is deductible, not the repayment of principal).
- If you structure the lease as such, you don't own the underlying asset that you are leasing at the end of the term. You can walk away from the asset and begin another lease.

In the computer industry, where innovation and new models are the norm, a computer that you own today might have almost no value in three years. If you lease the computer, you can just give it back to the leasing company at the end of the term instead of selling it for a value less than what you show it to be worth on your balance sheet.

Chapter 14 also contains a section on leasing companies.

Equity

Equity is ownership a person has in a corporation. There is no obligation to repay the equity investment. It is meant to stay in the company and generate a positive return for the shareholder. You can own a piece of a business and not have equity in it. If you are a sole proprietor (one person owns the business) or in a partnership (two or more people or corporations own the business), you own a piece of the firm instead of equity.

Equity can be structured in one of two general forms—preferred or common stock.

Preferred stock

Preferred stock is a lot like debt. Some people call it near-debt. It generally carries a certain dividend right to it (much like an interest payment) that might be paid annually or not (it might accrue for payment at some time in the future). Preferred stock is generally not voting stock. The shareholders do not have a say in how the company is run.

Common stock

Common stock is stock that doesn't carry a guaranteed dividend. It has voting rights within the corporation. Its holders can have a say in the way in which the corporation runs.

Depending upon how much equity you want to raise, you might be required to embark in a private placement to offer equity without stringent regulation by the Securities and Exchange Commission. Chances are, if you have more than a couple of investors and you need more than $25,000, you should seek the advice of an attorney to determine legal requirements for the equity you want to raise.

Equity sources

What equity sources are available for you? There are a host of friendly and unknown sources. If you deal with a friendly (known) or unknown source, protect yourself (see contracts under lawyers in chapter 14) against all possible events that can happen. Often, an investor will want to ensure that he or she is protected. He or she will draft contracts as they relate to the financing. Your legal counsel might be able to react to what is written. Make sure, in this one instance, that you have a proactive attorney who looks after your interests. Do not enter into any financing that you don't fully understand or with which you don't feel comfortable.

Family & friends   Family and friends are one of the best sources for capital. They don't check your credit history. They don't necessarily scrutinize your business venture to the extent a formal source would. These people know you. They respect you and what you have done with your life.

Although family and friends might be good sources of equity, they also might be relied upon for debt financing.

The upside to family and friends is that they can possibly provide you with better terms than might be available from the market. The downside to this source is that they are your family or friends. Many people quote the expression, "don't do business with family or friends." Although initially they might be an extremely friendly source of capital, family relations and friendships can often become strained. The closeness of the relationship and the competition that a business relationship can bring to an otherwise congenial relationship is often vexing. Although this source of funding might look intriguing, you should consider the entire impact that it might have on your relationship before you decide to enter into an arrangement.

Family and friends as investors can become too involved in your company and at the wrong times. At family gatherings, Aunt Millie might sit at the dinner table and expose your entire corporation to the family. She might then launch into criticism of the way you run the firm and handle her money. Embarrassing? You bet. Desirable as a way to run a business? No way.

Professional advisors & business acquaintances   This source is a little more distant from you than family and friends. Scrutiny of the potential investment is probably a little more objective. Professional advisors and business acquaintances will still invest because they have faith in you. But they will also take a harder line on an equity return from their investment than will friends and family.

Past employers   There are a host of major corporations who will look at business ventures that their employees suggest and decide that the market is not large enough for them to justify the investment. They look for businesses that can grow into much larger companies than those that might potentially be developed in the identified market. But these same companies might help you (a previous employee) to launch the business. Smaller companies, who don't want to lose focus, might have some spare cash that they can invest in an idea that they feel has merit. So they too might potentially fund a business venture by a previous employee.

In both of these instances, there is a certain level of comfort. The comfort comes from the fact that the potential investors know the individual in whom they are investing. And the known is often much easier to deal with than the complete unknown. For this reason, the known of the previous employee might be an attractive investment vehicle for a past employer.

Potential customers & suppliers   There might be certain unfilled niches in the market. There might be niches that are filled in an unsatisfactory manner in the eyes of certain customers or potential customers of that niche. They will often try to encourage development of a company that can either serve the market (because no company now exists) or serve the market better than a supplier who is not delivering satisfactorily. Potential customers might, therefore, invest in potential suppliers in order to have a product or service that they want and in a fashion they want.

Suppliers might want to increase their business. They might realize that by creating a company that could potentially buy product from them, they might be doing just that. Potential supplier funding can come with an accompanying contract to buy supplies from that supplier. Quite an interesting way to fund a business.

The key is to find a company that wants to see you in business. They want to put you in business and keep you in business (especially if you can either provide them with a critical product or service or purchase one from them). This type of funding can be either equity or debt, all contingent on what all parties in the transaction might want. Remember, these sorts of deals are not necessarily handed to you. You can't sit around and hope that some customer (or potential customer) will approach and ask to fund you. You might have to take a proactive approach to these types of sources. The best way to do so is to sit down and make a list of all potential sources. Then, either call (if you know them) or write to them in order to present your idea. You will probably not find people lukewarm on this sort of idea—they will either like it or hate it. As a result, these types of deals are either completed (or rejected) in a fairly short time.

Prospective employees   Prospective employees can be a good source of equity investment for your company. There are certain advantages and disadvantages, though.

On the advantage side, a person who invests some personal money should work hard to see that that investment grows. Someone who has a stake in a company can feel very loyal to it.

On the disadvantage side, an employee who has made an investment is an employee with whom you might be stuck. If you don't structure the investment with an escape or buy-out clause (by you), you might have an employee who you don't want to own a piece of the firm. You might have a partner through the simple act of selling some equity to an employee. If you structure this type of ownership, develop a well-thought plan to be able to buy out the employee. Leave yourself the right to get rid of the employee for cause and buy out the equity based on some formula (which should be based upon an independent stock valuation). When an employee has ownership, even if performance is good, you might soon learn that the employee feels justified in telling you how to run the company. A similar situation as is described in the family and friends investment route can easily develop. At inopportune times, your employee might tell you how you should run the company. Depending on the situation, you might be forced to listen. This scenario can develop if you have taken more money from an employee than you have invested in the business yourself. When this occurs, it frequently happens that the employee feels he or she has more of a right to run the business than you do and might try to take it over. Be extremely careful!

Wealthy business people & private investors   Check references. Check references? Of an investor? How and why? Often wealthy businessmen and private investors might seem to be just the angel that your business needs to get off the ground. Yet they also can be the source that can put your business into the ground. Hypothetically, assume your potential investors just made $10 million profit in the sale of some cable broadcasting stations. They structure an investment in your company in a multidimensional fashion. Every facet of their investment has some incredible tax consequences. They even structure the deal so that if they cause your business to fail, they will not only be able to write off this loss but still retain a host of the other tax benefits. Therefore, they stand to gain more if they put you out of business (from the aggregate tax consequences) than if you stay in business. This situation did truly happen. The company survived but not without much grief.

Make sure you understand the agenda of the investor before you take her or his money. Talk to other companies where she or he has invested. If the treatment of the other companies has been fair and the investor has a good reputation in the community, you should feel better but still proceed with caution.

Wealthy businessmen and private investors want a financial return for their investment. This return might be secondary to the central premise that they are building a company. If they are hands-on investors, you might be in trouble. Hands-on successful businessmen can attempt to take over the show. They might become so enthusiastic about the business that they might want to run your business. If you want this situation to develop, don't protect yourself against it. But if you don't want it to happen, build in safeguards in financing agreements so that it won't. You can benefit from experience, particularly experience of successful individuals. But, decide how you want this advice. Under certain conditions, where you have not performed up to the standards that have been set forth (the business is not meeting projections consistently), an investor might want to take over.

Wealthy business people and private investors will vary in the types of return that they seek when they make an investment. Again, ask them and the companies in which they have previously invested to see what sort of return they seek and over what period of time. Impatient versus patient investors can shed a completely different light on a company. If you can choose, choose a patient investor. In any instance, make sure you know what type of investor you have.

Experience is one of the most important attributes of wealthy business people and private investors as investors. Sure, they might have made some money or they call themselves a private investor, but have they ever invested before? If they have no track record, it is similar to you if you have no track record. They might not know what to expect. And you might be surprised at their reaction if they don't know what to expect. If you find an inexperienced wealthy business person or private investor, think twice about what might happen, especially if the company doesn't do well.

Professional venture-capital groups   Some seasoned investors can turn into incredible mentors. The best example is Compaq Computer. Ron Canion, who had worked for Texas Instruments, received his idea and money from Ben Rosen, who has helped guide Compaq to be the first company to reach Fortune 500 size in five years. You might not have the benefit of Ben Rosen as your investor or mentor, but if you choose correctly, you can benefit. Ben Rosen is a professional venture capitalist.

A *venture capitalist* invests in a company. She or he hopes that the company will do well. At some point in time, the venture capitalist liquidates the investment by either taking the company public, selling the company to another firm, or being bought out by another venture capitalist who might be putting more money into the company. Generally, the first two scenarios occur, hopefully for a profit.

A few of the characteristics of venture capitalists are:

- There are few venture capitalists who fund early-stage ventures. Early-stage ventures, although they have the potential for the greatest return, are the riskiest ventures because they don't have a track record. No one knows what to expect, especially from management. Management is the key element to make a company work. Many venture capitalists say that they'd rather have an okay idea with a tremendous management team than a great idea with a mediocre management team. Venture capitalists often feel that start-up and early stage businesses don't have a sufficiently experienced management team to make the company work. Frequently, the members of the management team will individually have a great amount of management experience. The team, though, might have little or no experience working together. Not a good sign, the venture capitalists often conclude, to ensure the success of a venture.
- Venture capitalists, as professional money managers, attempt to get a return on their entire *portfolio* (the money that they have invested) of an average of at least 35% per year. Although recent studies have shown that many venture capitalists have netted returns in the 2.5% per year area, venture capitalists still look for that home-run business to give them a great return. If your business realistically generates a 10% per year return, that might be too low for a venture capitalist.
- Many venture capitalists are like sheep. The bulk of the people who manage venture capital portfolios have little or no operating experience in

many of the industries in which they invest (especially from an entrepreneurial, run your own show, perspective). Therefore, like sheep, they follow a chosen leader and make investments either in the same company in which he or she has invested or in the same industry. If this one leader is wrong, time will show that all of the venture capitalists were wrong.

- Some venture capital firms are not sheep. They do invest in start-up and early-stage businesses. Many of these funds are state-sponsored groups that are encouraged to make investments in companies that are or choose to locate in their state. Check with your state's Department of Commerce to see if such a venture capital fund exists.

There are several listings of venture capital firms that invest in computer-based early-stage companies. The best source is *Stanley Pratt's Guide to Venture Capital*. You can get a copy of the book in your business library. The book includes a listing, by state, of venture capital firms. Included in these listings, in addition to each of the principals in the firm, is the amount of capital that they have available to invest, preferred size of investment, industries in which they like to invest, and stage of corporate growth in which they will invest. You can save yourself a lot of time by only contacting firms that will potentially want to invest in your company.

The National Venture Capital Association (NVCA), located in Alexandria, Virginia, will send you a list of their members (and principals in the firms) if you send them enough money to cover postage.

In addition to these guides, there are a couple of firms who are worth contacting based on their focus in start-up companies and their interest in the computer industry. They are Zero Stage Capital in Boston and NEPA in Bethlehem, Pennsylvania. These two firms like financing start-up and early-stage companies in the computer industry. Both of them will invest as little as $20,000 to $30,000 to test the feasibility of a concept and up to $400,000 or $500,000, on a staged basis, to assist with the growth of the firm. Both firms have a program where they place mentors in your company to help it grow. The mentors do not operate in an obtrusive fashion but in a way to truly assist your company achieve its goals.

Public stock offerings   Public stock offerings are the sale of stock to the public. They are regulated by the Securities and Exchange Commission. They are commonly thought of as a means to cash out or harvest an investment. Although it is true that public stock offerings are more frequently used by companies later on in their stage of development, you can also fund a company through a stock offering at its inception. Funding at inception generally takes place on one of the smaller stock exchanges, such as the penny stock exchange in Denver.

How do you find any or all of these equity sources? The first thing you do is re-read this section. Write down each category. Underneath the category name, list every single person or entity who you know who you could potentially approach for any funding. Once you have completed the first pass on the list, put it away. Later, go back to the list and confirm the validity of the names that are on the list. Then figure out who you forgot. Once you have gone through this process a couple of times, start adding dollar estimates to the names on your list. This will let you determine that Aunt Millie might invest $1000 and your brother Harry, $500. When you complete this exercise, prioritize the names of those who you want to approach.

Remember, it can be better to get money from fewer sources. You will have to deal with fewer people when you are running the business. When you prioritize, though, factor in all of the personalities behind these potential investors. You might recognize that Aunt Millie is not someone you want to deal with and even though she can potentially come up with $1000, you are not going to approach her as a potential investor.

Reason through your list of potential investors. Remember, especially with sources close to you (family and friends), that it is not only who you ask but also those who you don't ask that might become offended.

What happens if you get through this entire exercise and come up with no one? How do you find potential investors then?

One way is to advertise for investors. Crazy? Not hardly. There are sections of newspapers (such as *The Wall Street Journal*) that carry advertisements for potential investors. Different papers have specific days on which it is preferable to advertise. *The Wall Street Journal* has regional editions, so you can advertise in an edition that might only go to people in your part of the world. If you segment in this fashion, you will actually be able to get to potential investors. Choose your paper carefully. The more sophisticated the paper, the more sophisticated its reader. If you want an unsophisticated investor, select an unsophisticated paper. Through newspaper advertising, you can find firms that do public offerings, venture capitalists, corporate investors, and private investors.

You can ask your friends and business associates, who might not necessarily be candidates to fund your business, if they can identify sources of financing. They might help lead you to sources.

Government sources

Finally, there are a host of government financing sources. Explore them, even if you have other financing sources. You can look into government financing sources at the federal, state, and local levels. If you are a minority, the government can offer extra help at all levels.

Small Business Administration The SBA (Small Business Administration) sponsors a guaranteed loan program. This program is administered through regional offices of the Small Business Administration. A company must provide a business plan outlining the reasons why it needs financing.

A guaranteed SBA loan is executed by a bank. To receive an SBA guaranteed loan, you need to apply for a loan at three different banks. If all three of them turn you down, you are then eligible for an SBA guaranteed loan that might be placed with one of the banks that turned you down in the first place. The SBA guarantees 90% of the loan principal. The bank, therefore, has only 10% of the principal plus the accrued interest at risk of nonpayment. The criteria that the SBA uses to evaluate loans is not much less stringent than that of normal banks, though. So, if you were turned down by three banks, it is likely that the SBA will also turn you down.

In the guaranteed loan program, the SBA can also require collateral (as a bank would) as a normal condition to a loan. There are instances where the SBA will require your house as collateral for a loan. If you default on the loan, you lose your house.

Small Business Innovation Research The Small Business Innovation Research grant program is not equity nor is it debt financing. It is truly a grant program. You are given up to $50,000 to explore some innovative idea that the United States government feels has merit. You fill out an application for this program, which is administered by the Small Business Administration. If you are successful in completing the lengthy review process and you receive an award, you can also qualify for up to an additional $500,000. There are individuals who are expert in obtaining Small Business Innovation Research grants. You might want to contact the SBA to find them to help you go through the process.

Success is in no way guaranteed in this program. Success in initial financing can take a minimum of six months. If you need money now, this alternative might not be a viable one for you. Even if you have received money from the initial stage, you might not receive any money as a follow-on investment. Be prepared to find other money to finance the business.

These grants are awarded for research, not the operation of a business. Once you get to the commercialization stage of the business, this source is not going to be a viable one.

Different states have different programs. It is advisable for you to contact the Department of Commerce or Business Development Office in your state to see what types of debt, equity, and grant programs exist in your state.

Equity sources that exist at the state level might come through a state-supported venture capital fund. Debt and grant sources might be available to support various regions in a state where the economy needs bolstering.

Local sources

Just as state governments have programs to encourage location in their states, counties and cities have equity, debt, and grant programs to attract businesses to their area. Check with your city or county to see what they have available. You might have to go to the office of your county executive or mayor to learn what programs are available.

Minority funding sources

Federal, state, and local governments have long wanted to encourage women and minorities to run businesses. There are Minority Business Enterprise Associations at each of these levels of government. They have primarily equity and debt programs (generally at a lower than market rate for loans).

Evaluating sources

Evaluation of funding sources is a difficult subject to cover. Often you might only have one source of debt or equity available to you. Your decision in this instance is to either take or not take the money.

If you have more than one option, the question becomes more difficult. You have to evaluate all of the goals and objectives that you have set for the firm and yourself. Assess that financing vehicle that will best help you meet those goals and objectives. If you want to be able to grow your company into a $2 million company and you need product financing, you might have to accept the accounts-receivable financing that is available to you. If you can get a $250,000 contract, but you need to place a $50,000 bond in order to get it, you might use every financing source available to you, including lending the business money yourself.

At different times, what is attractive and what is not might change. Your perspective will change based on your company's age, the success you have been able to achieve, the success that you think you can achieve, and sometimes all opportunities that might face the company and you.

The best way to evaluate sources of financing is to be aware of as many of them as possible. Once you are aware of them, assess and reassess their applicability to the company. Financing is a dynamic process. Once you have one type of financing in place, you shouldn't necessarily be wed to it. Situations do change. The best example is interest rates on a loan. You might pay 14% interest on your loan. If you find a source that will offer you 10% with no additional financing costs (points on the loan's origination), is there any reason not to take advantage of the 10%? On the surface, the answer seems to be no. Yet this 10% financing is good for only $20,000, the 14% is on a line of credit for $50,000. If you can't get any more than $20,000 at the 10% source, should you still do it? The answer might still be yes, particularly if you can leave the $50,000 line of credit intact without using it. If you can't leave it intact, your decision criteria will change.

The answer to computer business financing requirements is to constantly keep abreast of any and all financing sources that might be available to you. Reassess all possibilities to keep your cost of capital—the overall cost that you pay for your financing—at the lowest possible level.

11 Potential roadblocks

What are the potential risks in your computer business that could make it fail? Roadblocks you might face include:

- Market risks
- Competitive risks
- Technology risks
- Operational risks
- Political risks
- Financial risks

How do you identify these risks and how do you minimize them? This chapter discusses them in some depth so that you can avoid many of them.

Overview of risks

It is the naive business person who looks at the world through rose-colored glasses and believes that running a business is a piece of cake. The naive individual believes that nothing really can or will go wrong. A cliché, attributed to a man named Murphy, tells you that whatever can go wrong, will go wrong. A caveat to this axiom is that it will go wrong at the worst possible time.

Those things that can and will go wrong are essentially the risks that you face when you plan and run your computer business. They are often critical to the path that the business will take.

You should take a positive, proactive approach when you plan and run your computer business. As part of this approach, you must recognize that critical risks might appear. You will then be able to plan your strategy if and when they do.

To understand all possibilities and guide your action accordingly is the key reason to list critical risks.

What happens if there is truly no market for your product?

Market risks

Assume you completely misread the market. You thought there was a market for your new product, but when you introduced it, no one wanted it. What do you do now? There is a way to protect yourself from committing many resources to a product or service. Before you take a product or service to market, do some market research. Complete an initial concept test to see what the market thinks of the concept.

Make sure you sample people who could use your product or service. If you want to see the market for a word processing training service, sample people who now have or are thinking about buying word processing software. Ask people in different size companies. And ask people in different job functions. Don't ask people if they'd use a word processing training service if they don't have computers!

Assume you've asked all of these different people. You find that no one wants to use your word processing training service. Did you ask questions like how do they now train people? If they said that they only use in-house trainers, there might not be a market for an external training service.

Make sure you properly interpret the information that you receive. Often people don't want to believe anything but what they initially thought. If you get information that tells you to go in one direction and you head in the other, it is your own fault if you err. Listen to the information you get and follow its direction.

Make sure you ask enough people about your potential product or service. Assume you survey one person about whether or not she or he would use a word processing training service. The answer is positive, so you stop surveying. Smart move? No way. Even 10 positive responses aren't enough to make you believe there is a market. Fifty people will give you a better perspective. Yet, depending upon the size of the market, you should probably ask at least a couple of hundred folks their opinion.

If you survey enough people and properly evaluate the results, you shouldn't be in a situation where you enter a market that just isn't there. If you enter the market after you've done market research that is positive, and you can't find any prospects for success, you might be marketing your computer product or service incorrectly. Maybe you're not getting the word out. Maybe you're not getting it out to the right people. Maybe you haven't given it enough time.

Maybe there is something about the time of year that doesn't point to market opportunity. I started my business on the 21st of December and was sure I had no market: Everyone only wanted to celebrate the holidays and not worry about business. Had I based my whole business on the reading I initially got, I would have quit by the first of January. Fortunately, I didn't. There are certain seasonal issues that you must consider. For the first two weeks of January, people frequently execute their new year's resolutions. They don't want to deal with outside product or service vendors. The summer months are a time when you find many people on vacation. You might have to endure extended times to get something done. Things either wind down or end up as last-minute year-end things to do in the last weeks of December. If you start your business during one of these periods, you might genuinely believe that there is no market for your service or product. Don't despair.

If, after you've done all of these things correctly and you still assess that there is no market for your product or service, you will want to see how you can either change your product or service so that there is a market. Also consider quickly finding another way to do something else to save the business. Early on, the senior staff of my company and I assessed that operationally we couldn't use optical scanners to convert information from hardcopy to magnetic media (based on technological constraints that were present). We decided to change the process to manual data entry in countries where labor costs were less than in the United States (to create a competitive advantage). At the same time, we added to the services we provided because we listened to the market—we added the conversion of information from minicomputer formats to microcomputers, because these computers became the preferred medium. The conversion service division of the company was born. The old adage that states if you are handed a lemon, make lemonade, is very relevant here. If, after you've done everything, you still face some critical risk, change the underlying elements that created the critical risk in the first place. This type of action takes creativity and speed. Act decisively, but only after you've reasoned through the entire situation.

What happens if the market dries up?

Another critical risk is that the market might dry up. This risk is a real one in the computer industry with the short product life cycles. You need to constantly monitor your sales and your competitors' sales. You can follow the product life-cycle curve by understanding what happens in the market. Watch advertising. If a competitor's advertising goes from a full page to a quarter page in six months, you can begin to see a shortage of funds. The reason could be cyclical (and economic), but if you begin to see alternatives to your product or service, beware. This happened with my company's conversion service division. More alternatives to using a service bureau began to spring up—many software conversion utilities created an alternative to our conversion service. This trend, coupled with a decline in sales dollars (although volume was still increasing) pointed to more of a commodity pricing that occurs in a mature market. When advertising expenditures began to decline, it was clear that the market was changing.

You must be keenly aware of the trends that occur in the market. You have to follow every sign that you see. Anticipate trends early or you will find yourself with a market that is dry. As you see trends develop, take appropriate action to harvest your business or diversify into an area where the market has not dried up. In the computer market, this process is ongoing. The critical risk is that you might miss some signs and get caught off guard.

What happens if competitors drop their prices?

When competitors drop their prices, and price is the most important issue in a market, it is a commodity market. Commodity markets are ones where price, not product or service attributes, are important. When many competitors drop their price and they have no additions or modifications to their products, this is not a good sign. Prepare for the market to change or dry up.

If prices drop due to decreased production costs (a form of product enhancement as happened in the computer chip market), it might not be a signal that the end is near. This might signal that more innovation has occurred and the market leader wants to maintain a competitive advantage. The price of the product is used to make it more difficult for competition. Intel, the computer chip manufacturer, takes the lead in pricing that lets them garner more volume, fuel further product research, and come up with innovative new computer chips. Old computer chips might be commodity priced as new chips are invented. These commodity-priced chips signal that more innovation will occur. The key is to anticipate these trends or, as is the case with Intel, actually control pricing trends by retaining a market leadership position. If you are the follower in a market, you are more vulnerable than the leader. Attempt to be the leader through innovation, especially because this vehicle might be the only survival mechanism in the computer industry.

What happens if a new, superior product or service is introduced by a competitor?

Hopefully, you will be prepared with your own competitive reaction. You don't want to be caught completely off guard. It is possible to do ongoing competitive research to see exactly what your competitors are doing. There is always someone in an organization who is so proud of what is being done that he or she is quite willing to talk about it. Survey competition either through open channels where you readily exchange information or through covert channels where you query competition as a potential customer.

If you are caught off guard because the competitor truly kept the innovation secret, the first thing to do is assess the situation. Buy the product and do what so many companies do—reverse engineer it and see what is going on. Or buy the service and see what is so special about it. Then, once you have a better assessment of the situation, plan a competitive reaction. Your reaction might be to give up. It might be time to sell your company. Or you might decide to come out with a product or service equal to that being offered. Remember that you must plan carefully and not act in haste. Do act swiftly, especially in the computer industry, or you might completely lose your window of opportunity.

Technological risks

What happens if the technology you use becomes outmoded?

A friend of mine ran a hot lead type typesetting business and all typesetting shifted to computer-based typesetting systems. What did he do? He scrapped the old technology and bought the new technology. If technology becomes obsolete in service businesses, all of the service businesses are in the same boat—they have to retool in order to shift to the new technology. Your best hedge against this risk is to have some type of a cash reserve that you can use if the technology changes. With this cash reserve in hand, you can purchase, lease, or rent the new technology as it becomes available. Your biggest risk is that you don't have enough money to get the technology.

If you are involved in a product-based company, your situation could be a little different. If the technology in your product becomes outmoded, hopefully you will have anticipated this through ongoing market risk assessment. And hopefully you will have innovated to keep pace with technology. If you are not prepared, you will want to try to acquire the technology somehow. You might be able to license the technology from a competitor. If you license the technology, though, you are dependent on the competitor, who will remain one step ahead of you. If you find yourself in this position, you might want to license the technology and try to innovate as well. Licensing will keep you somewhat competitive in the market. If you don't control the technology, though, you are in a position of weakness. You will want to attempt to play catch up, or better still, create your own innovations.

How do you anticipate technology trends?

You can give all your efforts to anticipating technology trends in the computer industry. You need to assess the issues, products, and services that are referenced in the trade press, the market (your customers and your potential customers) and your competition. The more information you can factor into your assessment, the better a conclusion you will be able to draw.

Tracking trends is the only way you can anticipate them. You want to establish as many information sources as possible so that you can understand what is going on in the computer industry. The industry is very fragmented and it is often very difficult to follow everything that occurs. Technological innovation can take place in academe, the government, corporations, and garages.

Innovation that takes place in academe is probably the easiest to track. Many academicians write papers and articles about their research and publish them.

The government is another matter. Much of the best technological research that occurs today takes place in the government. Some of this research is in civilian agencies but a lot is in defense agencies. Some of the research is unclassified but a great amount of it is classified. Unclassified information can be released. Many technology-transfer vehicles exist to release not only the information but the use of the technology to its creator. Classified information, on the other hand, is not released. It is therefore difficult to track.

Corporate research, if valuable to the corporation, might also be kept in the strictest of confidence until that research can be translated into commercial products. Once commercially viable products are released, it is easier to learn about the underlying technology. Many times, the technology will be kept in confidence even though it is used in the production of a product or the creation of a service.

Garages are the most difficult innovation arena to track. How do you find out what your neighbor is really doing inside the garage? Not easily.

Therefore, to track research in the technology area, the academe is the easiest, government-released information is probably the next best source, released products or services from corporations follow, and garage-type innovation is the most difficult to follow. This issue might disturb you, but you have the same disadvantages as everyone else. Larger corporations might be able to pour more resources into tracking information flows from more of these sources than you. But, these larger corporations might not necessarily be able to react as quickly to the information as you. Smaller firms, it is often said, can "turn on a dime." Once they get information, they can move quickly to deal with it. Smaller firms are generally much more malleable than are larger ones. After all, isn't it easier to steer five people in a new direction than 5000?

In conclusion, the best way to anticipate technological trends is to track as many sources as possible. The more information that you have in your arsenal, the more power you will have.

When and how do you change the technology you're using?

This can potentially destroy your company or catapult it into the highest level of success. Timing and understanding the market are absolutely critical.

This decision is inextricably linked to the market. If you change the technology that you are using too early in the game, the market might not be ready to accept this change. If you attempt to change the market, you will have to educate the market. Market education is necessary to increase awareness to create interest, purchase intent, and ultimately purchase in a product or service. Yet market education can be extremely expensive.

Market education is targeted at the innovators in the product life cycle. In the introductory phase of the product life cycle, only those who find out about the product or service and are truly innovators will try the product or service. As the product or service goes into the second phase of the product life cycle—growth—less education is required. Greater consumer acceptance will naturally take place.

To decide when and how you change the technology you're using is dependent on the position of the technology in the product life cycle, the type of technology that you have, and whether or not you have a product or a service.

If you have a new service that reads PAP smears via a computer, the biggest hurdles you face are market education and then finding the innovators who will use the service. Both of these steps can be quite costly. If you are a small firm, you might not be able to afford these expenses. If you attempt to undertake them, you might put your firm out of business. And even if you don't put your firm out of business, you might find that you've educated the market only so that another, more powerful competitor could enter the market and take advantage of all of the money that you have spent on education. (This situation increases in risk when the technology is less proprietary.) If you wait until another firm has introduced the same concept and educated the market, you might be able to piggyback this effort with new and improved service technology. You might not, though. What do you do?

One solution is to maintain proprietary protection on any new technology (such as the PAP smear technology) and concurrently establish a joint venture with a much larger firm that can afford to educate the market. You will then have the resources you need to spend once the market begins to accept the technology. In this situation, you hedge against the market risk while still retaining the rights to the technology. Although your gross margin dollar percentage (the percentage of every dollar of sales) might not be as high as if you had undertaken to market this service on your own, your absolute dollar sales might far surpass any expectations from a campaign launched on your own. For example, assume you sold the PAP smear service on your own, for $75 per PAP smear. Your gross margin (sales less variable costs) might have been $50. You might have sold 100 PAP smears a month for a total gross margin of $5000 a month. If you join forces with a larger firm and enlist their marketing support, you might receive $7.50 (gross margin) per

PAP smear. But, they are able to attract 10,000 PAP smears per month or $75,000 per month. Where are you better off?

This is only one way in which you can protect yourself against the technology product life cycle. If you have the resources to garner enough market share as you educate the market, to take advantage of the situation when the product or service catches on, then do it yourself. If not, find some type of partnering structure where you can take advantage of the situation and not lose your technological edge nor your shirt.

Once you have hurdled market and technological risks, you might not be at all free and clear. Many different types of risks occur when you operate your computer company.

Operating risks

What happens if your lead entrepreneur dies? Who will take over? The company could be completely ruined. Unless it has some type of key person life insurance policy in place. This key person life insurance would, at a minimum, pay the company a certain amount of money to enable it to find a new lead entrepreneur. Other members of the management team might buy key person life insurance so that they could buy out the estate of the lead entrepreneur to continue to run the company themselves. Understand what you and your company face and plan accordingly.

What happens if one of your employees becomes pregnant and retires next month? (This situation occurred in my firm only four months after I founded it.) It all depends, doesn't it? If she is your chief revenue producer, you've got problems. One solution might be to have business interruption insurance that covers this type of risk. Another is to have a pool of money that can tide you over until she is replaced. Another solution is to panic, which will accomplish nothing. In the instance in my firm, we had a pool of money that helped us survive until she was replaced.

What happens if your key supplier goes out of business? If you don't have a backup supplier for this product or service, you might have serious troubles. The best and only hedge against this is to have backup suppliers in place. If you don't, and the supplier is absolutely critical to your business, you too might find yourself out of business.

The list of operating risks is endless. So many things can possibly go wrong when you run your computer business. The key is to anticipate as many operating risks as possible. Every business operates differently. Consequently, every business will have different operating risks. Carefully analyze your business and figure out where the weak links are in your operation's chain. Figure out the most cost-effective solutions to the operating risks based on their position of priority on your scale of risks. These operating risks can be quantified in importance and given a probability of occurring. Based on this weighting, you can begin to prioritize the resources that should be devoted to hedging against them.

Political risks

Political risks are probably the most difficult risks to assess and hedge against. Political risks are those risks that somehow relate to governmental risks. Governmental risks can occur within the United States or outside it. In order to anticipate the political risks that face your firm, you must understand the way governments function in the countries you conduct your business. This understanding will give you some insights into what you might face. There are degrees of risk that might make the environment completely different from what you initially thought.

How do you anticipate and minimize the effect of political risk on the firm?

Identify them. This should occur on an ongoing basis. You need to get information from all possible sources—newspapers, radio, television, and other media. Government agencies are also a good source of information. If you deal with a foreign country, United States Embassies, the International Trade Authority (ITA) of the United States Department of Commerce (located in both regional offices in the United States as well as offices in the United States Embassies in foreign countries), and United States Embassies' general information sources all assist in this process. Trade associations that already do a lot of business with various countries and have faced political risks might have banded together and made information available. Professional resources (see chapter 14) are also good sources of information if they have a global presence. These professional resources include advertising agencies, attorneys, banks, investment banks, and insurance brokers. Banks and insurance brokers are probably your best source for assessment of political risks.

An example of a political risk is the railroad car that I attempted to run on a commuter basis between Philadelphia and New York City to ensure commuters would have a seat. Amtrak, a quasi-governmental organization, controls the terms by which you must operate a business if you use their railroad tracks and trains. If you have a contract with Amtrak, it is "at the pleasure of" the United States Government. This clearly creates a political risk. When Amtrak told me that they would only enter into a one-year contract for my railroad, I ran a great risk that they would not renew it. The political risk factor was so high that I decided not to buy a railroad car and enter into this business. What do you do with a railroad car that can't travel the railways? Create a restaurant?

Several years ago, when Toshiba gave some sensitive technology to the Russian government, the United States initially contemplated the ban of the sale of Toshiba computers in the United States. If that had happened and you were a reseller only selling Toshiba's computers, what would you have done?

Unlike the railroad car example, you had an alternative. You could sell computers made by another manufacturer.

The key to dealing with political risks is not only to understand what they are or might be but to figure out alternatives to deal with them. One alternative might be to diversify a source of supply or a source of distribution. As with other types of risk, you must look at all possible risks that might affect your company. Determine all the alternatives needed to address them.

Financial risks

Financial risks are numerous. Every time someone owes you money or you owe money, there is a financial risk. Look at examples of each and figure out the best way to limit the risk.

Collection risks

You've decided to do business across the country, someone on the other coast owes you $1000, and refuses to pay you. How do you collect? How could you have avoided a problem in the first place? This is a collection problem. In order to avoid collection problems, there are several things that you can do:

Collect money up front   Collect before any delivery of product or services is made. When you receive an up-front payment, you receive all of your money before you deliver any product or service. You can do this with a cash or credit card payment.

One way to get cash directly into your bank account is to have your customer wire the funds into your account. In a wire transfer, a bank electronically wires money from one account to another. Wire transfers occur between banks that have electronic funds-transfer capability.

If you accept payment via check, you still run the financial risk that the check might not clear the bank (due to insufficient funds in the account). If you require the funds up front in this manner, you can wait to make delivery on the product or service until the check clears the bank.

Collect money cash on delivery (COD)   Collection on delivery is entitled cash on delivery. You receive your payment when you make the delivery. If you use cash or a credit card, you obviously have no credit risk. If you use a check as the collection vehicle, and it either doesn't clear the bank or a stop payment is placed on it, you have borne a financial risk. If you get a check that is certified, the bank certifies that there are funds in the account to cover the check. The bank ensures that they are allotted to this specific, noncancellable check.

Ensure payment through a letter of credit   Letters of credit are issued by a bank with very specific terms. If you have a letter of credit drawn on a bank, the bank tells the recipient that the money is in the account. Letters of credit have many different attributes. They can be revokable or irrevocable. A revokable letter of credit means that the issuer can cancel it. As the recipient, you are not in much better shape than with a normal check. The irrevocable letter of credit is like the certified check. Once it is issued, it can't be revoked. Letters of credit can have additional terms attached to them such as product specifications. They can have delivery quantities, dates, and locations attached to them. Letters of credit can be your insurance of proper delivery and payment, especially if you are far away from your client.

Perform a credit check   The most lax form of financial risk reduction is a credit check of your client. You can use Dun & Bradstreet (be careful, it contains information primarily reported to Dun & Bradstreet by the company itself) or TRW (generally used to track individual credit). These services cost you something each time you use them. Therefore, many companies have their own credit application that gives them a list of references for their use in checking credit. When these credit applications are filled out, references are called or written to check the credit worthiness of the potential client. Based on the finding of the credit report, you can set the financial terms that you extend to your potential client.

All of these credit protection vehicles are different types of terms. Yet when the business people commonly refer to terms they talk about all credit terms. These include net 10, 15, and 30. Or 2/10 net/30. When someone talks about net 10, 15, or 30, they refer to the number of days that you have to pay for the product or service that you have purchased. The 2/10, net/30, term means that you can take a 2% discount if you pay within 10 days. If you do not pay in 10 days, you have to pay the full amount within 30 days.

Payment risks   Payment risks are the opposite of collection risks. If you, as a customer, have some type of credit terms in place with your supplier and they somehow change, you might face a credit risk.

For example, assume you work for your father who runs a business that you will inherit. The business has a $50,000 line of credit. Your father turns the business over to you. The bankers don't agree with your father. They don't think you are capable of running the business. They *call* your line of credit (they ask you to pay it back to them). What will you do now? You will either be forced to renegotiate the line with the present bank, another bank or private source, or if you can't negotiate any line of credit, you will be forced to file for bankruptcy protection. This last solution is quite extreme. But if you receive a mandate to pay off a callable loan or line of credit, you constantly face this type of financial risk.

Similarly, what do you do if you are one month late with your lease payment and your investor wants to call your lease? What happens? Again, you can try to renegotiate with the present lessor, find a way out of the lease and enter into some type of new financing, or, if you are not successful in any of these negotiations, you might be forced to file for bankruptcy protection.

When you are the debtor and debt is structured to either be callable or contain provisions (the most important ones are the default provisions), if there is some lag in payment or complete nonpayment, you open yourself to financial risk. If you are personally guaranteeing one of these debt instruments, you put yourself in a financially precarious position if indeed the loan is called or some default occurs. If you can't negotiate terms for repayment of the debt, you might be forced to personally pay for the debt. This situation can be very costly, especially if you don't have the assets to repay the outstanding debt. If you don't have the assets to repay the debt, you might have to file for bankruptcy protection.

There are a host of different risks that your business might face—market, operational, political, and financial. They all come in different forms and at different times. If you attempt to anticipate as many as possible, you will then be able to better cope with all risks as they surface. Thorough, ongoing assessment of risks is the key to minimizing their effects.

12 Cashing out

From the moment that you start your business, you should think about how you will cash out or *harvest* it. When you harvest a business, you reap a return from it. Some of the harvest methods are:

- Take cash from the business on an ongoing basis
- Sell part of the company
- Merge with another company
- Have the company acquired
- Sell the company outright
- Have the employees of the company purchase it
- Take the company public

Too many people start businesses without consideration for the harvest. They start or purchase a business and think that they will run the business forever.

There are a host of vehicles that you can use to get cash out of the business, without completely selling it (see the list above). Each method has its own merit. When you set the goals and objectives of the firm and incorporate your individual goals into them, you should constantly consider harvest alternatives. This planning is especially needed in the computer industry, where life cycles are short. If you don't constantly consider harvest alternatives, you might forever lose your opportunity to harvest.

Ongoing cash harvest

One of the most interesting ways to harvest a business is to do so on an ongoing basis. To the extent that you own your company and pay yourself a salary, you harvest the business. To the extent that your business might pay for your automobile, you harvest the business. If you take less than you could now, you hope to reap a greater harvest in the future. If you take more now, you leave less in the company to build the future of the firm. When you evaluate this harvest option, you ask yourself if the money is better left in the company to help it grow or if you should take it out yourself.

Computer-based businesses have an interesting way of eating cash. Because of the short product life cycles, innovation is constantly needed. You have to purchase new computers and innovate to keep up with the market. Consequently, you might want to leave all of the cash in the business and pay yourself nothing. Yet you need to live. The best way to handle this situation is to set some type of a salary for yourself, which you feel is reasonable. If times get tough or if you see a market opportunity, you might want to make some type of adjustment to it temporarily to compensate for this unusual occurrence.

It is not wise to be at either of the extremes—paying yourself nothing or paying yourself more than the company can afford. I know an individual who ran a computer company and performed an ongoing harvest through both a large salary and fancy cars for himself. The company is no longer. It couldn't afford the ongoing harvest.

I know an individual who doesn't pay himself anything. He pours most everything back into the company to make it grow. His ego suffers.

Moderation and balance are key. Just as farmers let the ground lay fallow every seven years, you have to know when to stop taking from the firm and give it a rest. Understand market conditions and you can more easily make this determination.

Partial harvest

A *partial harvest* is the sale of part of your company. The merits of a partial harvest are that you retain some of the assets of the firm and reap a return from others. If you have a microcomputer that is about to be outmoded by the introduction of a new system, and you own the system outright, you might want to sell it while you can still make some money from it in the secondary market. Although the sale of some computers doesn't seem like a harvest of the business, it is. It is a source of cash that you can use to either fund other operations or distribute to the owners of the company. This vehicle for a partial harvest of assets is best practiced with assets of the firm that have a market value but are not used by the company. It is not wise to arbitrarily sell assets of the company.

Selling one division of a company is a partial harvest. This sale is an example of more than just a simple asset sale. If you are large enough to distinguish between two business units in your firm and you find that one of the business units' value is diminishing, you might decide to sell that part of your business.

In order to prepare for a partial harvest, you have to be intimately aware of all of your businesses. If it is more than one business, understand it as separate businesses. Separate out the accounting records of the businesses and track them in the market separately. If and when there comes a time to consider selling them, you will have all of the vehicles in place to do so. If you have any employees or assets that are used by more than one business unit, be sure that you can allocate these people or assets over the remaining business units should you sell just one of them. If you can't justify this allocation, reconsider selling the business unit. Or figure out a way to sell the unit and reconfigure the assets. For example, assume you have purchased a $10,000 computer that is used for two business units of your firm. You now want to sell one of the business units and you conclude that you can't carry the $10,000 computer in the remaining business unit. You might want to consider a transaction called a *sale/leaseback* in order to make the sale work.

A *sale/leaseback* is a transaction where you sell the asset you own to another party and agree to lease it back from them for a certain term. They give you the money for the asset. You can then use the money they've given you from the purchase to pay the lease payments on it. In the example, you would receive $10,000 for the sale of the computer. You might then obligate yourself to a five-year lease that might cost you $175 per month. You would invest the $10,000, reap interest from the principal, and periodically draw down some of the accrued interest and underlying principal to pay the lease payments. You might be able to couple this amount of money with the actual allocation of the computer from the remaining business unit and more than cover the payments. If you structure this transaction between yourself and the business, where you purchase the equipment, it can have beneficial tax consequences. Check with your accountant, though, before you enter into such a transaction.

Mergers

Mergers are another way to harvest your business. Unlike the partial harvest, the merger generally takes place with the whole company. Although you can spin off a division of the company and have it merge with another firm.

Mergers occur when two or more companies decide to combine. Mergers can occur for a host of reasons—strategic, resource sharing, or harvesting. Although this chapter focuses on harvesting, it makes sense to mention the other elements.

Mergers for strategic reasons happen all of the time. One firm might have developed a marketing or distribution system in a specific market. Another company might have developed a research and development or manufacturing capability in that same market. The two firms decide that combined they will have all of the elements needed to run a successful business.

There are other strategic reasons to merge. For example, if two companies both have marketing strength in one target market, their combined forces might be able to achieve a competitive edge over any competition, so they merge.

Once mergers take place, resources of the organization—people, funds, and technology—are shared. Through resource sharing, the merged companies emerge stronger.

When mergers take place, very often the management of both companies are blended together to run the newly merged company. Political battles can occur and one of the management teams might prevail. Before you consider a merger, realize that you might not run the company in the future if a political battle ensues and you are not on the side of the prevailing management team.

These reasons are strategic and tactical reasons for a merger. Achieving a harvest can also be a reason for a merger. If one company is privately held and one company is publicly held, when the companies merge, one of two things can happen. The merged company can become a privately held company. In this case, the public company's stock is completely purchased by the private company. This is called taking a company private. It doesn't achieve much for the shareholders of the public company except to liquidate their holdings, which is a harvest technique. When this privatization occurs, the shareholders then have cash for the equity that they owned in the public company.

The cash harvest occurs unless there is a stock swap. If a stock swap occurs, the holders of the equity of the public company are given equity in the privately held company. They are then owners of a nonliquid (it can't be easily traded) equity. This stock swap doesn't achieve the goal of privatization—putting ownership of the corporation into fewer rather than more hands. It also isn't really a goal of the public shareholders to own nonliquid stock whose value can be arbitrarily set. Therefore, this type of stock swap isn't a vehicle that is used as a harvest option.

The neatest harvest option in a merger is with a private and a public company. The private company swaps its stock for the stock in the public company. What this transaction does is to provide immediate liquidity for the holders of the equity in the private firm. They now own equity in a publicly traded company. The harvest is complete.

There must be an underlying reason for any one of these stock swap harvests to take place. That reason is either a strategic reason or one of resource sharing. Harvests just don't happen. I spent about six months, once, trying to convince a publicly traded company that it wanted to merge with my privately held company. My reason to enter into this transaction was to provide liquidity for the equity holders in my firm. The deal didn't work because, in the end, neither firm could see any strategic value to a merger. Yet conversations did take place and there was interest.

If you become interested in initiating a merger of your privately held company with a publicly held one, identify companies that might be candidates for this merger. Contact their president or chief executive officer and express your interest. Either call or write a letter. It is better to call initially. If the head of the public company is receptive to a conversation (be somewhat vague initially, but explain why you're calling), meet in person to discuss prospects. You will have to find something that interests the public company. The best fit is if there is some strategic reason why the other company and your company should try to join forces. Try and find this fit. If you can't find the fit before an initial conversation, you are going to have a difficult time making a convincing case for merger.

Acquisitions

Acquisitions are tidy ways to harvest companies. One company buys another company. The acquiring company maintains control over the acquired company. The acquiring company will either blend it into its own operations or have its own management run the acquired company. In some instances, management might stay on to either run the company or assist in a transition of management from the old to the new company. If you are the company being acquired, you might be out of a job shortly. This condition might even be outlined in the acquisition agreement. Unlike a merger, where there is the thought of merging management teams, the acquired company is very aware that its management probably won't run the company in the future.

Outright sales

An outright sale of a company is a sale of the hard assets of the firm, a sale of the intangible assets of the firm, or a sale of both.

In selling the conversion service division of my company, I only sold the hard assets of the division (computers, mailing lists, and employees related to the operation, if desired). No way was the name of the company associated with the transaction (the intangible asset).

When Aberchrombie & Fitch, the famous sporting goods store went through a bankruptcy, there were no hard assets of the firm left to sell. The firm's name, an intangible asset, was eventually sold and used in an entirely new chain of stores.

When Fox Software, a producer of microcomputer database software, was recently sold to Microsoft, both the hard assets (all software and rights, some personnel, and any financial assets) were purchased. The intangible asset (the name of the firm) was also sold.

Outright sales will vary from one sale to the next. What form the sale will take is completely dependent on the interests and negotiating prowess of the firm doing the acquiring and the firm being acquired. Outright sales can be very effective for the owners of the acquired firm. They can receive cash for the transaction and be done with the company's management. The constructs will vary depending on what is sold (for example, management might be required to stay on for some period of time after the acquisition or stock might be swapped in lieu of some cash).

Employee stock option plans allow employees to slowly become partial owners of the firm. If the majority shareholder decides to cash out, he or she can opt to sell the rest of the firm to either some or all of the employees of the firm. This strategy might or might not work.

An example where it didn't work is an advertising agency whose principal shareholder instituted an employee stock option plan. Slowly, over the years, employees began to acquire equity in the firm. For purposes of the employee stock option plan, the equity of the firm was valued every year. At the point when the primary shareholder decided to retire, he asked the employees to buy him out based on the previous year's valuation. The employees couldn't afford to buy him out. He had to find another company to not only acquire his share of the firm but the employee's share of the firm. The strategy that was planned for years changed dramatically. The employees ended up owning none of the firm. This entire transaction took only several months. The result was that the lives of the principal shareholder and all of the employees were changed drastically in a very short time.

An example where the strategy did work is an architectural firm owned, initially, by one individual. He gave four employees the right to own equity in his firm. He outlined a five-year strategy where, year by year, they would buy out his share of the firm. After five years, the four employees would be the sole owners of the firm. The transaction was successful.

Why was the second transaction successful and the advertising example not? One reason was that the buyout occurred over time. In the advertising example, the employees had to come up with the funds to buy out the principal all at once. Because service-based businesses are not easily financed without a personal guarantee, and the employees of the advertising agency were not willing or capable of providing this guarantee, they couldn't raise funds for an equity purchase. The architectural firm's extended transaction time made the purchase possible for the employees.

When you want to sell your company to your employees, you have to plan the transaction in such a way that your employees will be able to participate. You can't expect that one day, your employees will each be able to come up with $50,000 to purchase your company. You have to know something about their present and future ability to buy your company. Then you need to come up with a purchase plan that will work for them and help you achieve your goal. Sale of the company to employees can take much more planning and much more time than other types of harvest. But it can also be the most effective for you to leave the company in the hands of the people who have helped to build it.

Sale to employees

Initial public offering

Everyone talks about taking a company public. *Taking a company public* means issuing stock to the public. The first issue of stock to the public is called the *initial public offering*. Many think that once the company is public, it will then offer liquidity to the shareholders.

Those that assist in taking companies public are investment bankers, accountants, and attorneys (see chapter 14). The resource organization that has the largest role in taking a company public is an investment banker.

The key to a successful public offering is to understand all the conditions that come with being a public company.

There are many costs that accompany a public offering of stock. There are legal and accounting costs to create offering memorandums and audited financial statements (even if they don't show anything) that can exceed $150,000 per offering. You have to want to raise a substantial amount of money or the costs can be disproportionate to the amount of funds raised.

Once a company is public, government reporting requirements can begin to eat up your time. Once you are a public corporation, no matter what your revenues might be, you are required to file all sorts of reports with the United States Securities and Exchange Commission.

One of the reasons many people take companies public is to provide liquidity for the shareholders in the company. Private companies do not provide easy liquidity for investors. How much, therefore, is your equity worth in a private company? Is it based on the valuation that you or your accounting firm has given the company? And how is that value realized? Through the sale of the company to another? Generally.

But if you are a publicly traded company, people buy and sell your stock. This stock trading allows you to sell $10,000 worth of your stock, if you want some money. It is not as if you have to sell the whole company to realize any value. Right? Well, if you are an unknown company on a small exchange, you might have no more liquidity in your stock than you had when you were a private corporation. To create liquidity in your equity can be such a great task that many who are faced with it forget about running their company. As a result, their company suffers because of the time spent making a market for the company's stock. These people are not always successful either. And if they are unsuccessful in making a market for their equity, they might be forced to go back to private individuals to get an investment in their firm. I have seen this occur numerous times. In fact, I've been asked to invest in many companies that went public on the penny stock exchange (an exchange where a company's stock sells for pennies). These penny stock exchange companies couldn't raise a dime through the exchange, after their initial offering, so they needed to go back to private sources to raise funds.

If you are fortunate to be on a larger stock exchange, such as the over-the-counter market (NASDAQ), your stock liquidity can be much greater than on the penny stock exchange. You don't even need to make a market for your own publicly traded stock. This scenario doesn't always unfold, though. Your stock might be traded on what is called the *pink sheets*. These stocks don't trade in enough volume or have enough shares (in terms of number and dollars) to be traded on a frequent basis. Although they might be listed on a major exchange, in order to stay listed, there must be a certain trading volume and a certain net worth requirement.

So, if you start out initially with a public stock offering or you enter into one later in the life of your company, there are a host of tradeoffs that accompany it. Evaluate them solidly before you decide to expose everything that your company does to anyone who wants to find out (this exposure includes your salary).

Harvest options are many. Plan now and on an ongoing basis to maximize what you can take out of your firm.

13 Choosing software, hardware, & peripherals

You might already have a computer that is completely equipped with software, hardware, and peripheral devices. You might have made your decision based on some price and performance criteria and then bought what you felt made most sense. Even if you own a system, you should read this chapter to understand what you will need to do to evaluate your future computer purchases.

Evaluate your needs

Before you decide to purchase any type of computer software or hardware, evaluate your computing needs. For what tasks will you use a computer? Word processing, database or file management, spreadsheet, accounting, communications? These tasks and others are referred to as *applications*. These applications are all software programs that run on a computer.

Define your applications

Applications include:
- *Accounting*
- *Communications*
- *Computer-aided design (CAD)*
- *Computer-aided manufacturing (CAM)* √
- *Database management*
- *Desktop publishing*
- *Drawing*
- *Electronic mail*

- *File transfer*
- *Graphics*
- *Integrated software programs*
- *Multimedia*
- *Networking*
- *Paint*
- *Personal information management*
- *Presentation*
- *Project management*
- *Spreadsheet*
- *Word processing*

This list serves as a representation of the types of software applications that you can purchase. There are many more applications, a host of which are discussed in chapter 3 and appendix A. Decide what applications you need in your business.

Once you've decided which applications are required, then you should begin looking at specific program packages.

Buying a popular application package isn't necessarily a bad idea. It's been tested. It has more written about it than a less popular package. You can read about its attributes and evaluate it more easily. Finally, it has a larger base of users who you can ask about its pluses and minuses.

It might be a good idea to view a list of the most popular selling software, but do these packages have the attributes that you will want or need? You can't tell from a list.

You get a better perspective on an application program by reading articles and reviews of it. The IBM PC (MS-DOS) and Macintosh press all carry articles, although somewhat sporadically, about different application software. There are buyer's guides in these publications. There are publications dedicated to nothing but reviewing application software. Most of the publications can be found in your public library.

Read articles in the computer press

Go through each application of interest. Make a list of the attributes that you feel are important for your use. Ensure that each program title or package that you are reviewing has these attributes. You might want to copy part or all of this list of price/performance attributes from one of the buyer's guides referenced.

Once you've narrowed down the number of programs to three, based on needed attributes, test drive the software. Go to your local computer dealer and try to use each application package. (If the dealer protests, tell him or her that without a test run, you'll buy from someone else.)

You, more than anyone, must feel satisfied that the program offers you what you want. Look at each software package in terms of its:

Power   It should be able to do what you want it to do. The software package should be robust enough to perform all functions needed in your specific application.

Flexibility   It should be able to operate in a host of different environments. You want it to be able to operate with different hardware platforms (Macintosh and IBM PC) as well as different operating systems environments (MS-DOS, OS/2, Windows, and/or Macintosh OS).

Ease of use   You should be able to do what you want to do and not have to worry about how to get the application running. The application should be user friendly. It shouldn't be intimidating but appealing to you.

Support   If you run into a problem, how well can the company solve it? You want to make sure that the company has a technical support telephone line, you can get through to it, and you can get your questions answered when you have them.

Documentation   If you are using the software, before you even call the company, how good is on-line help or written documentation? The software should be so self-explanatory that you don't need to call the company for technical support. If the help is on-line, you have a more expedient way to get answers to your questions.

Security   Can other users easily access the software or is it protected so that you have some measure of security? The last thing that you want is to have everyone snooping around your files by being able to use your application. If password protection is present, how well does it stop unwanted users?

If you are satisfied with the various applications that you have test driven, it is now time for you to choose the hardware on which you will run your software.

Choose your hardware

You should choose your hardware based on your software requirements. Your software might require certain minimum computer platform attributes or configurations such as:

The operating system   The operating system or *OS* is a program that virtually runs your computer, acting as both a scheduler and an overall traffic cop. It is the first program loaded (copied) into the computer's memory after the computer is turned on. The operating system might be developed and sold by the vendor of the hardware it's running in or by an independent software house.

The operating system is an important component of the computer system because it sets the standards for the application programs that run in it. All programs must be written to function with a specific operating system such as MS-DOS on IBM-type PCs and OS-Finder or MultiFinder on Apple Macintoshes.

RAM (random-access memory)   All program execution and data processing takes place in memory. The program instructions are first copied into memory from a disk or tape and then extracted from memory into logic circuits for further analysis and execution.

As data is entered into memory, the previous contents of that memory space is lost. Once the data is in memory, it can be processed (calculated, compared, and copied). Then the results can be output from memory to a screen, printer, disk, tape, or communications channel.

Memory doesn't usually remember. Oddly enough, the computer's memory doesn't remember anything when the power is turned off. That's why you have to save your files before you quit your program. Although there are memory chips that do hold their content permanently, they're used for internal control purposes and not for the user's data.

CPU (central processing unit)   The computing part of the computer is also referred to as its *processor*. A personal computer CPU is contained on a single microprocessor.

The CPU, clock, and main memory make up a computer. A complete computer system requires the addition of control units, input, output, and storage devices and an operating system.

Clock speed   *Clock speed* is the internal heartbeat and speed of a computer. A faster clock will speed up all processing operations provided the computer's circuits can handle the increased speed. For example, the same processor running at 20 MHz (megahertz) is twice as fast internally as one running at 10 MHz.

Monitor   A *monitor* shows the output of a computer. It might either be color or monochrome. Monitors come in various levels of resolution that include CGA, EGA, VGA and SuperVGA. The resolution is the degree of sharpness of a displayed or printed character or image. On screen, resolution is expressed as the number of dots per line by the number of lines. A 680 × 400 resolution means 680 dots across each of 400 lines. The same resolution looks sharper on a small screen than it does on a large screen.

Keyboard   A *keyboard* is a set of input keys. Keyboards on terminals and personal computers contain the standard typewriter keys in addition to a number of specialized keys.

Keyboard quality is critical for experienced typists. The feel of the keyboard (the amount of tension and springiness) varies greatly from one keyboard to another. Key placement is also important. Older keyboards might have awkward return and shift key placements.

Hard disk   A *hard disk* is a magnetic disk made of metal and covered with a magnetic recording surface that is used to store information that is used on computers. Hard disks come in removable and fixed varieties that hold from 10 megabytes (a million characters) to gigabytes (billions of characters) of information.

Diskette drive   A *diskette drive* is a peripheral storage device that holds, spins, reads, and writes magnetic or optical disks that contain information that will be used by the computer. A floppy diskette drive might come in either 3½ or 5¼ inch dimensions. The drive holds either high- or low-density diskettes that are either single sided or double sided.

Mouse   A mouse is a pucklike object that is used as a pointing and drawing device. As it is rolled across the desktop in any direction, the *cursor*, or pointer, moves correspondingly on the screen.

Desktop, laptop, notebook, & portable computers   Computers come in different sizes and shapes. A *desktop* computer is meant to fit on your desk; it isn't meant to be easily moved. Portable computers are easily transported from one place to another. Portable computers include *laptops* (those that are meant to rest on your lap while you are traveling in either a train or a plane) and *notebooks* (smaller than laptops, these computers can occupy only a portion of the standard-size tray in an airplane).

These factors should all be considered carefully before you purchase any type of computer hardware. Ensure that the applications packages that you have chosen will run on the hardware configuration that you have selected.

Choose peripherals

Before you buy anything, choose your peripheral devices. The peripheral devices must be compatible with not only the hardware that you just selected but also with the computer software that ultimately will drive each of the peripheral devices. Peripheral devices from which you can choose include:

Printers   A *printer* converts computer output into printed images. Some printers include:

- *Serial* printers print a character at a time from approximately 10 to 400 characters per second. Serial printers use dot-matrix and character printer (also known as letter-quality) technologies.
- *Page* printers, also called *laser* printers, print a page at time from approximately 4 to 215 pages per minute (400 to 14,000 lines per minute) and primarily use the electrophotographic technique used in copy machines.

- *Color* printers use impact dot matrix with multiple color ribbons, electrophotographic with multiple color toners, electrostatic plotters with multiple color toners, printers using the Cycolor technology, ink jet with multiple color inks, and thermal-transfer with multiple colors.
- *Character* printers are similar to Selectric typewriters, printing one character at a time. A *daisy wheel* (circular printing disk containing the letters and numbers near the circumference) or similar mechanism is moved serially across the paper. At the selected print location, a hammer hits the shaped character image on the wheel into the ribbon and onto the paper.
- *Ink jet* printers use a continuous stream of ink that is sprayed onto paper, or droplets of ink to generate a dot matrix image, usually in a serial fashion. Another technique uses ink in a solid form, which is melted just before it is ejected.

Modems   A modem (modulator-demodulator) adapts a terminal or computer to a telephone line. It converts the computer's digital pulses into analog frequencies within the audio range of the telephone and converts them back into digital pulses at the receiving end.

The modem handles the dialing and answering of the call and controls the transmission speed. Modems used on telephone lines transmit at speeds of 300, 1200, 2400, 4800, 9600, and 19,200 baud (or bps—bits per second). The effective data transfer rate is about 10% of the bit rate. Thus, 300 bps is equivalent to 30 characters per second. It would take a full minute to fill up a video screen at 300 bps; 15 seconds at 1200 bps, and about seven seconds at 2400 bps.

Using a modem with a personal computer requires a free serial port to hook it up and a communications program.

Scanners   *Scanners* read text, images, and bar codes from paper and convert them into magnetic data. Text and bar-code scanners recognize printed fonts and bar codes and convert them into a digital code. Graphics scanners convert a printed image into a video image (*raster* graphics) without recognizing the actual content of the text or pictures.

There might be other peripheral devices that you want to add to your computer configuration that are not included in this list. This list is not complete but only meant to serve as a representation of the types of peripheral devices that you can purchase to add to your computer system.

Once you've chosen all of your peripheral devices and are sure that they are compatible with both the software and the hardware that you have selected, you need to decide where you want to buy all of your computer equipment.

Choose your vendor

There are many dimensions on which people choose computer vendors. The most common dimensions are price, support, and reputation. You will have to make your own decision about the relative value of each one of these attributes in your selection process.

Borrow, rent, lease, or buy   Once you've chosen your equipment and your vendor, you have arrived at the day of reckoning. Borrow, rent, lease, or buy your equipment. Just remember the amount of effort that you put into your decision-making process. Remember that product life cycles in the computer industry are such that there is a high probability that all of the research that you have done might be completely invalid tomorrow because of a new innovation. Don't fret and don't start the process over. Just remember that based on the information that you had at the time, you made the best possible decision.

14 Where to find help

Many organizations and companies can help you start and run your PC-based company. Consider contacting these types of resource organizations:

- Accounting firms
- Advertising agencies
- Banks
- Brokerage companies
- Consultants
- Financial advisors
- Insurance agencies
- Investment bankers
- Law firms
- Leasing companies
- Market research
- Public relations firms

How do you choose the proper firm to help you with your needs? What are your needs and the needs of your firm in terms of resource organizations? When you sit down to decide what types of firms you will need, you should understand what they can do and what you want them to do for you. Prepare a list of questions. Extract from the capabilities and descriptions that follow in this chapter. Once you have completed your own set of questions, call all of the firms that you feel you should talk to before you make your decision on who to hire. Then, you interview them, not the other way around.

Choosing an organization

When you hire any professional resource organization, don't forget who works for whom. The resource organizations work for you. It is not the other way around.

When you interview a firm, go to their offices. You can tell a lot about a person by the way he or she lives and by the way his or her house is established. The same is true with a company. In a company, this notion is commonly referred to as the *corporate culture*. It is important to observe this feature. Factor it into how you feel about an organization. There are some that will be cold and standoffish; others will be warm and friendly. Obviously there are balances in between these two types of firms. You will have to decide how and where one might fit.

The initial interview with any firm should not cost you anything. You explore their capabilities, and they try to sell you. Most firms call this activity a business development expense. There might be one exception—the highly specialized firm whose advice or counsel you might truly need only for one or two hours. If a firm is so highly specialized, they might even have to travel hours to get to you or vice versa. Given that this scenario prevails, you might want to interview this type of company on the telephone and use your judgement from there. If you feel comfortable, hire them over the telephone.

Goodness of fit

Goodness of fit is the most important factor to consider when you choose any professional resource organization. How well can you work with the professional and nonprofessional members of the organization? If you rely on these people for assistance, you want to ensure that you can work with them. Do you like the members of the firm you are considering? If you can answer affirmatively, you have passed a critical hurdle. Do business with people who you enjoy and can rely on.

Size

How large is the firm? Is a small, medium, or large firm the most appropriate for your business? There are advantages to firms of all sizes. You should consider firm size based on the goals of your company. For example, if you always intend to be a one- or two-person company with a very straightforward business structure, you might never confront any complex business problems. If this description fits your situation, you might want a very small firm that has a good reputation in the community, doesn't really do work beyond your own town, and is very inexpensive.

If the goal of your organization is to grow and do an initial public offering (as a means of harvesting the business (see chapter 12), you might decide that you want a much larger firm that knows the ins and outs of all areas of their specialty. They will be able to solve all problems that might arise in your growth to an initial public offering.

The size of firm consideration should also consider area of specialization, global reach, and fee structures.

In all resource organizations, there are generalists and specialists. Generalists have a general knowledge and skill set. Specialists focus on one specific area within a certain field. As the world becomes more complex and the information revolution continues, more information evolves in every field. It is hard for any one human being to keep up with it all. This notion is the one that Alvin Toffler expresses in *Future Shock*. As a consequence, in every field, specialization occurs. There are attorneys who specialize in legal proceedings that relate to pharmaceutical firms that specialize in pediatrics. There are advertising agencies that only deal with clients in the environmental area. There are bankers who only deal with financing farm machinery.

Area of specialization

You should assess your present and future needs to figure out whether you can live with a generalist resource organization or if you need a specialist.

Global reach is tied into the geographic scope that a firm has. If a firm only deals with issues that take place in one small town, this scope might be fine for you. Yet, if you face situations that might have far-reaching geographic concerns, you might need an organization that has greater global awareness.

Global reach

A friend of yours says that he or she can put you in touch with someone to get your software distributed in Hong Kong. You will need many resource organizations that have global tentacles if you decide to go through with this deal. First, you will need an organization that can explain to you both cultural and business mores in Hong Kong. How should you do business? You will not find this information in the resource organization that has never operated, let alone traveled, to Hong Kong. You will also need a bank that can process foreign currency, and if you get large enough, letters of credit. You probably want the bank to have a location in Hong Kong. Don't forget the advertising agency. They must be familiar with Hong Kong in order to create appropriate advertising. The faux pas that can occur if this understanding is not present can be potentially disastrous. Finally, your law firm must understand Hong Kong's laws. This understanding is an important issue. For example, the firm might tell you that Hong Kong doesn't adhere to the international copyright convention. As a result, software copying occurs all the time. In fact, when I visited the largest computer mall on mainland Hong Kong, it sold software by the disc, regardless of its contents. Lotus 1-2-3 and WordPerfect both sold for $5 (Hong Kong) multiplied by the number of discs that the software occupies.

Fee structures can and should be very important to you. You only have a limited number of financial resources. You have to use them wisely. Know what and how firms charge for their services.

Fee structure

Some types of resource organizations charge on an hourly basis; others charge on a project basis. Make sure you know how you will pay, up front, or you could be in for a big surprise. Before I learned this lesson, I was once and only once confronted with a legal bill that was thousands of dollars more than

I expected. Don't be afraid to ask all resource organizations what and how they bill.

Payment terms are another consideration. There are some resource organizations that request up-front retainers off of which they work. You might need to shell out $5000 before you get anything in return. If you don't feel comfortable with this arrangement, tell them. Make an arrangement with which you feel comfortable. Some firms bill monthly, and others bill on completion of the project. You must keep an eye on cash flow. Know how they will bill you.

There are also resource organizations that will recognize that you don't have a lot of money and you might need assistance in payment terms. Some firms will let you pay the bill over time. Other firms might even negotiate equity (if you want to give it to them) or a percentage of your gross (or net) revenues in return for services. Don't be afraid to be creative with a resource organization, especially if you don't have a lot of money available to you.

Locating organizations

You will need to explore a host of sources to find resource organizations and then choose the one or several that are right for your company. Start in the most obvious place.

Friends

Ask your friends first. Friends can often recommend reliable resource organizations. Goodness of fit and trustworthiness are important elements in your relationship with professional advisors. But be careful; your friends might not be the best pool of talent for you to use.

An example might be if you are extremely successful. At some point you decide to sell your company. You find another company to buy your company for $2 million. You have been the sole owner of the company. You ask a friend of yours, an attorney, to handle all of the final negotiations of the deal for a fee. It turns out that this friend is actually somewhat competitive with you. The attorney drags his or her feet on the deal. He or she negotiates in a fashion that is not exactly what you had intended. You sell your company for $1.5 million. Your friend, the attorney, receives a $15,000 fee, and you get $1,485,000. You might read this and think that this is a lot of money, and certainly it is. Yet this friend, who was somewhat envious, actually lost you $500,000 in the process of the negotiation. You think it might have been intentional, and you are infuriated. You might have only gotten $1.5 million anyway. You think that because your friend was involved, you got less than you would have otherwise received.

Remember that friendships can be destroyed over misunderstandings. When money is involved, these misunderstandings get blown out of proportion.

Use friends as a reference source, given you trust them and their judgment. Deal with people you might know initially as acquaintances, or deal with people referred to you by friends. Over time, these folks become your friends. The professional relationship came first and the friendship second. This process has an interesting implication in the relationship.

Another source of professional advisors is the yellow pages. If you need a professional organization that is located in a specific locale, the yellow pages can be a perfect source.

Yellow pages

Often resource organizations will take out advertisements in trade publications that are relevant to you and your business. For example, urban planners have trade publications. Computer firms that specialize in this area advertise in their trade publications. Sailboat magazines carry advertising from organizations that specialize in marine law, banking, and accounting. So the list goes on.

Trade publications

Professional associations are a good source of information about resource organizations for their members or prospective members. When I tried to establish a high-end train service between Philadelphia and New York, it was the industry's professional associations that helped me locate support organizations in that industry.

Professional associations

There are things that you should know about different resource organizations that will help you determine the correct firm for you and your computer company.

Typical resource organizations

Area of practice   In accounting firms, there are primarily three practice areas. The areas are tax, audit, and consulting.

Accounting firms

Tax   The tax practice in accounting firms is what you traditionally think of when you think of accountants. You link accountants to compliance issues with the United States' Internal Revenue Service if you're located in the United States. If not, you tie this practice area to your country's taxing authority. In the United States, accountants in tax practice are known for the tax forms they complete. From about January through April of the year, tax accountants fill out tax forms for people and corporations.

When tax accountants are not filling out tax returns, they review tax procedures and engage in one area of consulting, tax consulting. Tax accountants assist their clients, both individual and corporate, with ways to minimize the tax burden imposed on them by the Internal Revenue Service (in the United States).

Almost every corporation needs a tax accountant to help it prepare its annual tax forms. If an accountant assists you in preparing your tax form, the accountant signs your tax form. Many think that an accountant's signature on the bottom of the tax form greatly reduces the chances of an audit by the taxing authority. They particularly hold this belief if the accountant is a CPA (certified public accountant). People become CPAs by passing a rigorous examination (given by the state in which the accountant wishes to practice and, in some states, practice for a certain length of time).

Audit   An *audit* is a review. In the sense that most people hear the word, they become terrified. When you hear you will be audited, you commonly think of an audit (or a review) by the Internal Revenue Service. As most accountants practice this audit, it should not have that stigma. Individuals and corporations hire accountants that specialize in auditing to review their books. The most common reason they perform an audit is to use it in the preparation of financial statements. As you can read about in chapter 8, there are a host of financial statements that bring meaning to the financial position of the firm. Accountants who perform audits use the information from these audits to prepare financial statements. Based on the audit and the firm's financial statements, these practitioners write opinions about the statements they prepare.

If you run or plan to run a publicly held corporation, you will be forced to have this audit work done followed by the preparation of the financial statements. When this procedure occurs, the eventual statement that is prepared is called an *audited financial statement*. Lending sources (such as banks) require, even if you are not a publicly traded corporation, that you have annual, semiannual, or evenly quarterly audited financial statements prepared for them to review your financial position.

If an accountant accepts the numbers that you provide to prepare your financial statements, these statements are called *unaudited financial statements*. They might be acceptable financial statements to some lending organizations or to report to shareholders of privately held corporations. They are generally not acceptable to report information for a publicly held corporation.

You will probably not need audited financial statements initially. If you plan to take your company public, you might have your financial statements prepared in an audited fashion so that you can then present these statements to the public. If you run a privately held corporation that has no debt, you might never meet an accountant that is in an audit practice.

Consulting   Generally, it is the medium- to large-size accounting firms that have consulting practices. Initially, accounting firms limited their consulting practice to tax and accounting issues. Tax and financial statement preparation was done by the tax and accounting practice areas, respectively. Consulting work that accompanied each one of those areas was placed into the consulting practice of the firm. As time went on and accounting and financial systems became computerized, the consulting practice expanded to help the accounting and financial staffs deal with the computer systems that ran their accounting and financial programs. This practice area grew. Many accounting firms developed their consulting practices into management information systems (or computer systems, in general) practices. Some of the largest computer consulting firms in the world are the consulting divisions of the major accounting firms.

This situation can present an interesting opportunity for you. As someone who is or wants to run a computer-based firm, you can enlist help from accounting firms' systems practices if you are stumped with computer questions. You can also perform subcontracting work for an accounting practice. For example, if you are a database developer, the consulting area of the accounting firms might be able to use your talents on contracts that they have.

As a result of this systems consulting, accounting firms have even expanded this practice to include complete computer systems integration tasks as well as hardware and software sales.

With the trust and strong reference that so many of these accounting firms have from the tax and audit practices, they have a natural pipeline established to receive business. As a consequence, many accounting firms have developed or bought consulting practices that do everything from manufacturing to marketing to strategy business consulting.

Industry specialization   There are accounting firms that specialize in different industries. If your business is highly specialized and has specific accounting procedures that govern it, specialization by your accounting firm can be beneficial. The highly specialized accounting firms will bill more for their services than their generalist counterparts.

Global reach   Accounting practices and procedures are different between the municipal, state, federal, and international levels. If you operate in the City of Los Angeles, you must comply with the tax issues of Los Angeles (municipality), California (state), and the United States of America (federal) issues. If you hire an accounting firm from San Francisco, the firm might understand California and the United States accounting issues quite well. When it comes to the City of Los Angeles, the San Francisco firm might have to start from scratch. You will pay this accounting firm to learn about Los Angeles tax issues. If you had chosen an accounting firm that was already familiar with Los Angeles tax and accounting issues, you would not have to pay them to learn about these issues.

At a state level, you might have an even more difficult issue. State tax laws are different. If you hire an accounting firm from Los Angeles, California, to handle your tax issues in Reno, Nevada, they might have a much steeper learning curve. State tax laws are generally more complex than local municipal tax laws. If you want to compound the matter even further, look at tax issues from country to country. If you have an accountant in New York state and your business is located in Canada, you might have two problems using this accountant. First, the accountant might not know anything about Canadian tax and accountancy issues. You might pay a steep fee to get him or her up the learning curve. Secondly, Canada might have laws that require either certain residency in the country or passage of certain examinations to practice in Canada.

The more global any of these issues becomes, the more you have to be concerned with the type of accounting firm with which you deal. Smaller firms generally deal with smaller geographic areas than do larger firms (especially larger firms with offices in multiple cities, states, or countries). Think this issue through to figure out where you should go based on your firm's growth strategy.

Size Accounting firms come in all sizes. They range from one man operations to firms with thousands of employees. You should probably interview firms of all sizes in order to see what each one offers you now and in the future. Until merger mania started, when all of the accounting firms began to merge, there were a group of very large accounting firms called the "Big Eight" firms—eight companies that were recognized to be the largest firms in the world. These firms are now called the "Big Six." Today these large firms include Deloite & Touche, Arthur Anderson, KPMG, Ernst & Young, and Coopers & Lybrand. Merger mania is also taking place in the medium-size firms. Because many of them are regionally based, it would take volumes to list them all. If you look up accountants in the yellow pages, you should look for clusters of individual names with the same telephone number. These clusters will give you some indication of the size of the firms with which the accountants are associated. Then start to interview small, medium, and large firms (if all are present in your global reach).

Fee structure Accounting firms have fee structures based on many different factors. Hourly rates can range from $35 to $500, depending upon the firm's size, specialization, geographic location, area of practice, and individual in the firm who does the work.

The hierarchy of a firm is different for firms of different size. The fees are therefore different. A manager with a specialty in a large firm might bill more than a partner in a small firm with no specialty. Ask the accounting firm who will work on your account and what they will bill. You probably should ask for written estimates (or formal quotes) as to the price of various types of work (that is, how much will it cost to complete my company's tax return?).

Advertising agencies Advertising agencies perform several services, based on their size. These services include marketing strategy development, creative advertising development, advertising placement, market research, and public relations. Starting out, you might need assistance in marketing strategy development, although you probably won't be able to afford it. The same is probably true with advertising placement and market research.

Area of practice   Advertising agencies often specialize in various areas of practice.

Marketing strategy development   Many advertising agencies, regardless of size, will assist you in developing a marketing strategy for your business. This strategy should include all elements of the marketing mix—product, place, price, and promotion. This type of strategy should include a sales force (sales) strategy. Depending upon the type of agency, you might decide to look elsewhere for assistance in the development of a sales force strategy.

To develop a marketing strategy, you will probably be billed on either an hourly fee or project basis. If the advertising agency has worked with marketing strategies in your area, they might charge you on a project basis. If they perceive too many unknown time requirements, they might opt to bill you on a straight hourly basis. If the agency believes that it can recoup fees in other ways, such as advertising placement, they might not even charge you for this component of their services. With a business just starting out on a shoestring, it is highly unlikely that they will charge you based on advertising placement.

To save money, you might bring in an advertising agency to check or endorse your marketing strategy. Independently develop a marketing strategy. Then take it to the advertising agency for their feedback. You should pay them strictly for their time, and it could be beneficial for you in developing the marketing strategy.

Creative advertising development   Typically when you think of an advertising agency, you think of the work from the creative side of the house—the creative department. The creative department in a small advertising agency might be one person, the owner of the agency. In medium to large advertising agencies, there are teams of people. These creative teams come up with creative campaigns for companies. These creative campaigns include work in print (direct mail pieces, newspaper and magazine advertisements, billboards, signs, and literature or brochures) and the broadcasting media (radio and television).

The sexy part of the creative department's work is the broadcast media campaigns, especially television. Television enables creative departments to let their imaginations go wild. The intent of this (as well as other) advertising is to gain awareness, interest, purchase intent, and eventually purchase. The more effective the advertising reinforces the message, the better it will be to drive people to the point of purchase (and repeat purchase).

Fees for creative departments are frequently absorbed because the advertising placement fee is so large that the creative fee is dwarfed by it.

This situation will not be the case for you or your company initially. It is most likely that the only part of an advertising agency that you will use is the creative department. You will often use them only for the creation of a product or service brochure or some other simple advertising that you might use in a magazine or newspaper advertisement. If you find yourself in this situation, there is a way for you to save some money. The advertising agency will want to charge you a fee for their work. On top of this fee, they will want to place the advertising for you. You might opt to place the advertising yourself.

Advertising placement   Typically, an advertising agency will get a 15% discount off of the advertising rate quoted by the media source, be it television, radio, newspapers, or magazines. If you tell the media source that you will give them production-ready television commercials, radio spots, or print advertising, and you are placing it through an advertising agency, you can get that 15% discount. You might, therefore, set up a division of your company that is there just to place advertising. You set up the advertising division by naming it. For example, The Computer Software Company's advertising division might be called "The Advertising Company, a division of The Computer Software Company." For many media sources, this type of activity is perfectly acceptable. The result for you can be a tremendous saving. If you take out $1000 worth of advertising, normally this vehicle will save you $150 on each placement. If you don't want the savings, you can certainly send them to me.

There are large advertising agencies that typically place millions of dollars of advertising for companies. On a $70 million media placement, the advertising agency would make $10.5 million. Do you now see why they might absorb some of the creative and marketing strategy work?

Market research   Chapter 6 discusses many of the dimensions of market research. The larger advertising agencies will have market research departments that can help to determine the appropriate overall marketing strategy. Usually, advertising agencies perform market research on a fee basis. They will look at the needs of the project and give you a proposal for the work. The market research departments of an advertising agency compete with stand-alone market research firms. Yet, they can often provide identical services to dedicated market research firms. Both of these firms might subcontract part of the market research, depending upon what the market research needs of the project are.

Public relations   Public relations is one of those misunderstood areas in marketing. The end result of public relations, if successful, is to create editorial coverage of news, features, or other events that relate to your company. Many medium-sized and larger advertising agencies either have public relations departments or own public relations companies. On a fee basis, they try to stir up awareness for their clients. It is often said that nonadvertising copy has much more credibility than does advertising copy. The goal of public relations is to create media coverage—newspaper, magazine, radio, or television. Credibility is increased by virtue of the fact that some editorial-type person has endorsed the news or event and deemed it viable for coverage.

Although you can create your own public relations campaign (see chapter 6), there are people within this area in advertising agencies or in stand-alone public relations firms (see the section covering public relations firms in this chapter) that have an industry specialization. They know all of the editors of the newspapers, magazines, radio, and television stations. These folks can make a simple telephone call and have your event covered. Although you can make these contacts on your own to achieve the same ends, you might not have the 10-year relationship built up between an editor that someone who focuses in on building these relationships might have.

Fees for this type of work are commonly hourly fees, although entire public relations campaigns can be priced out for you. If you intend to use this type of service, find out what other press the agency has been able to achieve for other clients.

A byproduct of this public relations is credible literature. You might have had a write-up on your product or service in *PC Week* magazine. You can now take that write-up and either make photocopies of it yourself or buy reprints directly from the magazine. You can then use these reprints for promotional purposes of your firm. Some magazines and newspapers have no reprinting capabilities. Therefore, they will tell you that you can make reprints. If you find yourself in this position, make sure you get written permission from the publisher to make these reprints. On the reprints (generally at the bottom), be sure to include a phrase that says, "Reprinted with the permission of xyz publisher." Be sure to include the masthead of the publication with the date and issue number of the publication. This attribution reinforces the credibility that you have gotten in print. Similar reprints are possible in radio and television with attribution. Essentially, you make statements such as, "Here's what XYZ radio stations says about our product."

Radio, television, and print endorsements can be used as a part of an advertisement you create. Always remember the attribution.

Industry specialization   Because so much can go into a marketing strategy and creative advertising work, advertising agencies frequently specialize in one or more industries. I still remember the small advertising agency (about six people) with whom my business started. They were and are tremendous people. Their focus, when I came along, was political and environmental advertising. They not only accepted my account but they found my first set of investors in an effort to ensure that they would be paid for their work (but also because they are good people). After they put together the initial service brochure, one of the principals came to me and said they would not be able to do any more work for my company. Initially, I was somewhat taken aback. After I listened to the reasoning, I understood completely. In order to keep up with the computer industry, it takes a lot of time and effort, they reasoned. (Something that any of us in the industry can easily understand.) They told me that they had attempted to get other clients in the computer industry to add this industry specialization to their focus. After six months, they were unsuccessful. They also could not see enough work coming from my company's account to justify the amount of time necessary to keep up with the industry. So they went back to their environmental and political work.

The lesson is simple. Pick an advertising agency that either has experience in the computer industry or will invest the resources to support it.

Global reach   Depending on the quality of the advertising agency's work and the industry focus that it might have, global reach might not be as important as it is in an accounting or law firm. You might be able to travel far and wide if the work and industry familiarity of the advertising agency is worth the trek. An advertising agency choice should take on a global perspective if your business is or becomes international. There are many cultural differences between countries and regions of the world. If you want to target a specific area and you do not take into consideration the various cultural mores, especially as they relate to creative advertising, you could find yourself not being understood. If you are or intend to conduct business globally, you should choose an advertising agency with this factor in mind.

Size   Advertising agencies come in all shapes and sizes. You must take all of the factors mentioned in this section into account before you choose a small, medium, or large agency. Interview all those agencies that will speak to you. You might find that really large advertising agencies might not consider you to be large enough for them to justify their overhead. They might reject your account.

Unless you can go to Madison Avenue in New York, you will probably deal with local or regional advertising agencies. Most of the truly large advertising agencies have some sort of presence in New York City.

Fee structure   Fee structures vary based on the size of the firm as well as the type of work done. Fees can be calculated on an hourly, project, or advertising placement basis.

Your big question should be, "How do I judge the quality of an advertising agency's work?" For different areas of practice, you will use different criteria. The best way, in all instances, is to ask to see samples of their work. If you need to judge how well they can create a marketing strategy, ask to see other marketing strategies and their results. Often, companies will not allow advertising agencies to release this type of information to potential clients. If you encounter this situation, ask to speak with the clients who the agency will give you as a reference.

In creative work, advertising agencies always have something called a *portfolio*. The *portfolio* consists of all of the work that they have done that they want you to see. If they work in print, you will see all types of print advertising. If they work in electronic media (radio and television), you should see all sorts of television advertisements and hear different radio spots. Even if you only want to have the agency do work in one medium, you should see and hear what they have done in other areas. Creative departments tend to be somewhat holistic. You can judge overall quality by the work they do in all areas, especially if an advertising agency has done an integrated media campaign. You will see how one theme has been translated to another medium.

If you like what you see, don't look further. If you don't, keep on looking. It can be a lot of fun shopping for an advertising agency. Enjoy it!

Banks

Bankers can provide invaluable assistance to you in areas where you might otherwise pay for services. Bankers can provide you with loans, estate and financial planning and cash collection services.

Area of practice   Even banks have different areas of practice. Some are discussed below.

Account maintenance   Probably the first and most common experience that you will have with a banker is a depository relationship. You will either have your money on deposit at a bank in a checking, savings, or money market account. The banker holds your money until you need it. For some checking accounts, the bank will not pay you anything for this right (although the bank will earn money from your money by lending it out or depositing it in interest earning vehicles). For a savings and money market account, they will pay you some interest rate for the use of your funds.

Brokerage   Banks serve as brokers for securities, both bonds and equities. They compete with brokerage companies (see brokerage companies) that buy and sell securities on behalf of their clients. Bankers provide this service for a fee, which is associated with the transaction itself.

Lending   Bankers are most often associated with lending money. People and businesses need to borrow money for a variety of reasons. Bankers provide money to them in return for their own return (an *interest rate*) over a set period of time (*term*). Lending decisions are generally made by a loan committee of a bank. They want to understand the reasons to make the loan and the source of its repayment. Bankers want to get back the money they have loaned to you in addition to a fair interest on that money. They have to ensure that the risk is not an unreasonable one. That's why borrowers are frequently classified into risk categories. People and corporations are either good or bad risks (or somewhere in between). Your risk assessment is based on your record of repayment.

If there is no historical record of repayment (which is very often the case with a new business), it becomes very hard for a banker to judge what will happen. The bank must look to the people behind the new corporation to see their credit worthiness. The personal credit history of the owner of a new company might or might not reflect on the future credit record that will develop in a company. For this reason, if the company has no history, or the banker doesn't like (or feel comfortable with) the credit history of the company, the individuals might be asked to somehow secure the repayment of the loan. This security can come from either a personal guarantee (where you guarantee that no matter what happens to the corporation, you will repay) or be insured for repayment by something called *collateral*.

Collateral is something that gives a banker a method of repayment. It is a financial asset that can be translated into money in order to repay a loan. Collateral can be pieces of real estate, computers, plant and equipment, or anything that can be translated into money.

When a banker feels that the credit of the individual or the corporation is a good enough risk, the bank will not need security in the loan's repayment. In this situation, the loan is called an *unsecured loan*.

If and when you need a loan for your business, you might find that you have to either personally guarantee the loan or put up your own collateral if there is no operating history to your business. Even after time, if you have a completely service-oriented business with no hard assets, you will still need to give a personal guarantee. The guarantee is necessary unless you have repeat revenues and your cash flow is so solid that your company is considered to be a good credit risk.

As a lender, a banker makes money through the difference between the cost of his money and what can be charged to you on a loan. Your bank borrows money (from the Federal Reserve Bank) at the prime rate (the rate at which the Federal Reserve Board will loan to the nation's largest and most reputable banks) at a certain interest rate. Assume the rate is 7%. They charge you 10%. Your bank's profit is 3% on the loan. This 3% is not all profit. All of the expenses associated with processing the loan have to come out of this 3%. In some cases, the bank will charge you something called a *loan origination fee*, which might cover some of the overhead involved in the origination of the loan.

Banks will lend money at different rates based on how much money you want to borrow, the nature of your credit history, and the term. If they can borrow long-term money more inexpensively than short-term money, you will probably get a better long-term rate. If your credit history is better than the next guy's, the rate on your loan will be lower than the other guy's loan (generally more the case with corporate loans). If you want to borrow $1000, and the next guy wants to borrow $500,000, the other guy might get a better loan rate. Actually, all of these factors go into the rate and term of your loan.

Lending varies tremendously from bank to bank. In some banks (large, medium, or small), it is still possible to get a loan based on your father's relationship with the bank. In other banks, it doesn't matter who your relatives are; your rate is assessed only on credit worthiness.

If and when you apply for a loan, you will probably need to present the banker with a business plan (see chapter 5) as well as personal financial statements. Your business plan should include the reason why you want the loan and your method of repayment. The loan committee (which might only be one person in the bank) will meet and decide your fate.

Estate planning   *Estate planning* is done to figure out what happens to your estate once you die. If you are the key person in your business and the bank has a $500,000 unsecured loan issued to your business, they want to be sure that they will get their money back. As a result, they might get involved in your estate planning. They might make you purchase a life insurance policy with the bank designated as the beneficiary.

They can also get involved in your personal estate to the extent that you wish. Bankers are often trustees of estates and assist in the settlement of affairs. In this instance, some type of a fee might be associated with this estate work, either on an ongoing basis or at settlement.

Initially, when you start your business, neither one of these relationships might be relevant. Although, there are instances where life insurance policies are necessary to create a lending relationship.

Financial advising and planning   You should plan your business well from all perspectives, but be especially careful of your financial picture. Bankers often lend financial planning assistance (both personal and corporate) in order to secure their present and future position with their lending relationship. After all, if they assist you in making sound financial planning decisions, you might need more money that, in turn, can generate more fees for them. In this role, they are in direct competition with accounting firms, brokerage firms, and financial planners. Very often, bankers do not accept a fee for this service. They view it as a cost of either advertising (for future loans) or an ongoing cost of processing the existing loans.

There are various types of loans. Please refer to chapter 10 to explore them more fully.

Cash-collection services   Banks want to get their money. One way that they can get their money is to ensure that you get your money. Therefore, they have a host of vehicles that can help you get paid. These vehicles range from letters of credit (letters that are written by banks that assure the recipient that the money is actually in the account) or lock box services (where a bill is paid to a post office box to which only the bank has access, as is the case with accounts receivable financing). Wire transfers of money are another vehicle banks use to assist in collecting money quickly. In my service-based computer company, we often require that a retainer be wire transferred (or *wired*) into our account before we will start work for a company, especially if the company is located far away from us. If situations are real tough, bankers might even help you collect money directly from the corporations who owe you money.

If you do business internationally, letters of credit are an invaluable tool. You can ship goods halfway across the world. Yet you can't as cost effectively collect the money owed to you on those goods. If you do business even 100 miles away, you might find it very helpful to have money wired into your account before you begin your service for your client.

Industry specialization   Traditionally, commercial banks executed loans to be used in commerce, and savings and loan associations (another form of bank) executed loans to be used in real estate. There is a change in this situation, especially with all the troubles that both types of banking organizations have had recently. Commercial banks now execute real estate loans, but the converse is also true.

Many lenders have chosen to specialize in one type of loan. It is generally the smaller banks that have chosen this practice. The benefit is that banks who are lenders to the boat retailing industry really know the nuances of that industry. The problem is that if boat retailers begin to experience difficulties, the entire loan portfolio of the bank could be in jeopardy.

If you want to find banks that specialize in lending to the computer industry, one of the best places to find them is in areas of a high concentration of companies in the computer industry (for example, the Route 128 corridor in Boston, Silicon Valley, and now pockets such as Boca Raton, and Route 202 in Philadelphia).

From your perspective, as long as a bank loans you money at favorable terms, you shouldn't care what their own diversification might be. If they know your industry, can make loan decisions based on their knowledge and help your company grow through the contacts that they have, so much the better.

Global reach   If you are manufacturing part of a computer you have designed in the Far East, you want a banker who is knowledgeable about international banking issues. If you think you'll expand your geographic scope, you will want a banker who can support you in your efforts. Very often you will find that a smaller banking organization just doesn't have the reach that you need to do business globally.

Size   A bank's size can be a factor in your choice. Small banks often have a much more personal relationship with their customers than do larger banks. Some perceive that small banks are not as sophisticated as are larger banks. Small banks might have to charge more for their loans because they don't have access to the same low cost funds (from the Federal Reserve) as do their larger counterparts. Yet small banks might also be lending private individuals' capital. Therefore, they might be able to loan money more cheaply because their cost of capital is less than larger organizations. The fees of smaller banks might be less than larger banks because their overhead might be lower. Smaller banks might have a greater specialization in a certain area than a larger bank. There are so many variables in size issues that you must determine what the bank will offer you and then you can make the decision as to its value.

Fee structure   Banks extract transaction-based fees. It is extremely rare to see a bank bill on an hourly basis.

Area of practice   Some of the areas of practice that you will typically encounter with brokerage companies follow.

Brokerage companies

Brokerage services   *Brokerage companies* or *securities brokers*, are companies that are licensed by the various securities exchanges in the United States to execute trades in bonds and equities (stocks). These companies make their money through the fees that they generate from their trades. If you have any extra money that you want to invest in some type of a security, you might turn to a broker to have the broker execute a trade for you to either acquire or dispose of equities or bonds.

Brokerage companies traditionally gave their clients investment advice. They told them their feelings on what they should or should not invest. These firms were and are called *full-service brokerage firms*. Today, there are brokerage firms that give no advice but just execute trades. These firms are called *discount brokerage firms*. Both types are licensed to execute trades. In the second type of firm, the firm has a lower overhead because they don't employ people to give you advice; they just take orders. As a result, fees of discount brokerage firms can be lower than those of full-service brokerage firms. Many full-service brokerage firms have been forced to react to this pressure and offer both advice and discount brokerage rates that can put the squeeze on their profitability.

You can benefit from this trend. Get advice from full-service brokerage firms. Then play the discount firms' transaction fee structure off the full-service brokerage firm to get the best deal going. (Apologies to all of my full-service broker friends.)

Some brokerage companies let you execute securities transactions via computer terminals. You can trade off of your account at any time of day from any place in the world over modems and telephone lines.

Financial advisors and planners   On a fee basis, just as with accounting firms and financial advisory firms, people within brokerage companies can serve as financial advisors. Selection criteria should be based upon past performance, which you ascertain from other clients. However, in the financial advising business, past performance is not necessarily an indicator of future performance.

Industry specialization   In order to execute trades for clients (both personal and corporate), brokerage companies often specialize in certain areas. There are brokerage companies that follow computer stocks and bonds, solely, and trade in them. Again, the problem for firms that specialize in a single industry is the issue of diversification of risk. If the industry in which they specialize fails to perform well, their entire business could be in jeopardy.

Global reach   With the advent of telephone systems throughout the world, all brokerage companies are now accessible from most anywhere. Via computer telecommunications networks, you can execute a trade any time of the day.

If you want advice on equities that are traded on global markets, you will need to talk to people who specialize in those markets. If you want to trade equities on the Tokyo or London exchange, you are best served by brokers familiar with those exchanges.

Size   Brokerage firms range in size from one person to thousands of people. You must assess what you want from a broker—advice, transaction fees, industry specialization, or global reach. Then assess your trust/confidence factor in the individual with whom you will be dealing. Interviews and reference checks can often help you in your decision.

Fees   Fees are transaction-based for the brokerage side of the house and hourly or project-based for financial advising and planning.

Consultants

Consultants come in all shapes, sizes and varieties. They range from generalists to specialists. There are strategic thinkers and those who implement the ideas of the thinkers. Some folks think that consultant is a catch-all phrase for people who are unemployed or between jobs. Consultants are people or firms who can offer you outside expertise to assist you to plan or implement a specific situation.

Area of practice   Consultants' areas of practice are as diverse as the people who make up the organizations within this catch-all profession.

Industry specialization   The industries in which consultants specialize are also diverse. You can find everything from computer to fine food consultants.

Global reach   A consultant's perspective can be extremely ethnocentric (provincial) or it can be geocentric (worldly). You must match your present and future needs in an area to your need for each type of perspective.

Size   Consulting firms vary in size from one person to thousands.

Fees   Fees might be hourly or project-based. The lowest hourly fee that I could find is $15. The highest hourly rate I could find was a strategic management consultant whose hourly rate is $3125.

Financial advisors

Area of practice   Like the financial advising arms of accounting firms, banks, and brokerage companies, stand-alone financial advisors and planners assist in both personal and corporate financial planning. Almost anyone can hang out a shingle and become a financial advisor or a financial planner, so be very careful if you want to use one.

Financial advisors can advise you in matters of accounts receivable, accounts payable, general ledger, inventory, and payroll. They can assist you with financial statements like profit-and-loss, cash flow, balance sheets, and break-even analysis. They can give you advice on debt versus equity financing. They can give you investment advice. They can be invaluable to you in your business, especially if this area is not your strength or any of the team members of your firm. Yet they can also create absolute misery if you entrust them and they are either wrong by giving you poor advice, not frequent enough advice, or unlawful advice. I learned this area cold so that I could judge advice that I receive, which is a good idea. There are more tales of companies going out of business because they entrusted their financial advising and planning to companies or individuals that either didn't know what they were doing or were incorrect in their approach. Choose your financial advisors and planners very carefully. Check their reputations out thoroughly with as many of their clients as you can possibly reach.

Industry specialization   Just as in resource organizations like banks and brokerage firms, financial advisors and planners can focus in on certain industries. If you want financial planners in the computer industry, you are best served by those pockets where the industry is located.

Global reach   Financial advisors and planners should be knowledgeable of more global issues if you perceive yourself or your firm to deal with them now or in the future. Choose your financial advisors accordingly.

Size   Financial advisors and planners come in all sizes. Reputation and trust are the most important elements on which to judge a financial advising firm. Size is probably irrelevant to you unless your matters are so complex that you need a team of advisors that you can only find in a larger firm.

Fees   Generally, financial advisors and planners work on an hourly or project fee basis.

Insurance agencies   **Area of practice**   Insurance agencies engage primarily in two things: placement of insurance (through what is commonly referred to as *insurance brokerage*) and financial advising (usually employing insurance as a financial investment vehicle).

Insurance brokerage   Insurance agents commonly sell four different types of insurance—property and casualty, life, health, and disability insurance. The risks are assumed by pools of individuals or corporations who underwrite the risk in return for the collection of the premiums on those risks.

Assess all insurance policies carefully for their costs and benefits before you sign up for any of them. It is wise to get competing quotes from a host of insurance brokers before you decide on one that makes sense for you or your company.

There are many companies that require that you have a certain size business before they will give you coverage, especially for health insurance. It's one of the reasons so many small companies don't offer coverage. It is not easy for them to obtain it. Vehicles do exist for small company coverage. They are pools established by either independent businesses, chambers of commerce, or municipal governments. The concept is quite simple: in isolation, there might be 100 businesses with two employees. None are large enough to receive coverage of any type of insurance by themselves. Their risk pools aren't large enough. When you take all 100 businesses and put them together, now you have one pool of 200 people that is an acceptable size for a risk pool. Risk is not the only issue. Processing fees for small groups might be too high for an insurance company to process. Often, an independent organization will do all of the paperwork and processing either for a fee (independent businesses set up to pool insurance) or as a benefit of membership (for members of chambers of commerce). Then, the insurance company can reduce its costs of processing the transaction so that it can now accept these risks on which it will make money.

- Property and casualty insurance (also called P and C) is insurance that covers items of property loss or casualty. The computer that you use in your business should be covered by property insurance. This insurance can cover such items as theft, loss of business, and errors and omissions. If you have property in your business, you want the basic theft coverage. If you could lose business because of a computer failure, you want business interruption coverage. If you run a computer service business and your client depends on you for crucial decisions in the client's business, you might want to have errors and omissions coverage. If you have the coverage, make a costly mistake with regards to your client and you are sued, you are protected to the dollar limits of the coverage, with respect to the client's recovery.

- Life insurance is coverage that pays out a benefit only if the individual who is covered (the insured) dies. You might be required to get key-man life insurance if you have an investor who wants a mechanism to recoup his or her loan or investment should you die. Life insurance is commonly a benefit that you will give to your employees. In doling out life insurance, companies often cover between one and two times the annual salary of the individual. For example, if you have an employee who earns $25,000 a year, typical life insurance coverage would be between $25,000 and $50,000. Companies frequently allow the individual to increase this coverage by paying an additional premium.

- Health insurance is becoming a common benefit in most companies. Coverage in this area falls into major medical, hospitalization, dental, and prescription drugs. Health insurance can be provided through what is called an HMO (health maintenance organization) or a medical insurance company. HMOs typically tell you who the doctors and hospitals are that you can use. HMO coverage might seem to be less expensive than coverage provided by the more common medical insurance providers (such as Blue Cross/Blue Shield). Under an HMO policy, they frequently dictate that you must see a doctor in their pool of physicians or you must go to a hospital in their cache of hospitals. This factor often deters people from these types of HMOs. Yet with the popularity of HMOs, more physicians and hospitals seem to participate in this coverage. As a result, you might not have any problem going to the physician or hospital of your choice.

- Disability insurance can be invaluable. It provides an income stream in the event that you become disabled and can't do your job. Although most people never think they will become disabled, it is more probable that you will become disabled than you will die in your working life. Even though this is true, many more people have life insurance than they do disability insurance.

  It is important that a disability insurance policy covers you if you cannot return to your regular occupation. Assume that you are someone who runs a data-entry service bureau and you actually do data entry. You now have an accident in which you are blinded and you lose eight of your ten fingers. Although you can still speak, you can't perform data entry nor can you adequately run your business. Therefore, you should be considered to be disabled and qualify for disability insurance. Although I am no legal expert and this scenario is completely fabricated, it might not hold up under certain policies. Someone can argue that you can still enter data with a voice-recognition input device. Check the language of any disability policy to make sure that you understand what events are covered. Ask any insurance broker to let you read the complete policy before you sign it. If you don't understand it, find someone who does understand it. Getting this assistance will help ensure that you will truly receive the coverage that you think you will receive.

Disability insurance is based on your income previous to your disability. Insurance companies ask for proof of income to enable you to get certain levels of coverage. The level of your coverage is almost always only a portion of your income, not the entire income. Tax planning strategies can assist in ways to reduce any tax burden of pay out. Make sure that you consult with a tax accountant or a tax attorney before you blindly accept the tax consequences as outlined by an insurance broker. Remember, they want to sell you insurance.

There is generally some time period before your disability insurance benefits begin. For example, you might have to be disabled for 90 days until the policy starts to pay you premiums. Therefore, a gap remains between the time you become disabled and the time that you start to collect on the policy. Many disability policies will let you cover part or all of this gap period with an additional premium. Carefully assess what you will pay to shorten this gap.

Financial advisors   Insurance can be used as an investment vehicle. Many insurance brokers try to differentiate themselves by offering a financial advisory service. Many insurance brokers take examinations to become certified financial consultants. When completed, they can offer two services: insurance brokerage and financial advising. When you are approached by insurance brokers who are also financial advisors, you should ask how they are compensated. In more cases than not, they are compensated if you purchase some investment vehicle from them. If they answer you in this fashion, you should immediately become suspect of their advice. They will suggest investment vehicles in which they receive a return. Can they be unbiased and objective? Will they tell you that you should purchase investment vehicles that they don't offer? No, they won't make any money this way.

Many companies who are the original offerer of an investment vehicle might compensate their agents with schedules that might be different from other companies. In this fashion, the agent now has an incentive to sell one company's vehicle over another company's if he or she makes more from it than another instrument.

Good financial advisors, as well as insurance brokers, will be quick to point out to you that insurance can be an investment. As you pay premiums on a life insurance policy, the cash value of the policy builds. This cash value, plus the accrued interest, is rightfully your money. You can lay claims to it, before you die, by borrowing from the cash value. There is a set interest rate when you borrow off a cash value of an insurance policy. This amount is established as a part of the policy itself. This amount is most always less than the prevailing rates in the market. As a result, many people borrow from the policy. If there is an outstanding borrowed balance at death, this amount will be subtracted from the amount that is paid to the beneficiary of the life insurance policy.

Industry specialization   To better understand risks, insurance brokers will also specialize in industries. This industry specialization is seen in the property and casualty area in most instances.

Global reach   Many underwriters need to have a global perspective because of the nature of their clients' international operations.

Individual insurance agents might not have this same global outlook as the large underwriters. There are large bands of brokers in firms such as Johnson & Higgins and Alexander & Alexander who have offices throughout the world. Therefore, they can handle risks for you or your business almost anywhere. Again, you must assess your present and future needs to determine the type of insurance broker you retain at different points in the life of your business.

Size   Size of insurance agents can determine the type of underwriters with whom they might operate. There are some large underwriters who don't want to deal with one-person agencies (as sole practitioners are called in this industry). Other large underwriters might target these small sole practitioners. Try and get quotes from small, medium, and large underwriters. Some of the larger underwriters (via their agents) might not want to accept your account because the processing costs involved with it are not justified by your premium.

Frequently with smaller agencies, the agency might specialize either in life and health or in property and casualty. Therefore, if you deal with a smaller agency, you might have to deal with two different agencies—one for your life and health insurance and one for your property and casualty insurance.

Fees   Insurance agents generally receive their fees as a commission. This commission is based on the premium of the insurance policy. As long as the policy remains in effect, the agent will receive a commission on it. Under certain instances (for example, financial advisorship), an insurance agent might receive payment on a fee basis.

Investment bankers

Area of practice   Investment bankers are companies that raise funds for both corporations and government agencies. They raise money in the form of debt or equity. Instead of lending their own money (or borrowed money) as commercial banks and savings and loans might do, they go out to the market to raise debt or equity. The market as they define it consists of both private and public sources. They might go to a group of individuals or corporations to create a private placement. A private placement is an equity offering where a group of individuals or corporations take a stake in a company. The offering is not subject to all of the laws and regulations of the Securities and Exchange Commission because of the offering size (in terms of number of participants as well as dollars). The offering is still subject to some regulations.

In all of these instances, investment bankers price out the deals (as they call all debt and equity offerings) based on similar deals that have been done in the market, the size of the deal, the size and credit worthiness of the firm, and the term of the deal (if a debt offering). Once the deal is priced, it is then sold to the private individuals or corporations or the public through another arm of the investment bank. The deal is sold, commonly on what is referred to as a *best-efforts* basis (the investment banker says that it will make its best efforts to sell the debt or equity). If it does all sell, the investment banker might have special provisions put into the deal for its own benefit (it might be able to buy equity at a cheaper than market price or debentures at a discounted price). When and if the deal is finally sold to the public, the investment banker will then promise to keep the offering somewhat *liquid*, which means that the debt or the equity can somehow be traded. In order to perform this function, they then trade the securities, unless there are restrictions on them that might be the case with privately held securities. In this role, investment bankers function much the same way that brokerage firms do.

Investment bankers should be involved in your company if you are or want to take your company public or if you just want to raise funds for your company through a private placement. If you plan to raise funds, you might want to place an investment banker on your board of directors to keep an eye on things to ensure that you are moving in the right direction for an eventual private or public offering.

Corporate finance   Investment bankers can specialize in corporate finance, the financing of debt and equity in both the private and public markets solely for corporations. The corporate finance department does everything that leads up to the placement of the deal. It makes assessments of the company and the market for various types of securities at any one point in time. It will set the terms of the deal that include the very last thing that is does, pricing the deal. Once the deal is priced, the corporate finance department turns the deal over to the sales department to sell it to private individuals, corporations or the public.

Municipal finance   *Municipal finance* is the financing of municipalities. The municipal finance department functions in the same role as does the corporate finance departments by placing both debt and equity to private individuals, corporations, or the public. The only difference between a municipal and corporate finance operation is the market that it serves. You will have no interest, probably, in dealing with a municipal finance department, unless you can benefit from some low-interest debt financing that takes place in a municipality and in turn is passed on to the companies that operate within that municipality.

Several years ago, a type of bond called an IRB (industrial revenue bond) was very popular as a vehicle to provide funds to municipalities. These bonds carried with them some tax benefits for the holders of the bonds. They also enabled the municipalities to pay a lower interest rate on them. The municipalities passed on this lower interest rate to finance industrial activities in its municipality. In Philadelphia, some of this money was used to purchase buildings (which were frequently accompanied by working capital) at an interest rate lower than what a company could receive from any other source. The catch was that the company had to locate in the city of Philadelphia. The city of Philadelphia benefited in a number of ways. It received the interest on the bonds, business taxes from the business (which were hopefully increased as a result of this financing) and additional wage tax from the increased number of employees that the company could employ as a result of this new funding. The company received the benefit of the funds for use in its growth.

IRBs lost their appeal with the changing tax laws but there are still some vehicles like them available within certain municipalities—ask your own city, county, and state for more details on what might be available to you. Because one of the primary goals of this activity was to add to the employment (and therefore tax) base of the municipality, money was often given (and even preference shown) to start-up businesses that would positively impact on the employment situation in the municipality.

Sales and trading/brokerage   The sales department of the investment bank picks up on a security once the corporate or municipal finance department has priced it. The sales department then endeavors to sell the securities at the best terms possible. The sales function corresponds to the brokerage firm's selling efforts and is rewarded the same way. The sales department receives a transaction fee on each sale. The sales department makes its securities available through traders who officially make the market in the security. They are the people who execute the trade or the transaction. If you are involved in a private or public offering with an investment bank, you are very concerned that these people execute their jobs well. You want to ensure that you sell as much debt or equity (as outlined under the offering) as possible at the best possible terms for the company. Your financial fate can rest in the hands of these people. For instance, if you try to issue equity and it is priced by the corporate finance department at $10 a share, you hope that the people in the sales department can sell the equities for at least $10 a share. If you offer 100,000 shares for an expected total sale of $1 million, if the sales department only gets $7 a share, your offering will only gross $700,000. If the sales department is stellar in performance and they are able to get you $15 a share, your offering will gross $1.5 million. Do you now see how these folks can make or break what you have worked so hard to achieve?

Financial advising   Investment bankers are often retained on an hourly or project fee basis to give financial advice. Although this advice might be similar to financial advice found in other resource organizations, it most frequently centers on potential debt or equity offerings. As such, it can also involve the valuation of businesses. You would probably receive this type of assistance from the corporate finance department.

Industry specialization   Because of the complexity of this business, there are a couple of types of specialization. There are firms that specialize in the computer industry such as Hambrecht & Quist and Alex Brown & Sons. These same firms also specialize in initial public offerings; specialization by offering type—another dimension. There are so many published reports in the investment banking area that you can tell by reading the *Wall Street Journal* what investment banks are working in what industries and with what types of offerings.

Global reach   Global reach can be very important in a firm's ability to make a market for your securities. If money is flowing in Japan but not in the United States, you want to be sure that your investment bank has access to this money (unless you, for some reason, don't want foreign investors in your business). You don't necessarily have to do business abroad to take advantage of the money that is available from abroad. Be mindful of this fact when you choose an investment bank.

Size   Investment banks are divided into three categories—*boutiques* (small firms), regional firms (medium-sized firms) and large firms. If your needs can be met by a specialized boutique (that only operates in the computer industry and might have access to only $100 million), then this firm might be the firm for you. Size can sometimes imply more access to capital, but size might not be a good measure of access to capital. Scope out firms' performances and reputations very carefully before you let size sway you in one direction or another.

Fees   Investment banks earn their fee through either transaction, project or hourly fees or by taking a piece of the deal. All of these structures are outlined above. Because many of the investment banker's fees are associated with the deal, it is imperative that you understand what your firm will and will not be responsible for in all instances. There are very often legal and accounting fees associated with these transactions. You might be responsible for these fees no matter what happens with the transaction. The investment banker might also have certain fees that you are charged no matter what the outcome of the deal. Be careful!

Law firms

There are many different areas in law practice and many different types of attorneys as a result. Attorneys are resource organizations who implement practices and procedures that are based on the law that is set by the legislature and interpreted by the courts. Attorneys set up vehicles for people and organizations to abide by these laws.

In many areas of law, contracts are put into place to establish practices and procedures in case certain events or directions might occur. Often these contracts are, or should be, an extension of a business concept or agreement, with clauses and constructs in them to protect all parties. You will probably deal with this area of the law—contracts—most frequently in your business. A contract is an agreement, either oral or written, in which at least two parties agree to something and in which consideration is involved. *Consideration* is present in a contract when one of the parties gives up something in order to get something. This definition is a general and partially complete definition of a contract. A complete and more specific definition would take pages. For that is what attorneys do on an ongoing basis—clarify, enhance, and play on nuances of meaning in order to protect all of those parties involved.

The law protects all of society's rights (and your rights in particular, in the area of a contract). Although it might do so, the more you try to protect your rights, the more you might put contracts in place to do so. Every time you attempt to protect yourself, you imply that you don't trust the other party or parties with whom you are dealing.

I have done the best business and had the best relationships without contracts. Whenever I feel the need for a contract between two parties, it seems, I feel that need because I am distrustful of the other party. As a result, I probably shouldn't do business with these parties in the first place. Trust, in any relationship, is the key element to success. The world has gotten so complex, though, that many argue that we need to protect ourselves with contracts. And as such, more frequently than not, we set up situations where we create distrust by throwing a contract in the way of a relationship. I am not advocating that you don't use contracts. I suggest only that you figure out when they are necessary—when you really need protection.

There are many contracts that can be put into place without attorneys. There are books in libraries (especially law libraries) and in bookstores that contain legal forms and contracts. The only concern that you might have (and an attorney will be quick to point out to you) is that these forms might not apply to your situation. If you are concerned about the relevancy of a generalized form, start with it and then have an attorney look at it to find the gaps.

Many attorneys feed on people's fear and need of protection. Because of people's ignorance of a situation, they will very often feel that they need overprotection. A good and honorable attorney (an oxymoron) will tell you when protection is or isn't necessary. Yet, you should always question what is or is not necessary, yourself. Experience is the only guide for this judgment. Initially, it will look as if you need a contract (or protection) for everything and that you should have an attorney review or draft any and all contracts into which you enter. Initially, this review might be a good idea. But as you gain experience in dealing with contracts, you will begin to see the areas where you need protection. You will begin to understand when you really need a contract and when you don't. You will also learn what you should and shouldn't include in a contract to give you the protection you need.

As you begin to learn these things, you might take the following steps. First, you might decide to take a stab at outlining what you feel should be in a contract. This practice can save you money (as attorneys frequently bill you by the hour). It will also ensure that your own intent is reflected in the legal document that eventually is drafted.

As you get even more confident, you might find contracts that you've either used before (which both reflected your intent and protected you) or you will find contracts that other companies use that you like. You can then begin to use all or part of these documents in other documents. You will save money on legal fees and reap the benefit of incorporating your intent through this vehicle.

If there is some dispute that arises and you want to settle it, you might look to the contract that you have in place. Given that there is an underlying contract that covers the situation and both parties agree to the settlement of the dispute based on the contractual terms, you are fine. There are many instances, though, where there is disagreement on contractual terms and the dispute can't be settled. Or there is no underlying contract and the governing body of law must cover this matter. In both of these instances, a process called *litigation* ensues. *Litigation* enforces contractual terms or determines the underlying intent of the law as it might or might not relate to specific instances. Where it is judged that a wrong has been done, this dimension can be reinforced by the litigation process. This process (a trial) takes place in a courtroom, presided upon by a judge—a man or woman charged with the interpretation of the law—or a jury (serving in the same role as a judge). The judge or jury renders some verdict (right/wrong or guilty/innocent). An award for damages that resulted from the wrongdoing will accompany the verdict.

One of the incentives layered into this system is an incentive for attorneys. If they do find themselves negotiating a settlement, an attorney might function on a contingency basis. This contingency basis means that if you attempt to receive a reward (of damages), and the attorney is successful to help you get this award, he or she will receive a percentage of the award (generally ⅓ of it) as a contingency fee. If the attorney loses the case, he or she will not receive any compensation. Many attorneys enjoy this type of work because it affords them a way to leverage their time. For example, if a case takes 200 hours and they bill at $150 per hour, their fee associated with the case would be $30,000. If they take the same case on a ⅓ of settlement contingency basis and there was an award of $3 million, they now made $1 million or $5000 per hour. More contingency cases are undertaken by attorneys where there might not even have been a case several years ago—attorneys see this vehicle as a means of making money.

Attorneys must pass a bar examination in order to practice law legally. This examination is generally taken after completion of law school in the state where the individual will practice the law. If the individual doesn't pass the bar examination, he or she can't legally practice law. If an attorney moves from one state to another, he or she might have to pass a bar examination in the new state. The bar association of each state polices the work of each attorney. If the attorney doesn't adhere to the ethical guidelines set forth by the bar association, he or she can be disbarred and not allowed to practice law anymore.

Conflicts of interest are an example that could cause a disbarment. If a law firm represents parties on both sides of a contract, this situation is a *conflict of interest*. The law firm is bound to live by a legal code, but they don't always do it. You should ask the question about conflicts of interest to protect yourself. Through experience, I can tell you that attorneys might not ask it themselves.

Area of practice   There are many areas of law. Below are a few that you will probably encounter as you run your computer-based business.

Corporate law   Corporate law involves all areas of law that might affect corporations (or sole proprietorships or partnerships). Most of the law in this area is involved with some type of contract.

Litigation   Litigation deals with the enforcement of specific contracts or general areas of the law via some type of court proceeding.

Estates and trusts   Estates and trusts involve contracts that establish direction and conditions of asset transfer. These assets might be personal or corporate. Estates and trusts deal with issues before or after death.

Industry specialization   If there is an industry segment, there is an attorney. Anywhere that the legal process might be aided through their nudging, attorneys seem to appear.

Global reach   Global reach of law firms can correlate with the industry segment that they serve as well as the area of the law in which they specialize. Small firms might need two offices, one in their home town and one in Washington if they specialize in lobbying for their clients on Capitol Hill. Large firms might only have one office in New York City if they serve the financial district of New York exclusively. For your type of computer firm, you might only need a firm that understands contracts. If you write software or develop hardware, you might need a firm that specializes in copyrights, patents, and trademarks as these rights relate to the computer industry. If you are setting up production facilities in the Orient, you might want a firm that understands the law in the Orient and has an office there.

Size   Area and industry specialists show up in firms of all sizes. Some firms specialize in one industry or area of law, and other firms might have such large staffs that they handle a host of different areas and industries.

Small firms are established in somewhat the same manner as the general practitioner in the medical field. They will do a little bit of everything. If they need a specialist for the situation, they will either oversee or refer you to the specialist when one is needed. Small firms, though, can have a specific area of specialization and not be involved in any general law practice.

Medium-size and large law firms can work on the same models as smaller firms, but they often set up practice areas of specialization.

Fees   Attorneys commonly bill on an hourly basis. Hourly rates range from $35 (for a *paralegal* professional, someone can do legal work but has not passed the bar examination of a state) to several thousand dollars an hour for highly specialized attorneys. Geographic location, firm size, and area of specialization all factor into hourly fees. Sometimes you can get them to consent to bill on a task or project basis. For example, you might get them to charge you $150 to incorporate your firm. As discussed, attorneys can also bill on a contingency basis.

You should be sure to keep a leash on attorneys and their billing. If you give them free rein, they will take it. Before you know it, they will have burned through thousands of dollars of your money, and they will do everything possible under the law to collect it. If you have an attorney who provides you with a discrete service, ask what it will cost. Tell the attorney what your understanding of the scope of work is. To protect yourself better, write this information in a letter to the attorney.

If an attorney represents you, he or she often bills you for time spent thinking about your case. Ask your attorney to let you know when you have spent a certain amount of money (perhaps every $500) so that you can tell him or her to stop or proceed. Also, ask for an itemized bill. Attorneys have a certain aura that they try to convey. As part of the aura, some might feel it demeaning to discuss money, especially fees for their professional services. Anyhow, they will often give you a bill that states, "For professional services . . . $1500." What professional services have they provided? Ask your attorney to explain.

If an attorney has or wants to avert a cash-flow problem or is distrustful of your credit worthiness, he or she might ask you for a retainer. Although this retainer is good for the attorney, you might not be able to afford it. If he or she won't negotiate it to a lesser sum (ideally $0), you might want to find yourself another attorney.

Leasing companies are companies that finance assets. They purchase an asset that you want to use, hold title to it, and let you use it for a certain period of time in return for a monthly lease payment. At the end of a certain time period, depending upon the structure of the lease, you can either purchase the asset for some predetermined price or return the asset to the company that leased it to you.

The advantages of leasing to you, the *lessee* (the person or company that leases the asset) are:

- You don't have to allocate funds for an entire asset at one point in time.
- The entire lease payment is deductible as a business expense (as opposed to a loan where only the interest is deductible, not the repayment of principal).
- If you structure the lease as such, you don't own the underlying asset at the end of the term. You can walk away from the asset and begin another lease. You don't have to sell the asset that might have a reduced market value from that which you've shown on your books.

In the computer industry where innovation and new models are the norm, a computer that you own today might have almost no value in three years. If you lease the computer, you can give it back to the leasing company at the end of the lease.

Area of practice   Leasing companies can lease physical assets ranging in size from a personal computer to a jet plane. Truly, any asset that has value and is of use to an individual or corporation is potentially leasable.

Industry specialization   Many leasing companies specialize in certain industry segments. IBM has its own captive leasing company that only provides computer leases to IBM customers. Apple Computer, Inc. works with a company that specializes in handling leases on Apple Computers, and the list goes on.

Global reach   Except for those countries that don't allow leasing, leasing can be found in most parts of the world. Yet many countries have different regulations on leasing.

Size   Leasing companies come in all sizes. You should only be concerned with the credit worthiness of the leasing company. If credit is in jeopardy, your lease might be in jeopardy.

Fees   Leasing companies make their money by purchasing an asset either with cash or borrowed funds. If they purchase the assets with cash, they need to get some rate of return on it. If they borrow funds in order to purchase the assets that they lease, their gross margin will be the difference between what they charge you and the cost of their funds. Their return will relate to the riskiness of the lease. The criteria then for risk assessment is qualify/not qualify as it relates to the lease.

Market research

As discussed in chapter 6, market research can be an invaluable tool to better understand the attributes of the market. Firms in this industry provide both secondary and primary market research for their clients.

Area of practice   Focus groups, questionnaire design, and questionnaire implementation and analysis are all things that a market research firm can do (see more detail in chapter 6). Firms often specialize in one of these practices. For example, there are a host of firms that do nothing but focus group studies.

Industry specialization   There are market research firms that specialize in certain industries. The most visible area of specialization is the political market research firms. Within the computer industry, there are a host of well-known firms that specialize in various components of market research. They include Computer Intelligence Corporation, Dataquest, The Diebold Group, Frost & Sullivan, The Gartner Group, Link, and Arthur D. Little.

Global reach   The computer-based market research firms that are listed above primarily concentrate on the United States market, although many of them have expanded their practice worldwide. For the computer industry, most innovation and initial selling starts in the United States, then moves to Europe, and finally reaches the Far East. The market researchers often follow these trends in their own development.

Size   Market research firms can range in size from one person to hundreds of people. Quality is key in this area, especially because so many of the components within market research can be subcontracted. If you go to a market research firm of one person, can it provide good project management and work with other firms whose specialty it will enlist? In essence, you want the one-person shop to be able to be the equivalent of a good general contractor.

Fees   Market research firms earn their fees on either an hourly or a project basis. If you have a choice, ask them to quote you their fees on a project basis so that you will have a greater certainty as to what you will pay. If they will not go for this arrangement, you might want to put a ceiling on what you want to spend on any given segment of the project.

Public relations firms

In the advertising agency segment of this chapter, also refer to the discussion of the public relations function of advertising agencies.

Area of practice   Public relations firms can assist in the area of print and televised media coverage.

Industry specialization   Firms do specialize in certain industries. In the computer industry for a very long time, Grays Strayton and Regis McKinna were considered to be the industry's two largest public relations firms. Many of the people in these firms go out on their own, taking their knowledge and contacts with them. These people can be valuable industry specialists at a fraction of the cost of the larger firms.

The firms in the computer industry often use specialized computer press mailing lists that they purchase from mailing list brokers. Be aware of this fact. A firm that says its press list is 1000 editors might have absolutely no rapport with any of those 1000 editors. The firm simply might have purchased a mailing list of their names. You want to ensure that the public relations firm really can and does have the contacts that it says it has.

Global reach   Boutiques in the computer or any industry probably don't have the global reach that larger firms might have. The key is the individuals behind the firm. Reach is determined by three things—contacts, contacts, and contacts.

Size   Public relations agencies come in all sizes, shapes, and varieties. Choose one based on capabilities, merged with the present and future needs of your firm.

Fees   Public relations fees can start out as low as $50 an hour and go as high as $20,000 a month (with no time commitment outlined). Make sure you know what you will get for your money. In general, fees are either hourly or project-based.

A PC-based companies

Ideas on many businesses you might consider are presented in this appendix. Some are appropriate businesses to consider in all economic times, and others have a better chance of succeeding in good economic times.

For all economic times

Many businesses are necessary in all economic times. It doesn't matter how the economy is doing — people and companies will always need these services. Although no business is truly recession-proof, the following businesses should be able to survive some tough economic times.

Bar coding system development

This business is based on the notion that coding any type of repetitive text entry is best done with bar coding. Typically, you see bar coding used on products for inventory control. It also can be used in order forms, employee names or numbers, fixed asset accounting, clients, and a host of other applications. This business idea sets up a bar-coding system housed in a microcomputer for a company to use.

Your best target market is smaller companies. You can best reach them through yellow pages advertising (list yourself under *bar-coding service*) and through direct mail. Your competition is other bar-code systems development operations and in-house development. In order to run this type of business, you need to be methodical. You need to be able to develop systems that are logical. You need to know how to market and run a business. This business has a legal liability that the system is not properly in place and inventory or one of the other vital processes of the company is disrupted. There is also a possibility that the technology will fail—generally for only a short time. A real risk is the market. The market might not want the service.

You can do all of the processing or install the capability in a company (make sure you write a maintenance contract to generate recurring revenue). In either case, all you need is a microcomputer, a dot matrix printer, and products such as the Barcode Label Maker ($99) and the Barcode Scanner Wand ($299), both from Disk-Count Software, Inc. You can expect to bill systems either on a complete system basis (not suggested until you really learn how much time is involved in developing a system) or on an hourly basis (anywhere from $35 to $95 per hour).

Business plan development

A computer-based service to develop business plans for companies that need them to either plan their businesses or attempt to raise funds for the business. These business plans should include an executive summary, marketing, operations, financial, and management sections of the plan.

Your market is individuals who want to start corporations and need assistance in planning them, corporations that are in need of funding and therefore must write a business plan, and corporations that want to develop a coherent business plan, even if they do not need funding.

You can find these businesses through new business registrations that are recorded in both county and state offices; through accountants, attorneys, and bankers who advise people and corporations that are in need of planning; through the Small Business Administration and its Small Business Development Center network that extends throughout the country.

Your competition is other individuals and corporations that do business plan development. This includes some accountants, attorneys, bankers, and financial consultants.

You'll need to market yourself to a group of professionals (for example, accountants, attorneys, and bankers) as well as individuals who are or have started businesses and are in need of planning. You'll also need to logically work through the process of developing a business plan. Often, specific industry experience is helpful in the development of the plan.

To run the business, you need a microcomputer, a software package like Biz Plan Builder ($99.95), and a letter-quality or laser printer.

Business plan development can be sold for as little as $2000 or as much as $25,000 per plan.

Computer-aided design (CAD)

This business requires a microcomputer, computer aided design software ($99–$999) and a printer or a plotter. You need to have an understanding of design and preferably have some type of drafting background.

The target market is architects, interior and kitchen designers, and builders and contractors. They are best reached through personal contacts but also through mail and telephone solicitations (find them in the yellow pages). Competition is in-house CAD operators as well as other services.

In addition to an understanding of drafting and design, you might also need to understand building codes so you will adhere to them with your drawings. There are two primary risks in this business—market and performance. The first is that you are unable to reach or convince the market to use your service. The second results from reliance on your work. If you were wrong in understanding the building code, for example, you could be liable and a lawsuit might ensue. Insure yourself against this risk (errors and omissions insurance).

Design service is billed as a professional service. Minimum hourly fees are $50 with $125 not being unreasonable.

Computer application evaluation

In this business, you evaluate computer applications on a contract basis. The best market for this service is computer trade press publishers and corporations. Telemarketing is the best way to reach the editors of the publications or the management information services (MIS) manager of the corporation. Competition comes from internal staff and other services that provide contract evaluation.

You need to have a technical understanding of the applications that you are testing and an ability to write up a summary of the evaluation. You must be able to market the service in order to run it successfully. The risks in the business are primarily market risks. All you need is a microcomputer and a printer to run this business. The client will always provide you with the application to evaluate. You can expect a minimum of $500 and a maximum of $2000 per evaluation.

Computer-based art development

Clip art is commercial art that you can sell to writers, publishers, and other customers who need art to use in their articles, books, software programs or other products. Clip art has become a big business. If you have artistic skills, you might want to create clip art and sell it. Clip art can be sold retail for anywhere from $19 to $99 for a set of images. The target market is users of computers who want to create pictures. Clip art can be targeted to specific groups—there is religious, military, and business clip art, to name a few. When you are in the clip art business, you are in the software business.

Distribution is critical. You will want to have a major distributor sell your product for you. If not, you might be faced with taking out advertisements in computer publications and trying to sell it yourself. You might also attempt to have computer retail stores sell the product. Competition for your clip art product is other clip art. In addition to your artistic skills, you will need marketing capabilities in order to get the distribution for your software. You will need your computer, a printer, floppy diskettes, labeling, and packaging (including documentation) in order to run this business.

More and more young children are learning how to use computers. As this educational market expands, so does the need for software for children to use educationally. The Apple II and Commodore have long been favorites of this market. If you are looking for a platform, you might want to choose either one. All types of educational software are thriving. Software based on age group (for example, early learning skills, ages 2–4; reading, writing, and arithmetic, ages 5–7). If you have a special interest, you might consider converting it into an educational software program. Many of these programs resemble games in order to make learning fun. Either way, you will need to be able to take the information that you want to present, figure out how to present it (the system design), and then either program it yourself or have someone else program it. As a result, you will also need a programming language on your computer. You will need marketing skills to get the program to market. The technical and marketing risks are the biggest risks that you face.

Computer-based educational software development

Define your target market well and attempt to reach them through the company whose hardware you will run (Apple Computer publishes a book of educational software). If you can't get into a manufacturer's catalog, find a distributor for the software (Apple Computer publishes lists of educational distributors). If you can't get a distributor for the software, take out advertisements in educational publications to sell it yourself. Competition is all other educational software producers. You are all competing for the same dollars. If your product is successful, you can make a lot of money. Educational software products usually retail for anywhere from $9.95 to $99.95.

In computer-based game development, you target the same group that you do in computer-based educational software development. The creativity needed to conceive a game might be much greater than that needed to develop an educational software program. Another difference is the marketing channel. You need to find computer game distributors (who are more likely toy distributors). Figure out how to sell the game in toy stores and book stores. Competition is obviously other computer games. The retail price for which you should expect the software to sell is $9.95 to $99.95. If you have a distributor, you might be lucky to get one eighth of the retail selling price as your share. Don't start this business without a creative, well thought game. Also, remember that a big risk to this business is a short product life cycle— your product might be perceived solely as a fad.

Computer-based game development

If you have a MIDI (musical instrument digital interface) on your computer, it is attached to an electronic keyboard, and you have the proper music scoring software on your computer (ranging in price from $300 to $1500), you can score music for people.

Computer-based music scoring

The target market is primarily musicians, music publishers, and recording studios. You can be paid by the musician (although they never have much money unless they're very successful), the music publisher, or recording studio that wants to create a musical score. Attempt to get paid by the hour ($10 to $50) and score away. You reach your target market through lists of publishers and recording studios. Let them know that you can perform this service. You can even rent your equipment to both the recording studios and the music publishers. Competitors are companies that do exactly what you do. Competition also can come from those who score music without a computer. Skill in scoring music is a prerequisite of the business.

You also need to understand the music business and how to market to it, or this is not the business for you. The risks in this business are primarily market and technical skill risks. You might not be able to market your services because you don't understand the business or you don't have the proper technical skills to score music.

Computer dating service

This business can take one of two forms. It can be a database that has different fields of information stored with personal information. If a minimum of a certain number of fields match between two individuals, it might be concluded that they are compatible enough to go out on a date. This business can also have images of the dates scanned into the computer along with a profile. The potential dates then choose the profile that they find interesting.

The target market is single men and women, generally within a certain geographic boundary. You can reach them through advertising in the yellow pages, newspapers, radio, and television. Your competition is all other dating services in your area. You should have good interpersonal skills to run this business. The biggest risk with this business is that you will not be able to sell the service.

You can start the business with a computer, a database management package, and a program to match people (that you either write or contract to have written). Or you can start with a microcomputer, a scanner, and a database management package (for the image/profile business). Fees are either charged for a period of time or a number of dates. Ensure that you are competitive with other services in your area.

CD-ROM mastering

This business involves taking data, either in printed or electronic form, and converting it to a format that is compatible with a CD-ROM (compact-disk read-only memory). The process is complex technically, so you need to know what you are doing. There are many companies that now have either paper or electronic databases that see a need to get their databases on CD-ROM. This mastering service is preproduction. It is not stamping out the disks.

You can find a market with any company that has a lot of information that they want to place on CD-ROM, including publishers, corporate libraries (they have money), and public libraries (large ones). You can reach these people first by telephone and then in person. Competition comes from other CD-ROM mastering services. You might want to learn the trade from one of them. Good resource organizations for this business are the SIGCAT (the Special Interest Group on CD-ROM headed by Jerry McFaul at the U.S. Geological Survey), duPont, Phillips, Microsoft, and Meridian Data. All these companies can inform you more about the process.

You can charge thousands of dollars to provide this service to your customers.

You will need microcomputers and a host of peripheral input devices (scanners, tape drives, and disk drives). The most important skill for you to have in this business is technical ability. The risk is that you don't possess the skill, will botch the data, and will be liable for your mistakes. The other risk is that you are unable to creatively penetrate this growing market.

Database conversion

A database conversion service takes information that was created in one database package and converts it to another package. Although there are tools that can partially facilitate the process, most of the conversion that is done in this area requires either partial or complete manual intervention. As a consequence, this business is not for the novice computer user.

There are two types of competitors—companies that specialize in database conversions and those who do database programming and who could, therefore, develop the capability of performing database conversion. To run this business, you'll need an ability to market, both proactively and reactively, a database conversion service. You'll also need an ability to develop databases in all database applications for which you are offering database conversion capabilities.

Database conversions can either be priced on a contract or an hourly basis. Price the contract yourself by using an hourly billable rate and estimating the number of hours required. Billable hourly rates that are reasonable range from $35 to $125. Annual sales volume, if you are billing 40 hours a week, 50 weeks a year, ranges from $70,000 to $250,000.

Data entry

A service that provides the entering of data, not necessarily into a word processing software package but into databases for use in applications such as accounting, finance, information retrieval, marketing, and sales.

The target market includes large-scale public-access databases, as well as corporate databases that require updating, such as accounting, finance, marketing, and sales databases. These databases are generally used by corporations and government agencies on a fairly frequent basis (daily or weekly). For public-access databases, there is a directory published by Datapro Reports (of Delran, New Jersey) titled *On-Line Services*, which lists the more common public-access databases. In corporations, the department that should be contacted is the data-entry department. If there is no data-entry department, contact the data processing or management information systems department. They probably maintain the data entry task for the corporation. In the government, you can get on actual bidders lists on a state-by-state basis. These government agencies generally give preference to in-state companies. For the United States government, there is a daily publication called the Commerce Business Daily (CBD) that lists all of the requests for quotations (RFQs) and requests for proposals (RFPs).

You can reach these folks best through direct mail and telemarketing. Competition is both local and off-shore data entry operations as well as in-house data entry operations. The most important skills required to run this business are marketing skills, an ability to perform or manage data-entry operators, and an ability to run a business. The biggest single risk to this business is that of price competition.

This business is very much like a commodity business. The pricing threat is omnipresent. Also, changes in technology in terms of optical character and speech-recognition technology threaten to reduce the size of the market. Data-entry services are billed by the thousand characters. Prices range from $0.35 to $5 per thousand characters.

Diskette duplication

In a diskette duplication business, you duplicate information from one diskette to another. Essentially, you are in the diskette-copying business. Additionally, diskette duplication services might provide other services such as labeling. Custom packaging and copy protection are also services that you can offer. Some of the more sophisticated services even provide printing on the shutter of each 3½ inch diskette or the jacket of each 5¼ inch diskette. Also they can provide printing directly on diskette sleeves, labels, binders, and slip cases, and they can print documentation pages. Most of the duplication services only offer duplicating services for diskettes along with labeling and packaging.

The target market for duplication services is any individual or company who wants to duplicate magnetic media. Generally, the best potential candidates for this service are companies who want to distribute software that was created for internal corporate use or for resale to the commercial market.

Where can you find companies who want to distribute software internally or resell it externally? One of the best vehicles is to look at computer trade publications and mail-order catalogs. Identify the companies whose names you see in these catalogs. Another source is catalogs that are distributed by both hardware and software vendors. Finally, don't forget both nonprofit and educational institutions that might publish software lists that represent their particular cause.

There are three ways you can contact potential customers—direct mail, telephone, or direct cold-call visit. Many duplication services advertise in the classified section of popular computer publications.

To run this business, you'll need an ability to market a duplication service, both proactively and reactively.

You'll also have to be able to complete a repetitive duplication task. The skills required to run this business are an ability to place a floppy diskette into a diskette drive, copy the contents of it onto a hard disk, format a floppy diskette, and then copy the contents that had just been copied onto the hard disk back onto the floppy diskette. You also need to be able to label the diskette and package it.

The following are the critical risks of this business:
- Lack of a market for your service
- Rejection of your work by a customer
- Customer refuses to pay for work done
- Customer holds you liable for media that was somehow "damaged"

You can start this business with one MS-DOS computer with a 10 MB (megabyte) hard disk and a 3½ or 5¼ inch floppy diskette drive. If you choose to do so, you can purchase a high-speed diskette duplicator.

A diskette formatting business creates formatted computer diskettes and sells them. Anyone who has a computer and doesn't enjoy formatting diskettes is in the potential market. You can find these people through trade publications and mailing lists that enumerate the corporate individuals who "own" microcomputers.

Diskette formatting

Diskette manufacturers and companies that might specialize in the service are your competition.

To run this business, you'll need to be able to market a formatting service, both proactively and reactively. You'll also need to repetitively complete a diskette formatting task.

The critical risks of this business are:
- Lack of a market for your service
- Rejection of your work by a customer
- Customer refuses to pay for work done
- Customer holds you liable for media that was somehow damaged

The minimum you will need for this business is an MS-DOS computer with a 10 MHz hard disk and a 3½ or 5¼ inch floppy diskette drive.

You can expect to charge $0.39 per 5¼ DS/DD (double-side/double-density) diskette; $0.69 per 5¼ DS/HD (double-side/high-density); $0.67 per 3½ DS/DD (double-side/double-density) diskette; and $1.39 per 3½ DS/HD (double-side/high-density) diskette.

On average, it takes one minute to format a diskette. If you can format all 3½ inch DS/HD diskettes and you have the business, you can format 60 in one hour. You can set up your computer so that it beeps when it is done formatting a floppy diskette. You can even do something else while running this business.

Electronic voice mail

You can set up a voice mail system on your computer and have incoming telephone lines connected to it. The software for this electronic mail system can be found for under $500. Target markets for this business are small businesses who might now be using an answering machine or an answering service. Use a directory of the small firms in your area (which you might be able to get from the local chamber of commerce) and telemarket them.

Your competition is in-house voice mail services, no service at all, answering machines and services (like Bell's Answer Call). An electronic voice mail system requires little more than purging the messages after a time. The selling of the service is key. A yellow pages advertisement will clearly aid your sales effort of this annuity revenue stream business. The greatest risk you run is a market risk—that you won't be able to sign up enough customers. You can charge a monthly fee plus a per call rate. A flat fee of $50 to $100 a month and a per-call fee of $0.05 to $0.10 would be reasonable. Make sure you are competitive with Bell's Answer Call service.

Facsimile services

A facsimile service sends and receives facsimiles. The facsimile transmission can either come from a facsimile machine or a microcomputer (with a scanner and a printer attached to it). With the latter configuration, the scanner inputs outgoing facsimiles and sends them to the recipient via a facsimile board housed in the microcomputer. In order to receive facsimile transmissions, the board receives the facsimile, sends it to the microcomputer's hard disk and then prints it out on a printer attached to the microcomputer. In all instances, the facsimile board is attached to an external telephone line to both send and receive facsimiles.

The target market is businesses that don't have facsimile machines and businessmen who are traveling. Many of these facsimile services have a retail store front and depend upon walk-in traffic. If you get a listing of businesses from either a list broker or your local chamber of commerce, you can target those smaller businesses that probably don't have the funds for a facsimile machine or the capacity to install and plan a facsimile board-based service. Hotels are good locations to target for businessmen who need facsimile services, but hotels are becoming competition by offering this service themselves.

The best way to reach these market segments is through direct mail to the smaller businesses and a point-of-purchase display in hotels. Hotels, other facsimile services, and in-house facsimile machines are obvious competition to this type of service. An ability to market and run a business and operate a facsimile machine or a computer with a facsimile board are critical to running this business. The critical risks in this business are competitive threats and technological change that will reduce the price of facsimile machines and boards to a point where it becomes much less expensive to buy the machine or the board than it is to use a service.

You will need a facsimile machine or a facsimile board, scanner, printer, and a microcomputer, along with a dedicated telephone line in order to equip this business. You can charge from $1 to $2.50 per page for transmission and receipt of faxes. Your gross receipts will depend upon how well you can penetrate your target market.

Language translation

MicroTac Software produces products that translate computer-based text from English to German, English to French, and English to Italian. Their products sell for less than $80 per package. And there are a host of other products that translate language.

With these products, you can target businessmen and attorneys who do international work. You can become their translation service. You can even subcontract to translate for companies like Berlitz (which has its own translation package). One easy way to find businesses that do business internationally is to look in foreign telephone books. Find the names of companies that you also recognize to have offices in the United States. For example, you might want to get the telephone book from France and look at all of the accounting firms. Those firms that have locations in the United States are possibilities for business. You might also want to target businesses and law firms that operate in cities that are known to be somewhat international (for example, New York or Washington D.C.). You can then either direct mail or telemarket these companies in order to attract their business. Competition comes from translators (freelance), in-house personnel with the ability to translate, and other translation services. You can use all of these vehicles yourself, as potential sources for work by offering to freelance for them.

In order to run this business, you should be fluent in the source and target languages you translate, even if you use translation programs. You also need to understand the foreign cultures that you are targeting so that you can better market to them. Your risks are both legal and market risks. First, if you don't translate the documents properly and another meaning is given to the original information, you could be jeopardizing the way the company does business. You might be held responsible. Secondly, there is a market risk that your service might not be needed in the market that you have targeted. There is a need for this service, you just need to target the market correctly. Translation services are generally billed by the word (anywhere from $0.05 to $0.25).

Forms design

Packages such as Per: FORM enable you to design any type of business form that a business could need. There are businesses that do in excess of $100 million each year in sales of forms that they design and print.

The target market for this service is any business that needs forms designed. The market includes smaller firms who don't have their own in-house design capability. You can most easily find these businesses by using either mailing lists that you've purchased or chamber of commerce listings of businesses.

You can best reach them through direct mail. Send them copies of the forms that you can design for them. Competition comes from graphics design companies, desktop publishing firms, and in-house graphics design departments. Although most of the forms design packages come with at least 100 different forms, it is helpful if you have design skills. Additionally, you will need marketing and business operational skills. The biggest risk is that the market is not the size that you think it might be. Survey the market first to determine if you have a market opportunity. Another risk is a legal one. If your forms have any legal overtones, you might or might not be complete and accurate in what is expressed on the form. Your best bet is to get the terminology from the client, directly, and not risk creating "legalese" that might come back to haunt you.

In order to run this business, you need a microcomputer, forms-generation software, and a good quality printer to produce the output. You can bill anywhere from $15 to $1000 for one form, based on its complexity and what competitors charge.

Grammar correction

How many people ain't able to speak or write with the correct grammar? You can establish a service to check grammar based on a host of different manufacturers (for example, SoftKey Software Products, Inc.). For generally less than $100, you can become an editor. And you should be able to bill between $15 and $50 an hour for your service.

Your target market is all people who write documents—college students and professors, authors, and businessmen to name a few. The most easily reached are college students and professors. Simply post notices on kiosks and bulletin boards on college campuses, distribute flyers, and take out advertisements in school papers to reach them. Competition is the individual who can correct her or his own grammar. Other grammar correction services also are your competition.

In order to operate this business you should be somewhat of a grammarian. You should at least be familiar with the rules of grammar. You also need the skill to market and operate a business. The greatest risk is the market risk in your area; before you start this business, ensure that there is demand in your specific geographic location. You can run this business with a microcomputer, grammar checking software, and a printer (optional). You should accept input on magnetic media and ideally return it to your client on magnetic media.

Legal forms generation

In the legal forms business, you create legal forms for people who can't afford or aren't inclined to go to an attorney. There are computer software packages that sell for $49.95 that are templates of legal documents. You load these forms on your computer and fill in the blanks for your clients. The only concern with this sort of business is the legal liability issue—you might not match up the correct forms for the right situation, the forms might be incomplete, or the forms might include extraneous information. Therefore, the best way to posture this business is to visit an attorney. This first stop should reduce the legal fees in drafting legal documents and can and should be sold to clients as such.

The market is individuals and corporations who want to save money on their legal fees and need a fairly straightforward contract. Individuals with more complex legal drafting needs are probably not your target market, unless you have legal skills to work with them.

The best way to reach this market is through yellow pages, local newspaper, and word-of-mouth advertising. Your competition is law firms, legal clinics, and other services like your own. In order to best operate, you are wise to have a legal background (being an attorney who has passed the bar is most preferable) and an ability to understand the law. You also need to know how to work in concert with attorneys. Being able to market your services and run a business also are critical skills. Probably the most critical risks center around legal ones—that you will be liable for doing something improperly or that you might be perceived to be practicing law.

In order to start the business, you need a microcomputer with legal document software, and at least a letter-quality printer. With attorneys billing rates ranging from $50 to $1000 per hour, you can easily charge $50 to $250 per legal form that you generate, even if it is necessary to have an attorney check the document.

Mailing list service

This service takes a list of names and performs contract mailings for companies, government agencies, and individuals. The business can take handwritten mailing lists and input them into a computer system. It can create databases for sorting names, street addresses, cities, states, and zip codes. It can generate labels, lists, and letters on magnetic media. Finally, it can actually print, stuff, and mail the materials.

The target market is companies, government agencies, and individuals who don't want to or can't perform any of the above services. One of the best ways to reach prospective clients in this business is through a yellow pages advertisement. Competition is other mailing houses (either geographically or industry segmented) and in-house mailing operations.

You need marketing and general business skills, skills to perform all of the operations mentioned above, and a clear ability to communicate and understand the needs of clients. This service can be a tremendous opportunity for repeat business and annuity revenues (especially if you charge your clients a maintenance fee to maintain their databases). Competitive threats do exist. This business can be much like a commodity business, where price is the key element. If you don't keep your costs under control, you might find yourself noncompetitive in the marketplace. Good technology, right down to the database management system you use to maintain the database, is absolutely critical.

This business can be run with as simple a setup as one computer, a database-management software package, and a dot-matrix printer (best suited for mailing label generation). You can use optical scanners (for input of mailing lists), extremely high-resolution color laser printers, folding and sorting equipment, and a postage meter. Scope of technology is completely dependent on how simple or extensive you make the business. Sales volume in this business varies from thousands of dollars to millions of dollars each year.

Multimedia service bureau

A multimedia service bureau creates *multimedia presentations*, which are nothing more than the communication of information in more than one form. These forms include audio, text, graphics (both still and animated), and full-motion video. These presentations can be used for business, educational, and recreational events. Therefore, the target markets consist of all of these categories. The best way to reach these markets is on a reactive basis through advertisements in the yellow pages and through point-of-purchase displays in computer retail outlets. Notifying advertising agencies of your capabilities and giving seminars and lectures on the topic (of course, with the assistance of multimedia presentations) can let the world know of your capabilities.

Competition is found in in-house multimedia service bureaus (generally audio-visual departments), advertising agencies (the larger ones), and other multimedia service bureaus. Production companies are also direct competition. In order to run this type of business, you need to be able to understand the capabilities of a host of different types of technology. You must be able to creatively apply the technologies. You must also know how to market and run a computer-based business. The critical risks in the business relate to the market, first. Because multimedia microcomputer-based presentations are rather new, your geographic area might not be ready for it. Make sure your market is ready before you make the investment. Technology risk is the second type of risk. This segment of the computer market is changing so rapidly that you might find your technology outmoded rather rapidly. Be prepared to make financial investments in new technology and play guinea pig to technology that might not be completely debugged. If you rent multimedia equipment when you need it, you protect yourself from the technology and market risks—if you don't have work, you don't need the equipment.

You should have a computer, sound input, video input, scanner input, MIDI interface with a keyboard input and the highest resolution monitor possible. If you also use your equipment for presentation purposes, you will want to be sure that you have a large monitor and probably a projection unit. In many ways, you are now making movies or commercials. You can charge what many production houses charge, if you have the setup that warrants the fees. These fees can range from a low of $250 per hour to as much as $50,000 an hour, depending upon how you are configured.

Newsletter creation

It is possible to receive anywhere from $500 to $5000 for a 10- to 20-page newsletter that you create monthly. This business might require more than just writing skills. It requires you to create mechanicals and full layouts of newsletters. The target market is any business that wants a newsletter but doesn't want to or have the skills to create it in house. You can telemarket or write to all of your local businesses, nonprofit associations, and religious groups. For some of these organizations, you might have to handle the printing, but that is easily done with a full layout.

Competition is any other business or freelancer who creates newsletters. This includes public relations firms and advertising agencies. The skill set you need to run this business consists of writing, editing, and layout skills, primarily. You also need to know how to run a business. The critical risk is a market risk, but once you've locked in clients, that risk converts to a performance risk. You can run this business with a microcomputer, a word processing application, a desktop publishing application, and a laser printer.

On-line information research

If you have research skills, this business is for you. All you need is a microcomputer, communications software for accessing on-line information services, a modem, and a telephone line. On-line researchers can charge a minimum of $10 per hour. Some charge as much as $75 per hour (plus database connect charges). As long as you have the skills to wander through on-line databases, you can become the research arm of a corporation, a nonprofit organization, or an association. You can identify each through the telephone book or other available business directories. You reach them through direct mail or telemarketing. Competition comes from internal research organizations, individuals who are inclined to do research themselves, and other services like yours. The largest risk is your inability to capture the market. It is there. Be persistent!

OCR (optical character recognition)

The OCR business takes paper-based information and scans it into computer-based magnetic media. The input of paper-based information can be either originals or photocopies of information. The output magnetic media can be either digital ASCII or EBCDIC representations or bit-mapped information.

The target market is businesses who either can't afford an optical scanner (because they don't use it enough) or those who have such a high volume of work that they need to off-load it. The market includes database producers, graphics arts studios, word processing service bureaus (both in-house and outside services), and law firms.

The easiest way to reach these target markets is via direct mail, telemarketing, and sales calls. Competition is other optical scanning service bureaus and in-house scanning operations. As with most of the businesses discussed, you need marketing and business operations skills, an ability to operate an optical scanner, and an ability to edit the output of the scanner to ensure that a high-quality product is delivered.

Critical risks in the business are the overestimation of throughput of the optical scanner because of a lack of understanding of the technology. A lack of a market in your geographic locale is also an issue (move elsewhere or target elsewhere). Finally, technological change in this market can cause your pricing to no longer be competitive.

In order to start this business, you need an optical scanner, which can range in price from $1000 to $60,000, a microcomputer, and software to which you are outputting for your clients. You might also want a printer. Pricing can be anywhere from $0.20 to $5 per thousand characters scanned.

Payroll service

A payroll service is similar to a bookkeeping service in that you are performing an accounting function for companies on a contract basis. Some bookkeeping services even do payroll accounting. The nuance in payroll accounting is taxes. When you do payroll accounting, you need to account for and pay payroll taxes at the local, state, and Federal level. With the changes in tax laws, many companies realize that it is difficult to calculate and recalculate all of the local, state, and Federal taxes for its employees. The service generates all of the tax information on each employee. It also cuts payroll checks for the company and fills out all needed payroll tax forms. To do this one, you really need a background in accounting. For the computerized end of things, if you find a good accounting package, you need only know how to operate a computer. The most important skill in running this business is building up trust in your customers so they will allow you to perform this task.

Your target market is all companies, small to large. You need to reach either the company president, office manager, or payroll manager, depending upon the size of the company. You can best reach them through direct mail or telemarketing followed by an office visit. Your competitors are the large payroll services, ADP (automated data processing) groups, many small payroll services and accounting firms. In-house processing of payroll by the payroll department is also competition. You can start this business with a microcomputer, a program like Quicken™ (Intuit—$39) and a dot matrix printer (which can print payroll checks). You can expect to charge anywhere from $0.50 to $2 per check, each pay period (an annuity revenue business).

Spreadsheet conversion

A spreadsheet conversion service takes information from one spreadsheet to another. Many of the popular spreadsheet packages enable the importation of information from other dissimilar spreadsheet applications packages. One of the problems is that many of the cell definitions, as well as the macros defined in the original spreadsheet, might not pass through to the new spreadsheet. As a consequence, if cell and macro definition are a needed part of the conversion, a specialized service such as a spreadsheet conversion service might be necessary. In essence, this service involves the conversion (or rewriting) of both spreadsheet cell definitions and macros.

Telecommunications

This business sends and receives information from one computer to another. Information can be sent in the form of an ASCII or EBCDIC file format or a binary data file format. For people who don't have the ability or capability to send information over the telecommunications network, this service can be invaluable. This service can focus on sending information to certain electronic networks for people (such as CompuServe, AppleLink, American On-Line, and Prodigy). This business can take one of two directions. It can communicate information for people from one computer directly to another one (point-to-point communications). It can also communicate directly to certain public electronic computer networks. This telecommunications service can either send files or electronic messages.

The target market is individuals and businesses who need to communicate via these means and either can't or don't know how. The target market potential includes virtually all microcomputer users and individuals who are not microcomputer users but need to communicate to someone who is. This target market is not easily reached.

The best way to reach it is through advertising in computer-based publications, which includes user group publications. Competition is users who have access to all of the electronic computer networks or are capable of communicating directly from one computer to another. In order to run a business of this nature, you must be a creative and persistent marketer of the service. You also need to know how to communicate with a host of different computers as well as a host of electronic computer systems. The biggest risks in this business are technology risks with the point-to-point communications—the communication might not work. The other major risk in this business is the difficulty in finding clients.

In order to start this business, you will need a microcomputer and modems along with microcomputer software that enables you to access various computer networks. You will also need a dedicated telephone line. Revenues will vary based on volume. You should be able to charge either on an hourly or a transaction basis. If you charge on an hourly basis, the minimum you should charge is $10 per hour with a maximum of $175 per hour (if you are performing a point-to-point transfer). You might become well equipped to estimate the amount of time involved in a transaction and be able to charge by the transaction.

Transcription

A transcription service takes voice input and types it into computer media for output either on computer media, telecommunications, or paper. Input is either via a dictating machine cassette or a telephone system.

The target market includes businessmen who travel and don't have their own offices available to them, doctors and lawyers who need speedy transcription and don't want to do it in-house, and large governing bodies that need transcription of records (for example, courts and court reporters, state, and local government organizations). Another market is businessmen who don't have any secretary but need to have letters, memorandums, and reports generated.

The market is best unearthed through hotels who target business travelers and shared office space facilities who target small businesses that don't have secretarial support. Competition comes from other transcription services and in-house clerical staff. In order to run this business, you need primarily marketing and communications skills, transcription skills (which includes typing), and business skills. The largest risks in this business are competitive threats that include price competition and technological obsolescence (as voice recognition improves).

The minimum capital equipment needed to start the business is a computer and a transcription device that accepts microcassettes. Sales volume can range anywhere from $500 per year to hundreds of thousands of dollars, if you can land a large enough account.

Word processing diskette format conversion

Word processing format conversion is probably the most straightforward type of format conversion that can be undertaken. The process involves moving textual information from one application to another (such as from Microsoft Word to WordPerfect).

Many applications packages have their own built-in conversions. But for those that don't, there are many tools that you can buy to run your business.

Law offices, accounting firms, manufacturing businesses, and service businesses are where you'll find people that want to move information from one word processing application to another.

There are two good vehicles to reach people who have the need to convert word processing formats.

- Computer hardware and software vendors. The time of greatest need of word processing format conversion is when an individual or a corporation is purchasing a new computer system or word processing application.
- Advertising in the popular computer press. One of the best places to advertise is the classified section of the computer trade press.

There are three types of competitors to this service business—the applications themselves, word processing conversion utilities, and other services that perform word processing conversion.

To run this business, you'll need an ability to market, both proactively and reactively, a word processing conversion service. You'll also need to repetitively complete a word processing conversion task. Finally, you need to be able to use many different word processing applications so that you can perform the required *cleanup* (taking care of the format conversions that did not take place automatically).

To run the business, if you're using a software-only word processing conversion utility, you'll need one microcomputer with a hard drive and a 3½ and 5¼ inch floppy diskette drive.

You can expect to sell this service for between $10 and $75 per converted diskette.

For good economic times

The following businesses and services are not considered absolutely necessary by most people and companies. These businesses have a better chance at success in good economic times than in hard economic times.

Computer-based bulletin board

If you have a special interest, you can buy software that enables you to set up a bulletin board ($250–$1000).

The target market is all people who have the same special interest. The special interest might be driven by events, vocations, or avocations. You target your market through trade publications, seminars, meetings, and newsletters in the narrow niche. Competition might be nonexistent, if no one else is running a bulletin board in this market. You need some computer skills to load the bulletin board program, set it up, and hook a modem up to both your computer and your telephone line. You will want to make sure that your computer has a large enough hard disk to handle the bulletin-board activity.

The largest risk is the market risk. No one might want to use a bulletin board to communicate or access reference information about their special interest. Do your market research wisely! If volume is great enough, proceed.

You can bill either with a 900 number listing (if volume is great enough) or by charging members a monthly fee, probably best charged to a credit card. You can attempt to set this business up on a transaction fee basis. You might need additional software, unless your bulletin board software program has that capability already built in. The fees will be determined solely by your feedback from the market. Different special interest groups will pay different amounts for information and conversation.

Computer-based glossary development

You can use your computer to develop computer-based glossaries. The target market is computer users or potential computer users who want to understand the meaning of computer-based terms. You can create the glossary in print or on electronic media. If the glossary is created in print, you will need to do everything that a writer does in order to get the book published. On the other hand, if the glossary is created in electronic form, you can attempt to get distribution through electronic services (for example, CompuServe). You can also attempt to get computer software and hardware manufacturers to include it as a part of their product distribution. Try to sell both a book and an electronic version via advertisements in the computer trade press. Probably your biggest competitor is *The Computer Glossary* by Alan Freedman. This business requires an acute understanding of the computer industry so that you can develop definitions for computer terms. It also requires that either you or one of your colleagues in the business know how to write well to clearly articulate the definitions that you establish.

The greatest critical risk in this business is that you might not be able to come up with the definitions of computer terms and therefore not be able to publish a glossary. You might also not be able to market it well. A final critical risk is product liability. The best way to deal with this risk it to be sure that your definitions are clear and accurate. You might put some type of disclaimer in a book or on your electronic media. You can expect to sell the book for a retail selling price of $34.95 in hard cover and $24.95 in soft cover. An electronic version can sell for $59.95.

Computer embroidery

A computer embroidery service can transfer letters and pictures through a computer interface to a sewing machine; the output of the sewing machine is embroidery designs on fabric. Meistergram™ is a completely self-contained unit for computer-based embroidery. The system includes a computer and a sewing machine that are connected. The system sells for under $20,000. There are less expensive systems on the market.

If you decide to run a wholesale business, you can target a host of retail stores to embroider for them. Generally, sporting goods and novelty stores are good candidates for this service. If you decide to create a retail operation, you can buy merchandise on which you can embroider. As with any retail business, you need to make sure that you have the right location for your business. Competition for this business is other businesses that embroider. The skills that you need relate to marketing and running a wholesale or retail business. You should also have some perspective to figure out how embroidery patterns can be laid out. The greatest risk is that the market doesn't accept the service.

Cookbook development

This business is perfect for the person who has many recipes and wants to put them on a computer. Why not put your recipes in an application like Hypercard (a series of file cards on computer) and sell them? Your target market is people who like to cook and who own the type of computer on which you have written the application (home PC or Macintosh).

Write the application and try to have a larger software company market it for you. Take a royalty of anywhere from 2 to 15%, depending on the software company. If you can't get distribution this way, you might want to send your software to the larger distributors (for example, Ingram/Micro D, Softsel, or Corporate Software) and try to get them to sell it for you. At worst, you can always take an advertisement out in cooking or food-related magazines. Offer the cookbook yourself for a retail price of anywhere from $9.95 to $29.95. Competition is cookbooks that appear in print and other computer-based cookbooks. In order to write the cookbook, you need to know how to cook, document what you've done, and record it on a computer.

You will need some design skills (or hire them) to make your cookbook on disk visually appealing. You will also need to know how to market and sell the product. The worst critical risk is that the product won't sell. Also, there is a risk that a recipe might not turn out as you planned; someone might get ill from one of the recipes. They might decide to hold you liable as a result (slim risk). You need one microcomputer, an application environment in which you can create the cookbook, and floppy diskettes to copy the recipes. You will also need to design some type of labeling and packaging for the product.

Employee manual development

You can go into business developing employee manuals for corporations. There is actually a company called JIAN/Tools for Sales, which created a software product called Employee Handbook Builder. Using this tool, or similar ones, you can develop the elements of an employee manual. The basis of the manual is a template established by the software product. Topical areas that it should cover include policies such as equal employment opportunity, sexual harassment, job classification, compensation policies, introductory period, unacceptable performance/disciplinary action, severance allowance, employee performance appraisals, introductory period—new employees, and employment of relatives. You can also include company rules and regulations such as absenteeism and tardiness, safety, substance abuse, consideration for smokers/nonsmokers, dress code, outside employment terminations, security/loss prevention and personnel files. Finally, cover benefits that include vacations, holidays, sick leave, leaves of absence, voting, group insurance, workers compensation, employment development, and pension and profit sharing.

The target market for this sort of service is companies who probably have less than 100 employees and are not inclined to write their own employee handbook. You can find them through business directories, especially those put out by your local chamber of commerce.

You can best reach these businesses through the mail with a small sample of an employee handbook. This shows your capabilities but doesn't enable the targeted company to create its own handbook with your sample. Follow up your sample with a telephone call to the company. Attempt to get an appointment to discuss their needs. In smaller companies, you might want to send this solicitation directly to the company president. In larger organizations, you might want to go to the human resources director. Human resources directors might be your competition. They are very often the people who are responsible for creating these documents. If you play your cards right, you might be able to subcontract the task from the human resources director. Other competition is services identical to your service and human resource consulting firms. A background in organizational behavior is very helpful to this type of business. An understanding of people and organizational needs is critical. The ability to communicate (both listen and express yourself) clearly are very important. Probably the biggest critical risk is the one you face by helping to shape the policy of the corporation whose employee manual you create. You should do one of two things (if not both) to protect yourself against this risk:

- Have a good contract that limits (if not eliminates) any liability that the corporation might incur as a result of the employee handbook. This should be a high priority for you.
- Take out insurance. You should carry something called errors and omissions insurance to protect yourself against any possible errors or omissions that you might make in the handbook. Liability insurance will assist you in the area that is allegedly covered by the contract that you have in place.

Your start-up equipment needs for this business are a computer, the employee handbook software, and a good printer. It is not unreasonable to charge from $5000 to $20,000, based on complexity and length, for an employee handbook.

Home design   Even if you are not an architect, there are computer packages that you can use to operate a home design service for individuals as well as contractors. Packages such as Floorplan and Dream House Professional by ComputerEasy enable you to plan or remodel floor plans of rooms and calculate dimensions, square footage, and perform room labeling. The packages commonly carry a library of common fixtures for inclusion in your planning. And they enable you to draw walls, boxes, circles and polygons. Rotating, magnifying, copying, erasing and inverting objects are features that you can perform for your clients.

The target market consists of people who want to redesign part of their home, build an addition or build an entirely new home.

The market is most easily reached by getting leads from interior designers and kitchen and bathroom showrooms. Approaching friends to let them know that you can perform this service is another vehicle. Taking out advertisements in community papers and local metropolitan newspapers can help you reach the appropriate individuals. Posting signs on bulletin boards in the local lumber yards, home supply stores, and hardware stores is another vehicle to use to find leads. You can even reach these people through realtors who might need your service to help them sell a house or just after the sale has been made when people want to redesign some of the interior (or exterior) of the house.

Architects, kitchen and bathroom designers, interior designers, other computer-aided designers, and other firms like yours are your competitors.

You'll need an ability to market, both proactively and reactively, a home design service to run this company. Most important, you'll need to be able to listen to clients and translate their thoughts into designs that are aesthetically pleasing, functional, and can be built. Some architectural and drafting training is extremely helpful.

You'll need an MS-DOS computer; a software program like Floorplan ($49.95) or Dream House Professional ($79.95); and a dot matrix, letter-quality, or laser printer.

Sales volume and revenues will probably be project based. A kitchen design can vary from $250 to $5000, depending upon who is doing the design and the size of the kitchen. You can look at your revenue possibilities based upon what architects bill for their time. It varies from a low of $35 per hour to $175 per hour.

Home inventory

How many people do you know who have an extensive listing of the items that they own in their home? How many people don't know exactly what they've lost when a robbery occurs? You can run an inventory service that takes an inventory of the homeowner's belongings. People don't take inventory of their belongings because of the time that it takes. If you are there to do it with them, then it will get done. If you perform this service with the homeowner, you probably want to charge $10 to $25 an hour. If the homeowner doesn't want you to know what possessions they have, rent them the computer program for use on their own system. You would be wise to rent the system by the day ($15 to $25 per day).

The market for this business is every household in the United States. You can find them through cross-reference directories that give the names of families by each block. You can reach them with a door-to-door campaign, distributing flyers. If you want to reach them more professionally, use the cross-reference directory and send them a letter. Your competition is the homeowner who could do this inventory or another company that does the same thing that yours does. The skills that you need to run this business are the ability to develop trust with your clients, to be methodical and follow through on tasks, to tolerate repetitive tasks, and to sell and run a business.

The greatest critical risk is that if a house is burglarized, you might become a suspect due to your knowledge of the inventory. You probably want to insure yourself against this risk. There is also the market risk that people don't want this service. In order to start this business with a microcomputer, you need software such as HomeInventory (SoftKey Software Products, Inc.) and any type of printer. You might also want a mouse to make the software easier to use.

Novelty creation

You commonly see this business in shopping malls. Microcomputers can be used to make novelties such as the *News of the Past* that gives you a description of what happened on a specific day in the past.

The target market can easily be a wholesale market. You can sell this service to, for example, balloon shops. They can then sell it as an adjunct to their balloons. It can also be a retail market if you choose to set up a kiosk in a mall. You will be least successful if you try to run this business as either a store front (unless you have a host of novelties) or as a business that is advertised in the yellow pages. The target market is either a wholesale or a retail market. In the case of the balloon-type novelty stores, the easiest thing for you to do is look in the yellow pages, assemble a list, and solicit them in person, with samples in hand. Look for the owner or manager of the store to give him or her a sales pitch. If you choose to sell something like this novelty in a mall kiosk, you might want to test market the idea when the mall has a special event where you can rent a kiosk for only one day. If your novelty sells well, try to determine if it was the event or if there is staying power to the idea. If the latter, set up a kiosk.

Your competition is other novelty companies, even if you are selling directly to them. People often aren't wed to a single novelty but might switch from one to another. The biggest skill that you need in this business is the ability to market and run a business. The single largest critical risk is a market risk— that either the market won't buy the product or that some competitor drives down the prices and the business becomes unprofitable.

You can start this business, depending upon the novelties that you create with a microcomputer, a package such as News of the Past ($49.95) and either a dot-matrix, daisy wheel, or laser printer. Even if you only make $5 per novelty, you have a positive return on investment of your software after 10 sales.

Organization chart development

For less than $100, you can buy a program such as Org Plus Advanced (Banner Blue Software). It runs on a microcomputer with either a dot matrix or laser printer to create organizational charts. You can create these organization charts, probably best for medium-size and large corporations, and let them use them for presentations.

You can reach your market through business directories. Once you get the directories, you probably want to target reaching managers in organizations by sending them a letter with a sample of your output. Competition is in-house art departments, graphics arts studios, and maybe even the customer manager. Just follow the directions of the software package you choose in order to operate this business. Your most important skill will be your ability to locate and sell the right people on the idea. Once you get a client, the client has potential to be a repeat business customer.

The largest risk in this business is a market risk. If you don't know how or can't penetrate the market, you might not have a business. Also, once you get started, if your customers decide to perform the service, in-house, your market could dry up. You can probably sell organization charts at the rate of at least $50 per chart. You can pay back on your software investment after you've done only two charts.

Real estate listing

A real estate listing service uses a computer-based database to keep track of real estate listings. These listings can vary based on your target market. Because there are so many local (or county) realtor boards, they often sponsor what is called a *multiple-listing service*. These listings frequently only include houses and commercial real estate that are for sale. Many multiple listing services don't offer computer dial-in services. If they don't, you can strike a deal with them to take their database and offer this service to the local realtors. In this instance, you only approach the one board of realtors and strike a deal with them.

Another more sensible way to approach this business is to include listing of rental properties. Many multiple-listing services don't keep track of rental properties. You can go to all of the realtors and track these properties, and have them update your database (via a dial-in service). You could have an annuity revenue business, targeted to realtors and individuals looking for rental property. You reach the realtors through telemarketing, direct mail, and personal solicitation. You reach individuals through yellow pages and local newspaper advertising.

The risks in this business are that a real estate board might perform the service itself. Another risk is that realtors might not be inclined to use the technology (dial-in lines to your database). Finally, a risk is that the individual market might not want the service. You make money by charging the realtor for a listing and the individual user on a use basis. You probably will charge a monthly fee to the realtor (probably $1 per listing) and the individual a transaction fee ($0.25 per match). You need to know how to use a computer (maybe even do some programming if you can't afford a programmer). You need to understand the real estate market.

Seventy-five home-based computer businesses

Abstracting service
Answering/voice mail service
Association management services
Astrology charting service
Backup service
Billing and invoicing service
Bookkeeping service
Bulletin board services
Business plan writer
Clip art service
Collection agency
Computer-aided design service
Computer-assisted instructional design
Computer consulting
Computer programming
Computer sales and service
Computer training
Computer tutoring
Construction and remodeling estimating and planning service
Copywriter
Coupon newspaper publishing
Creativity consulting
Data conversion service

Database marketing service
Desktop publishing service
Desktop video
Diet and exercise planning service
Disk-copying service
Drafting service
Electronic clipping service
Employee manual development and writing service
Event and meeting planning
Expert brokering service
Fax-on-demand service
Financial information service
Form design service
Indexing service
Information brokering
Inventory control service
Law library management
Legal transcript digesting
Legal transcription service
Mailing list services
Market mapping service
Medical billing service
Medical transcription service
Missing person/skip tracer service
Mortgage auditing service
Multimedia production
Newsletter publishing
Notereader/scopist
Payroll preparation
Personal organizing services
Professional practice management services
Professional reminder service
Property management
Proposal and grant writing
Publicist
Publishing services
Referral service
Real estate brochure service
Repairing computers
Résumé writing service
Reunion planning
Scanning service
Self-publishing
Sign-making service
Software location service
Software publishing

Sports league statistics
Technical writing
Temporary help service
T-shirt design and production
Used computer broker
Word processing service

These businesses are profiled in the book *Making Money with Your Computer At Home* by Paul and Sarah Edwards, 1993, Tarcher/Perigee. Copyright 1993 by Paul and Sarah Edwards.

Index

***Boldface** page numbers refer to art

***Boldface** page numbers refer to art

***Boldface** page numbers refer to art

*__Boldface__ page numbers refer to art

*****Boldface** page numbers refer to art